THE WALL BOOK

THE WALL BOOK

The interior walls of your home and how to build them, move them, and tear them down; how to decorate them with paint, paper, panelling, mirrors, tiles, carpets and hundreds of other things.

by STANLEY SCHULER

Illustrated by Marilyn Grastorf

M. EVANS AND COMPANY, INC.
New York, New York 10017

M. Evans and Company titles are distributed in
the United States by the J. B. Lippincott Company,
East Washington Square, Philadelphia, Pa. 19105
and in Canada by McClelland & Stewart, Ltd.,
25 Hollinger Road, Toronto M4B 3G2, Ontario

Library of Congress Catalog Card Number: 73-87709
ISBN 0-87131-143-7 (cloth)
ISBN 0-87131-150-X (paper)
Manufactured in the United States of America

9 8 7 6 5 4 3 2 1

Contents

1

Getting into Wall Work

Just about the first thing a family does when it moves into a new-new or new-old house is to go to work on the interior walls.

In a new house, even though the walls may have been given a final finish, they command attention because they do not suit your personal feelings and needs.

In an old house, the walls are a mess: dirty, scarred, water-soaked, broken, perhaps falling down.

Furthermore, in both new houses and old, inside walls may need to be moved; to be newly installed; to be altered to accommodate a longer doorway or a new closet or something else; to be ripped out; to be surfaced, as in the case of

an unfinished upstairs bedroom or basement playroom; or to be soundproofed so you can't hear the lights being turned on and off at the other end of the house.

Yes, inside walls are demanding. Other features or lack of features may be equally demanding in some houses. But of the 67,699,084 dwelling units in the United States today, I am willing to bet that in 67,599,084 the walls will be the first order of business when new families move in.

Consider a few case histories:

When my wife, Elizabeth, and I bought our very large, old house four years ago, it needed so much work that we had to hire a general contractor to get the worst of it done in the four weeks we had before moving in. Building a new bathroom and installing plumbing, cabinets and flooring in the kitchen were the biggest jobs; but wall work was the most extensive. The contractor resurfaced the walls in two rooms; patched plaster in a third; closed doors in two rooms and opened new doorways in two others; built an entirely new wall in an eighth room and rebuilt a bookcase wall in a ninth. Meanwhile, the first job we undertook ourselves (we always do much of our own remodeling and all decorating) was to tear ancient coverings and excrescences from the walls in a tenth room and apply no less than three coats of paint.

Today, the walls in every room except two have been completely renovated once—and in several cases, twice.

My friends the Utleys went through the same process in their brand-new house. It happens that another friend and I had built the house on speculation; and we had painted all the walls off-white, except those in the bathrooms and kitchen. We knew that builders rarely satisfy the decorative tastes of buyers; but we figured that anyone who bought this particular house could live with off-white walls if he didn't feel up to redecorating them immediately. And the Utleys proved us right, except that they went a little further than we expected and redid almost all the walls.

Then there were the Finnerans. They bought the first house my wife and I owned—another relic that we spent years revamping (again most of our work involved walls). But while the Finnerans liked the house well enough to give us our price six hours after they first saw it, they wasted no time in tearing things apart. Two walls, one of them a bearing partition, were torn out; every wall that was covered with composition board was re-covered with gypsum board.

Young Charlie and Cary Hull were equally ruthless when they purchased a 35-year-old Royal Barry Wills-type house. The previous owners, who had been in the house for about 15 years, had had a penchant for dark plywood paneling; and they had lined the living room, dining room and kitchen with it. The paneling was cheap; the workmanship, bad; and the results, hideous. So Charlie and Cary undid the atrocity; found the walls underneath in better shape than they had dared to hope; and did them over with bright paper and paint.

So it goes.

There are three obvious reasons why inside walls stir families like the Hulls, Finnerans, Utleys, Schulers and 67,699,080 others to action: (1) They are so prominent that if anything is seriously wrong with their appearance you cannot help noticing it. (2) They make you feel confined—perhaps uncomfortably so. (3) They may restrict the way you live in and enjoy your home.

Faced with any or all of these problems, you say to yourself: "Okay. Let's do something about it."

Right here in this positive let's-get-going attitude is the fourth reason—not so obvious—why inside walls provoke action: People are not afraid of them. I know lots of homeowners who are afraid of kitchens, bathrooms, heating systems, roofs and leaky basements because they don't understand them, don't know how to cope with them and are sure that whatever is done to them is going to cost a fortune. But inside walls are not frightening, because there is nothing terribly complicated about them. Furthermore, since a high percentage of people have painted walls with their own hands and found the work fairly easy and inexpensive, their fears of doing other work on walls have faded to a considerable extent.

As an old do-it-yourself advocate, I'm happy about this development. For one thing, it's a positive answer to the shabby treatment homeowners have been getting from the building industry in recent years. More important, it means you will no longer hesitate to take advantage of some of the beautiful, durable new wall-surfacing materials and treatments that are now available.

This doesn't mean, of course, that you can

jump into a wall project without some study. The hasty approach too often backfires even on simple jobs. For example, when we moved into our present house, I rushed into the papering of the living room simply because the whole house was in an uproar and we wanted to get at least one of the downstairs rooms in livable condition. The day I saved then has just cost me three days of unnecessary work and expense, because the room had to be papered all over again to make it look right. My initial mistakes were all elementary: I didn't completely remove the wallpaper which was already on the walls. I didn't feather out the patches in the plaster far enough. We had bought a plain, solid-colored paper which did not conceal the imperfections in the walls as a more patterned paper would have. Finally, while I knew the room had a mildew problem, I didn't stop to consider the effect mildew would have on a nonwashable paper.

On big wall projects, haste may cause more serious problems. The Finnerans, for instance, ran up a huge bill because they were in a hurry to get into their new house (he was being transferred across the country into a handsome new position) and she was adamant that the bearing partition between the kitchen and pantry had to come out. I don't know why their contractor didn't warn them they would run into trouble. Some contractors aren't as smart as they make out; others are pretty cavalier with the homeowner's money. I think the latter was the case here. In any event, when the wall was knocked out, the pipes and drains leading to a bathroom upstairs were exposed. Relocating them proved to be a tricky and costly job.

What are the things you should consider when you are about to work on a wall?

● *Your own limitations, if you intend to do the work yourself.* I am not concerned about your knowledge of the work to be done and your skill with tools. I honestly think that if you are given proper directions and if you do not have a crippling physical handicap, you can complete any wall project successfully. But you may have other limitations.

Take Tom Rooney. He's a bright young government scientist who grew up without ever using tools. But now he feels he must because he has a family to support; and looking ahead to the time when he will put his children through college and graduate school, he is not eager to contract out work he should be able to do himself.

Recently, Tom and his wife bought a century-old house in need of extensive remodeling. When they asked me for advice about the work, I pointed out that the plaster walls and ceilings in several rooms had (as the Rooneys were well aware) cracked loose in large sheets from the wood lath. "They really should be knocked out and replaced with gypsum board," I advised. "Is that the only alternative?" Tom asked. "It's the best in this case," I answered. But I could see he was worried.

It turned out later that his paint dealer had another idea: fasten the loose plaster to the lath with screws driven through special, perforated, slightly concave washers; then patch the cracks and cover the washers with gypsum board cement. Although this obviously would not produce such a smooth or durable surface as gypsum board, Tom preferred it for two reasons: He lacked confidence in his ability to work with gypsum board, and he did not have the time for such a big reconstruction job.

Lack of time is a limitation that deters many do-it-yourselfers, and it is one no one can argue with. Hence you should try to determine roughly how much time is going to be required to carry out a wall project with the surfacing materials available to you. If this depended only on the materials themselves, it would be possible for me to give you a list, rating them from easiest and fastest to apply to hardest and slowest to apply. But such a list would be meaningless, because speed of application also depends on several other things: the dimensions, contour and plan of the wall in question; the amount of preparation the wall requires; and how much follow-up work must be done to complete the project. These are variables I can't even guess at. However, in the chapters describing how different materials are applied, you will find guidelines to help you make a rough comparison of the time each takes to apply in a given situation.

A second limitation on some do-it-yourself projects is the strength of the worker as opposed to the weight of the materials used. Gypsum board panels, for example, do not look very hard to handle, but they turn out to be surprisingly heavy. I doubt that even a strong man could apply a ½-inch-thick panel at the top of a two-story partition without an equally strong helper. Other materials are just as heavy —or more so.

● *The qualifications of whatever contractors you employ.* Service—competent service—is just as difficult to get today in building and remodeling as it is in other fields of business. So your chances of securing the kind of help you are entitled to if you decide to have your walls built, remodeled or redecorated by so-called professionals are not very bright. The only things you can do to protect yourself are the following:

1. Before hiring a contractor, subcontractor or ordinary workman, check him out with some of his previous customers: Was his work satisfactory? Did he complete it on the schedule he had agreed to? Did he stay within the price he had set? Did he come back promptly to correct whatever mistakes he had made?

Since the great majority of complaints directed against men and firms in the building, remodeling and wall-decorating businesses fall within these four areas, you have probably found a gem if the answers you receive to all four questions are, "Yes." But if you get some "No's" along with the "Yeses," proceed with caution. And if there are too many "No's," find someone else.

2. If you can't find out very much about a contractor, check the Better Business Bureau. As a rule, this organization is unable to give any positive information about a contractor. All it can tell you is whether it has received complaints against him. But such a negative report can serve as a valuable warning either

to steer clear of the man or, if you still like him, to dig deeper into his background.

3. Secure several bids. This is especially important on large jobs; but it is a good way to protect yourself on small jobs, too. Getting bids is the only way to find out what your project is really worth; and it gives you a range of costs as well as a range of personalities to choose from.

In asking for bids, the most important thing is to make sure that each contractor is bidding on the same project. This means that all the contractors must come to your house and examine the walls you want to work on; and you must then describe to them—preferably in identical typewritten specifications—what you seek to accomplish. Thus you give yourself the most accurate possible basis for comparing the cost figures that are submitted for your consideration. You know, in effect, that you are comparing apple with apple, not apple with orange; so, if you find that one bid is much lower than the others, you can feel fairly safe in accepting it. (Nevertheless, to be perfectly safe, you should check again with the contractor to make sure he has not misinterpreted the project.)

Of course, this approach assumes that you have figured out—or that you have had an interior decorator, architect or knowledgeable friend figure out—exactly what should be done to your walls. What if you don't have any such blueprint? In that case, when you talk to contractors, you are really asking for ideas with price tags; and in the end, when you award a contract, you compare apple with orange, not apple with apple.

Many, many, many homeowners work this way; and since most are happy with the results, the approach cannot be called wrong. But it has two flaws.

First, the price you pay may be out of line with the work involved; but there is no way to tell this because only one contractor is bidding on his own idea. To be sure, you can take the idea and go back to the other contractors and request that they now bid on it. But to me that's unethical. A person who comes up with a good idea deserves to profit by it.

The second flaw is more serious: Contractors—I use the word loosely to cover all people who work, with their hands, on walls—are not noted for their good taste and sense of design. They know how to attach plywood paneling to studs, apply paint, hang wallpaper or whatever they do; but this doesn't mean that the particular paneling, paint, wallpaper, and so on that they suggest you use is going to add to your happiness and the beauty of the house.

Neither are contractors noted for objectivity or breadth of imagination. If you ask a man who sells hardboard what he suggests doing with a wall, he will recommend that you cover it with hardboard. If you ask another man who has no particular product ax to grind for his suggestions, he will nevertheless stick faithfully to materials he is familiar with and will ignore the materials he has never used.

Asking contractors for ideas about wall treatment is, in short, a good way to get a passable job, but not the very best job. I do not contend that this is not all you want or all you need. Few wall projects require the touch of a New York interior decorator or the equivalent. Just be warned.

4. Have a written agreement or full-blown contract with the contractor you hire. On major projects it's advisable to have a lawyer draw up a contract; on others, a less formal agreement drawn up either by the contractor or by you is probably enough. In any case, the document should include the following:

The name and address of the contractor.

A short but complete description of the work to be done and the materials to be used (be precise about name, grade, weight, style and so on).

The completion date.

The total cost and the schedule on which you are to make payments.

Guarantees on workmanship and materials.

A statement that the contractor carries workmen's compensation and liability insurance and is responsible for any claims for damages resulting from his work.

A statement that the contractor indemnifies you against liens on your home.

Before signing any agreement, read it carefully and make sure you understand every part of it.

• *The appropriateness of the wall-surfacing materials to the room and house.* It will be a long time before I forget our first visit to our present house. It was vacant and in disrepair; but what caught our eyes was its livability and fine Colonial lines. Elizabeth and our youngest daughter had wandered off into one wing in the tow of a real-estate agent while a second agent and I tarried behind to inspect the damage that had been done by water and time. Suddenly there were screams of amazement: "Stan, come here!"

My daughter rushed back to me: "You've just got to see this room."

I went scurrying. The reason for the excitement was apparent even before I was through the doorway. It was a large, high-ceilinged, sunken room—handsomely proportioned, with big windows, a good fireplace and two beautiful antique corner cupboards. But it was an absolute monstrosity. The walls were covered from floor to ceiling with dirty brown boards full of cracks, knotholes and knots. There were wide gaps between many of the boards, and in some places chunks had been knocked off the corners. And the fireplace wall looked as if, after it had been built, someone had cut openings in it willy-nilly and then filled them with boards that didn't line up with those above and below.

"What in the world ever happened?" I asked.

"I've heard Mr. Albert and one of the handymen he employed did it themselves," one of the real-estate agents said. "I don't know what they were trying to do."

"But the rest of the house is so well done. The details so perfect," Elizabeth protested. "This room doesn't belong at all. I mean the room itself is beautiful, but the walls are hideous—all out of place."

It was, in truth, a classic case of inappropriateness. If the house had been a remodeled barn, the crude board walls would have been acceptable (not desirable but pardonable). But in a well-detailed Colonial house—or in any other house of refined lines—they were incongruous.

(After four pints of spackle, one coat of stain-killer and two coats of paint, the eyesore was improved to the point where almost everyone who enters the room now exclaims over its beauty. But it will take major carpentry work on the fireplace wall before Elizabeth and I will be fully satisfied.)

I have seen many other walls which were inappropriate for the same reason—because somebody exercised poor taste. And I have also seen walls that were inappropriate because the surfacing materials were not suited to the ways the rooms were used or because they presented maintenance problems. For example, it is utter folly to build a child's room with gypsum board or insulating board on the walls within about 30 inches of the floor, because the child will sooner or later crash holes right through either material. It is also folly to cover kitchen walls with cork—as a famous magazine did recently—because the surface cannot be kept clean and unstained.

Unfortunately, it is impossible to set down rules that would keep you and other homeowners from making mistakes like these. But you can avoid the inappropriate if you make a practice of asking and answering certain questions before you decide how a wall should be treated:

Is the basic feeling imparted by the material traditional, modern or undated? If we think of materials strictly as materials—wood, stone, paint, glass—some are modern but most are undated. None is decidedly traditional. But when we look at materials as they are fabricated at the factory or handled in the house, we find stronger differences.

Wood, for instance, is suitable to any architectural style; but raised wood paneling of the type associated with the White House and other great early American houses is for traditional houses only. Plain board paneling, on the other hand, goes in modern houses as well as many traditional ones.

Similarly, wallpaper and vinyl wall coverings are universal materials; but only some of the patterns are universal. Most lend themselves either to traditional or to modern homes.

Hardboard, on the other hand, is a modern material; but whereas some designs of hardboard paneling are limited to modern architecture, others can be used in both modern and traditional architecture.

What is the style of the house? Fitting the wall material to the house depends, of course, on knowing the style of the house. It may be clearly traditional, clearly modern or nondescript. Of the three, modern gives the least trouble, because, while there are various schools of modern design, wall materials suitable to one are suitable to all. This is also generally true of traditional houses. But if you have a bona fide historical house, you have little latitude if you want the house to be an accurate reflection of its period. One of my close neighbors, for example, owns a small, simple New England farmhouse almost 250 years old. He is somewhat chagrined that when his parents bought and restored the place long ago, they covered the fireplace wall with raised paneling of pine. "It's lovely," Ham says, "but it's all wrong for a house of this type and period. It should be much simpler board paneling."

It can be dangerous to be too slavish to architectural style, however. One of the best examples of this I have seen (in a magazine) is a 1972 beach house more or less in the style of the gargantuan, Neo-Gothic ugly frame houses built in the famous beach resorts of the 1880s and 1890s. The interior walls and ceilings are covered with the same vertical tongue-and-groove wainscot boards (with small bead moldings down the center and edges of each board) which were often used in those old houses. This may make for sprightly conversation, but the effect is unfortunate. The boards were not attractive in the 19th century and they are not attractive today.

The same statement can be made about nondescript houses of all ages. They are rarely attractive, and for this reason they all too often have a depressing effect on their owners. In some cases, in an effort to compensate for the defects of the houses, the owners use wall treatments that are too grandiose. In other cases the owners are so discouraged that they unwittingly accentuate the nondescriptness of their houses by using too many different kinds of wall treatments.

Many traditional wall treatments are simply too formal, too refined, for houses lacking any architectural style. Simple modern treatments are better.

What is the shape and size of the room? Your choice of wall materials can have an influence on the appearance of the room. Dark materials will make it seem smaller; light-colored materials will make it seem larger. If you use a dark material on one wall, the wall is drawn in closer to the middle of the room, whereas if you use a light material, the wall recedes.

Materials with vertical lines make a room appear taller; those with horizontal lines make it wider. In two-story rooms, some people use both to good effect—horizontal materials in the lower half; vertical in the upper half. (What materials with diagonal lines do, I am not certain. Usually the effect is jazzy and cheap. I have thought it appropriate only to a few ultra-modern, multilevel mountainside homes with steep, angular roofs.)

Strongly textured or patterned materials help to conceal changes in a wall surface—whereas smooth, plain materials accentuate such changes.

How is the room oriented and how much light enters it? If a room faces south or west, it receives maximum sunlight; and the light itself is warm in color and temperature. Most people like this feeling so much that they choose wall materials and colors to accentuate it. But frequently a room receives so much sunlight—particularly harsh western light—that it is too warm and needs to be toned down with materials that give an illusion of coolness: tiles and plastic panels, or any light-blue or green-colored material.

A room that faces north or east represents a reverse situation. The light entering the room is cool, so the usual desire is to make the room feel warmer by covering the walls with materials suggesting warmth—natural wood and brick, for example.

A more practical question related to room exposure is what effect the incoming sunlight will have on the wall materials themselves. The power of the sun to fade fabrics is everyday knowledge. But many people fail to realize that it can also fade other, tougher materials. Paint, wallpaper, all other flexible wall coverings, wood, plywood and particleboard lose color quite rapidly if exposed for hours to the sun; and you must consider this fact when surfacing a sunny interior wall.

Is the room used more during the day or the evening? There is a great difference not only in the color of natural and artificial light but also in its intensity. For this reason, a room used mostly during the day may feel more comfortable if it has rather dark walls or strongly textured walls which absorb light than if it has bright, smooth walls. A room used mostly at night, however, should almost always have rather light, smooth walls.

Who uses the room—children, adults or both? By and large, children do more damage to walls than adults; so a room which is mainly for them should have exceptionally durable wall surfaces. The next most durable surfaces are required in a room used by adults and children. And the least durable surfaces are required in an adult's room.

But obviously, these statements are generalities. Some adults are much harder on a house than some children; and some dogs are harder than both. We have a big golden retriever named Joshua who delights in sleeping in a living-room corner behind a wing chair. We can't change his habit. Neither can we persuade him that if he wouldn't wedge himself into the corner, he wouldn't dirty the wall. In short, the only way we can cope with Joshua is to cover the wall with a material that can be readily cleaned with a damp sponge.

How is the room used? This affects wall-material selection in several ways. To begin with, if a room is used primarily for work, it must have light-colored walls, so you can see what you are doing. There is some sort of feeling on the part of Americans that, while they need excellent lighting in offices and factories, they don't need it in the home. Even architects, who need a great deal of light in their drafting rooms, seem to feel this way. They are all wrong. If low light levels save money on the electric bill, they cost money by causing injuries, breakage, losses and so on. And as for the architect- and decorator-sponsored idea that rooms with low light levels are most attractive —nonsense!

Rooms in which you need light, smooth walls so you can see better to work better, are —the kitchen, laundry, sewing room and any other room in which you do a lot of reading, writing or handwork.

But the main reason for analyzing how a room is used is to reduce maintenance. Home maintenance, like factory maintenance, is tedious and costly. It involves not only keeping the various parts of the house clean but also keeping them in sound, safe and attractive condition and replacing them if they are not. Most maintenance is corrective—fixing up things that have gone wrong. But the best maintenance is preventive—designing and building your house so that future trouble is averted or minimized.

I make no claim that the inside walls require more maintenance than anything else in a house. Floors, doors and stairs are just three of several areas that rank ahead. Even so, walls require a lot of attention. So it is of great importance that you build them properly.

Kitchen walls—particularly those nearest the range and sink, above work counters and in the immediate vicinity of a wall-mounted exhaust fan—must be surfaced with materials that are slow to soil and easy to wash when they do. This means, first of all, that they should have a smooth, textureless surface as free as possible of grease-catching joints. And they should be durable enough to withstand repeated washing with detergents or other cleaning compounds.

Bathroom walls must be unaffected by moisture and, behind the lavatory especially, they must be resistant to soap and drugs. But it is in a shower or tub enclosure that they take the worst beating—not just from water and soap but also from chemicals in the water. When Elizabeth and I built our previous house, we took pleasure in having all the bathroom walls covered with ceramic tile because in the house prior to that they had been plaster—and a headache. But, alas, the new tile walls in the tub enclosure proved to be anything but a joy, because our well water was full of iron and it stained the grout between the tiles badly. Only by hard scrubbing could we eradicate the stains —and then, in no time, they would appear again. That's why the new bathroom we built in our present house has laminated plastic walls around the tub.

As noted earlier, all children's rooms should have walls that resist battering—and, of course, abrasion. They should also be easy to clean. Family rooms should usually be treated in the same way.

Since walls in halls, especially narrow halls, and stairways are subject to a great deal of abrasion as well as soiling, they should be surfaced with materials which are resistant to both. Furthermore, since these walls are scratched laterally—parallel with the line of movement—the materials used should have a horizontal pattern or texture that would tend to conceal the scratches.

Is anything to be gained by mixing materials? Our forebears had the common though not universal habit of dividing interior walls horizontally into two parts. The lower part, usually about 30 to 36 in. high, was called the wainscot or, sometimes, the dado. Significantly, this was originally constructed of oak because its primary purpose was to reduce home maintenance by resisting damage caused by people banging into it, kicking it, scratching it and slamming furniture up against it. The upper part of the wall was usually covered with some less durable, contrasting material such as paint or paper.

Today, although wainscots are as practical as ever—particularly in children's rooms and heavy-traffic areas—they have largely gone out of fashion except in bathrooms, where ceramic tiles are used behind lavatories to a height of about 4 feet to protect the walls against splashing. It is, however, common practice to finish one wall in a room differently from the others and to cover a projecting fireplace and chimney breast in a material different from that on the adjacent walls. Such things are done primarily for aesthetic reasons—perhaps to relieve the monotony that might result from use of the same material on all walls; perhaps to make a special feature of the single wall; perhaps to change the apparent size or shape of a room; and so forth.

The effect thus achieved is often delightful; and this leads many a homeowner to think, well, if two materials are good, three should be gorgeous, and four—! Here's where trouble starts.

Even in a room with four matching walls, there is a wide assortment of materials: wood in the doors and trim; another kind of wood or some totally different material on the floors; glass in the windows; carpet; draperies; furniture upholstery and so forth. If these go well together, it is in good part because the walls act as a unifier. Making one or more of the walls of some new material therefore complicates the picture and simultaneously reduces unity.

This is not to say that a lovely room with walls of several materials or treatments is impossible to create. But it's best to leave the job to a skillful architect or interior decorator—and even that is risky. The simpler the wall treatment in a room, the more likely the room will be attractive.

This is also true of the walls throughout a house. The fewer the wall materials from room to room, the fewer the sharply contrasting patterns, the fewer the strong color contrasts, the more unified and restful is the effect. I am not suggesting that all the walls in your house should be smooth gypsum board painted the same color or covered with the same wallpaper. Heaven forbid! If you want to use natural-wood paneling in one room, paint in several others, wallpaper in several more and tile in the bathrooms, go ahead. There is no reason why you shouldn't also use different colors and different wall-covering patterns in the rooms. But as you move from room to room, you should not be assailed by startling contrasts in the wall surfaces.

The cost of the walls when completed. Although I give this as the final point to be considered when you undertake a wall project, it is highly possible that most homeowners think of it first. No matter. First or last, it is a point of considerable concern to everyone except the very well-heeled.

But unhappily, all building costs in the U.S. are extremely variable. They vary from region to region; from community to community within the same region; from building supplies firm to building supplies firm within the same town; from contractor to contractor; and from project to project. In short, the only help I can offer in this book is rather general.

The approximate cost of erecting the framework of a nonbearing stud wall is given in the next chapter. Costs of surfacing walls with the various materials available are given in Chapters 5 through 20. In all cases, the figures cover the cost of materials. Labor is omitted on the assumption that you will do the building.

2

Understanding Interior Walls

Interior walls are easy to understand. Yet as I start this chapter, it suddenly occurs to me that they are also a little confusing.

To begin with, walls that divide a house into rooms and other spaces may be called either interior walls or, simply, partitions. But there is another kind of interior wall which is not known as a partition, and therein lies one of the terminology problems we run into when discussing interior walls.

So, for the moment at least, let's forget the word *partition* and speak only of interior walls. There are four kinds:

1. Bearing walls. These are the walls that hold up the house. They bear the weight of the structure above. All the exterior walls of a house are bearing walls, but they are never known as such. It is only the interior walls that support the structure above that are called bearing walls; and as a rule, there are not many of these. Many houses, in fact, have no bearing walls at all because they are one-story buildings in which the roofs are supported by trusses resting on top of the exterior walls. Thus all the weight of the roof is borne by the exterior walls, and inside bearing walls are unnecessary.

2. Nonbearing walls. These, obviously, are inside walls that do not hold up the structure —you can knock them down if you want and the house will still stand as strong as ever. In houses with truss roofs, all the inside walls are nonbearing; in conventional houses, most inside walls are.

3. Dividers. These are a special kind of nonbearing wall. They got their name because, whereas nonbearing walls (and also bearing walls) are most often built with 2x4-in. studs sandwiched between the wall surfaces, dividers do not have this central timber framework. They don't need it because their only purpose is to divide rooms into two or more parts; and you can do this with just a single sheet of plywood, hardboard or the like.

Actually, dividers are built in countless ways. Some extend from floor to ceiling; some extend only part way to the ceiling (and perhaps only part way to the floor); some are made of glass (usually translucent, but occasionally transparent) or of pierced, honeycomblike materials which you can see, hear, blow and smell through. Other dividers have closets or cabinets at the base; open shelves for books and decorative accessories above.

There are even dividers that can be opened and closed. The most common are big, flexible units hanging from ceiling tracks that can be pushed open and shut. Laymen usually call them accordion doors, which is a perfect description. But while such doors *may* be used in homes—perhaps to separate the kitchen and dining areas or to divide a children's room into sleeping cubicles—they rarely *are*. So we'll ignore them.

We'll also ignore another kind of movable divider, but only after I've described it, because I have always been intrigued by it. You can see it in the Whitfield House in Guilford, Connecticut. Built in 1639, this is the oldest stone house in New England. The divider is a huge panel of wood across the middle of the living room. It is hinged to the ceiling so that it could be drawn up against the ceiling when the Whitfields wanted a big, open room; dropped down when they wanted to cut the room in two, to make it cosier on a winter night or to accommodate an oversupply of guests.

4. The interior surfaces of exterior walls. These are the interior walls which are not partitions. Strictly speaking, if you interpret the word *wall* to mean a structure with two sides, these are not walls at all—they are only surfaces. But most of us are in the habit of calling wall surfaces walls; and since these are the inside surfaces of the exterior walls, what are they but interior walls? Anyway, when you decorate a room, you are usually as much concerned with the inside of the exterior wall as you are with all the honest-to-goodness interior walls.

How to tell bearing walls from nonbearing walls. Most wall projects do not require that you differentiate between bearing and nonbearing walls. But any time you decide to rip out or move a wall, you must determine first—before you make any other move—which type of wall you are dealing with. The reason is obvious but bears emphasis: If you take out a bearing wall, part of the house may fall in. To prevent this eventuality, you must replace it with some other kind of support—usually a steel beam.

The difficulty in identifying a bearing wall is that it looks exactly like a nonbearing wall. What, then, do you look for?

If you know for a fact that your house has a truss roof, you have no worries, because, as I said earlier, none of the walls is a bearing wall. But if you don't know how your house is constructed, you might as well assume the worst until you can prove otherwise.

The joists in the house—the large horizontal timbers supporting the floors and to which the ceilings are attached—are the key to the puzzle. If the joists are parallel with the wall you want to remove, the wall is not a bearing wall; the joists are supported at the ends by the exterior walls. But if the joists are at an angle to the wall in question, and if the ends rest on top of the wall, it is a bearing wall. On the other hand, if the ends do not rest on the wall, it is a nonbearing wall.

To identify a bearing wall, in other words, you must see how the joists above it are laid.

One possible way to do this, if you have a one-story house or if the wall to be removed is on the top story of a multistory house, is to climb up into the attic and take a look.

The only other reliable approach is to make a hole through the ceiling next to the wall. Then poke a long, stiff wire through this, parallel with the wall. If the wire goes in several feet without striking an obstruction, it means that the joists are running parallel with the wall and the wall is nonbearing. But if you strike an obstruction, and if you then turn the wire around and poke it in the opposite direction and strike another obstruction, it means the joists are at an angle to the wall and that the wall may very possibly be a bearing wall. To settle the question once and for all, you must enlarge the hole enough so you can look into the joist space and see whether the ends of the joists are above the wall (it's a bearing wall) or whether the joists continue beyond the wall (it's a nonbearing wall).

Types of interior walls. Let me cover the unusual types first. Of the group, the most common are concrete block walls. These are used for all sorts of interior partitions in some houses in warmer climates; and regardless of where you live, you find concrete block walls in basements. Generally, the blocks, which measure 8x8x16 in., are laid up in a staggered pattern called a running, or common, bond. The blocks in the second course are centered directly over the joints in the first course; and from there on up, the blocks alternate. They are held together, of course, with concrete mortar.

I have never seen brick and stone used in interior partitions; but both are used to a limited extent in solid exterior walls. Thus you have an inside surface of brick or stone as well as an exterior surface.

In condominiums and other multifamily housing, walls between the dwelling units are very often of fireproof design, with a core of hollow building tiles cemented together and covered on the sides with plaster. Concrete blocks, which may or may not have plaster

surfaces, are used in the same way.

Interior walls within each dwelling unit in multifamily housing may be ordinary stud walls or constructed in various ways of steel and plaster or steel and gypsum board.

Stud walls. This is the way the vast majority of residential interior walls are built and it is also the way the vast majority of residential exterior walls are built (even when houses are covered with brick or stone siding). The walls are easy to construct; go up quickly; are strong enough to bear heavy loads and also strong enough to resist lateral pressure; have a hollow space through which pipes and electric cables can be run and serve as an excellent base for all wall-covering materials. The materials used in the framework only cost approximately $1.50 per ft. of wall.

Stud walls are normally built of 2x4-in. softwood timbers set at right angles to the face of the wall to make a framework with a nominal thickness of 4 in. Note that this is the *nominal* thickness. Actually, 2x4s measure only 1⅝ x3⅝ in., so the framework of a normal interior wall is really only 3⅝ in. thick.

Stud walls of other thicknesses are also built. Sometimes 2x3s are used to save a little money and space. If plumbing drains are made of cast iron rather than copper, the walls must be made with 2x6s to provide enough space for the pipe. If you need only a very thin wall, 2x4s are set parallel with the wall to make a framework with a nominal thickness of 2 in.

A stud wall rests on a horizontal timber called the *soleplate* or *sole*. In new construction, this is nailed to the subfloor, but in an existing house it is nailed over the finish floor.

The vertical timbers, studs, stand on the soleplate and are toenailed to it with 3½-in., 16-penny common nails. In construction parlance, the studs are usually spaced 16 in. on centers. This means the space from the center of one stud to the center of its nearest neighbor is 16 in. (The actual open space from the side of one stud to the side of the next is 14⅜ in.) This 16-in. spacing is used because all wall panels, such as plywood, are made in

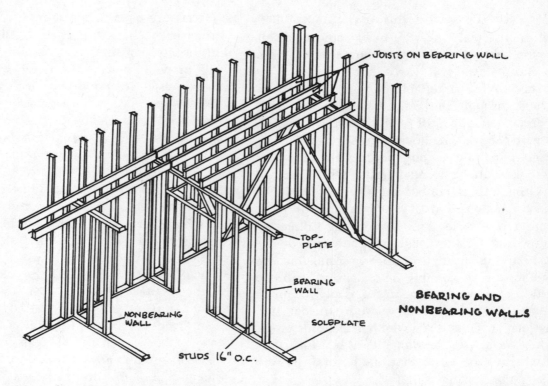

JOISTS ON BEARING WALL

TOP-PLATE

BEARING WALL

BEARING AND NONBEARING WALLS

NONBEARING WALL

SOLEPLATE

STUDS 16" O.C.

16-in. widths or multiples thereof. Occasionally, however, nonbearing walls are made with studs spaced 24 in. on centers while bearing walls are made with studs spaced 12 in. on centers.

The studs are held in place at the top by a horizontal timber called a *top-plate* or sometimes a *wall-plate*. In new construction, nails are driven through the top-plate into the ends of the studs, and a second top-plate is nailed above the first to give the wall extra weight-bearing strength. In an existing house with ceilings, however, the top-plate is erected against the ceiling and nailed through it to the joists; then the studs are toenailed to the plate.

If there is a door in a wall, a stud extending from soleplate to top-plate is placed on either side of the opening, and a second stud slightly higher than the door is nailed to each long stud on the door side. Two short pieces of 2x4 nailed together are placed across the tops of the short studs to form a header supporting the framework above. (*See drawing on page 29.*)

Windows are framed in the same way. However, in addition to the header at the top of the window there is a header at the bottom.

3

Building and Rebuilding Interior Walls

The hardest wall remodeling I ever undertook was the smallest. I wanted to close up an existing doorway from the front hall to the kitchen and open a new doorway through another wall. On the surface, the job looked easy; and the closing-up actually was easy. But making a new door opening was another matter, because as soon as I had removed the plaster I discovered that the wall had originally been an exterior wall and was framed with great ancient oak timbers put together with mortise and tenon joints. They clearly were not meant to be taken apart; and my attempts to whittle them down to make an opening of normal size were stymied by the steely hardness of the wood. In

the end, I had to settle for a doorway which was so low I ducked every time I went through.

Every once in a while an old wall presents complications like this. But it's foolish to waste time worrying about the possibility. Most walls are put together in routine fashion; and the problems encountered in those which are not can usually be solved.

How to knock out walls. If you are dealing with a bearing wall, call in a carpenter to take it out. It's a tricky business and requires a lot of muscle to set in the steel girder or heavy timber that must replace the wall.

But nonbearing walls are easy to handle. All you have to do is get yourself in a good savage mood and have at it. Be warned, however, that the lady of the house isn't going to like it. Taking out a wall makes the dust fly—especially if it is surfaced with plaster. So clear the area of furniture, rugs, draperies and pictures. Cover the floor with a heavy tarpaulin. And close the doors.

Remove the baseboards, ceiling moldings and other trim first. Since they are usually made of good wood, it pays to coax them out rather than rip. Furthermore, you must remember that it is virtually impossible to find in lumberyards new moldings which exactly duplicate old—and you often want to save the old. (However, I am happy to report a recent discovery: The Driwood Moulding Co., P.O. Box 1369, Florence, S.C. 29501, can supply accurate reproductions of almost every ornamental molding ever made. These are normally produced in poplarwood, but can be specially produced in walnut, oak, mahogany and so on. Prices for poplarwood moldings range from about 25¢ to $4.50 per lineal ft.)

Removing the wall surfaces is destruction pure and simple. You cannot save gypsum board or other composition wall panels any more than you can save plaster. Wood paneling, plywood and hardboard paneling are the only things that come out more or less intact—and after you have wrestled with them for a while, it is usually a case of less rather than more.

Studs are more readily salvaged, but still it's a tedious job, because you must pull the nails, securing them at, say, the bottom before you can twist them loose at the top. For a nail puller, use a wrecking bar with a claw. But even if you get all the nails out without too much of a struggle, the studs are weakened by the holes left in them.

When the studs are out, remove the plates.

One rule I urge you to follow when you are destroying a wall is to pull all the nails from each piece as you take it out. I know it seems a waste of time: You are eager to get the wall down as quickly as possible. But it is an excel-

lent safety practice. I once stepped on a nail sticking out of a board and, I can tell you, it was no fun. Besides, if you leave the nails in studs and the like, you will almost certainly scratch up the house as you carry the material down to the basement or out to the garage.

Electric cables and pipes that you find in a wall must, of course, be relocated. Sometimes this is easy—particularly in the case of cables, which bend and may have considerable slack. But don't count on it. That's why it isn't wise to rush into removal of a wall that you know to contain cables and pipes.

The final step in taking out a wall is to fill the gaps left in the ceiling, abutting walls and floor. If the ceiling and abutting walls are plaster, you can patch them with plaster (*see Chapter 10*). But I favor an easier repair which is equally applicable to ceilings and walls made with other materials. Nail strips of gypsum board into the gaps flush with the existing surfaces; then cover the repaired surfaces with several coats of gypsum board cement.

Gaps in a floor are much more difficult to fill so that they are not eyesores. In fact, you can accomplish this trick only if the finish floor is made of boards paralleling the wall removed. In this case, all you have to do is cut new flooring boards to fit and nail them down. But if you have floor boards running at right angles to the removed wall or if the floor is made of any kind of tile, you're out of luck. The only thing you can do—short of laying an entirely new floor—is to fill the gap with any kind of boards of the appropriate thickness and then carpet the floor wall to wall.

Building a new stud wall in a finished room. The important thing to remember in building a wall is that it must be firmly anchored at top and bottom. Because most floors are wood, bottom anchorage is usually easy. But at the top, unless the ceiling happens to be made of wood (which is unlikely), the wall must be attached to the joists; it cannot simply be nailed to the plaster or gypsum board. If the new wall is at an angle to the joists, it is attached to each of

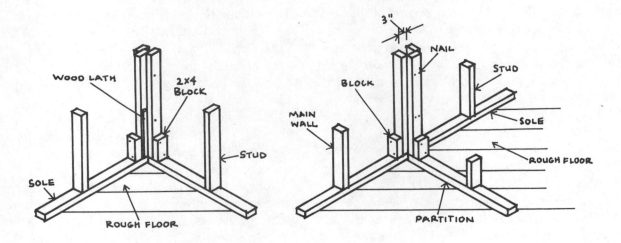

the joists. But if a wall parallels the joists, you should, if possible, build it directly under one of them. This means that before starting construction, you must locate the joists by tapping the ceiling with a hammer or drilling small holes.

Pry the baseboards and ceiling moldings from existing walls which the new wall will butt against.

Draw the outline of the top-plate on the ceiling; then drop a plumb line from this and mark the location of the soleplate on the floor. (Use of a plumb line assures that the wall will be absolutely vertical. Making measurements with a rule is unreliable, because the walls, ceiling and floor in a room are almost always out of square.) Cut the two plates to the required length and nail one to the floor with 3½-in. nails. Use 4- to 5-in. nails, depending on the thickness of the ceiling surface, to attach the top-plate.

Starting at either end of the wall, mark the location of the studs on both plates. (If the last two studs are less than 16 in. apart, don't eliminate the next-to-last one.) Then cut the studs to fit between the plates, and toenail them in place at each end with three 3½-in. nails. You

are now ready to surface the wall and—the very last carpentry step—install baseboards and ceiling moldings (if any).

As this description indicates, construction of a new inside wall presents little trouble. Special steps are taken in only four situations:

1. If you build two new walls coming together at a corner, the studs at the corner must be installed so that you can nail up gypsum board or another type of wall panel to form a sound outside corner and also to provide a nailing base for gypsum board inside the corner. This is accomplished with three studs nailed

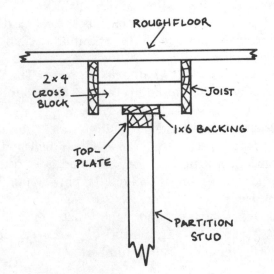

together as in drawing on page 23 at top left. Drawing on page 23 at top right shows how the studs are arranged when one wall is built perpendicular to the middle of a second wall.

2. If you build a wall parallel with but between two ceiling joists, cut out the ceiling between the joists and nail 2x4 cross-blocks to them. The bottoms of the blocks are 25/32 in. (the actual thickness of a 1-in. board) above the bottoms of the joists. A 1-in. board about 6 in. wide is then nailed to the bottoms of the blocks to provide a nailing base for the ceiling surface, and the top-plate is nailed to this. *(See drawing on page 23 at lower right.)*

3. If the wall is erected in a basement or a room with a masonry floor, the soleplate should be fastened with screws driven into hollow lead anchors set into the floor. The alternative is to embed the soleplate in silicone-rubber adhesive spread in a thick strip on the floor; but this should be done only if the wall will not be subjected to lateral pressure.

4. If the room in which you build a new wall is not too cramped, and if you are certain that the floor and ceiling are parallel, it is easier to construct the framework for the wall on the floor and then to raise and nail it into place. When doing this, however, you must make the wall ½ to 1 in. shorter than the height of the room and 1 to 1½ in. narrower than the width of the room; otherwise you cannot set it in place without getting it wedged at an angle or without scraping the ceiling and walls. Once the wall is erected, jack it up on blocks or boards so that it touches the ceiling. Similar wedging is necessary at one or both ends.

Building a divider in an existing room. There are so many ways to build dividers that I limit myself to just a few "for instances."

Screen walls. These are nothing more than a single thickness of material such as plywood, translucent plastic or glass, installed as a rule in rather large panels. To hold the panels, build a framework which consists, in essence, of a top-plate, soleplate and studs between the panels. Since the framework is exposed, it should be made of select lumber.

Attach the top-plate to the "studs" with nails driven through the plate into the ends of the studs. Thus the nails are concealed. Then nail the top-plate to the ceiling joists as when building a conventional stud wall, and toenail the studs to the soleplate. To hide the nails, drill small holes for them, use finishing nails, countersink the heads and cover with an appropriate filler.

Center the panels in the framework and hold them in place with small quarter-rounds or other moldings nailed around the four edges on both sides.

Storage walls. The easiest way to construct these is to build boxes of plywood, set them in place in the room and screw them together. The boxes can be tall and closetlike, or they can be made in smaller sizes and stacked. Nail or screw the boxes directly to the floor or raise them off the floor to the height of the baseboards. Attachment to the ceiling is unnecessary because of the wall's thickness and weight. Many storage walls are, in fact, only 6 or 7 ft. high. On the other hand, if you want a wall to appear built-in, install moldings or soffit boards between the top of the wall and the ceiling.

Shelf dividers. These are made with telescoping posts wedged between the floor and ceiling. Brackets which lock into slots in the posts support shelves on one or both sides of the posts. Complete systems for erecting shelf dividers are sold in department stores.

Closing door and window openings. This is a quick-and-easy project. To close a door opening, remove the trim around the opening and the door jambs. Cut a 2x4 the width of the opening and nail it to the floor between the studs. Then cut a new stud to fit between the newly installed soleplate and the header, and erect it in the center of the opening.

Out of ½-in. gypsum board, cut two pieces to fill the opening on either side of the wall. If the existing wall surfaces are ½ in. thick, the new gypsum board panels are nailed directly to the studs, plate and header. However, if the wall surfaces are thicker than ½ in., you must first tack thin wood strips to the framing. Seal

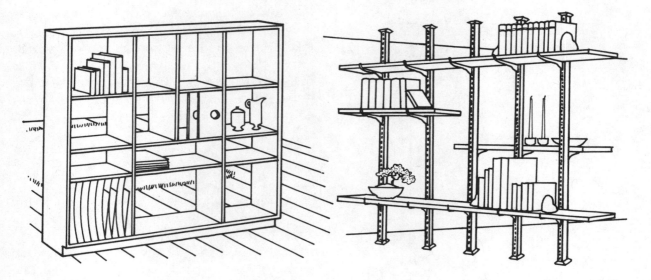

the cracks around the new panels with gypsum-board cement and tape. See Chapter 9.

Window openings are closed in the same way after removal of the trim and window frame. Depending on the width of the opening, install one or more studs between the top and bottom headers.

Hanging a door in a new wall. Interior doors come in standard widths of 24, 28, 30, 32 and 36 in. The usual height is 6 ft. 8 in. Before constructing a door opening, you must decide which size of door you are installing. The rough opening should then be made the width of the door plus 1½ in. to allow for the two side jambs, plus 1 in. to allow for adjustments. The height of the rough opening should be the height of the door plus ¾ in. for the top jamb, plus 1 in. for adjustments. In other words, the rough opening for a 30-in., 6-ft.8-in. door (the commonest size) should measure 32½ in. by 6 ft. 9¾ in.

To install a door of this size (or any other size), build a new stud wall as described above. Nail the top-plate and soleplate into place and mark the location for the rough door opening on the top-plate; then drop a plumb line and mark the location on the soleplate. Measure 1⅝ in. to both sides of the opening and install studs extending from the soleplate to the top-plate at these points. Now cut 2x4s to a length of 6 ft. 8⅛ in. (the height of the rough opening less the thickness of the soleplate). These are called cripple studs because they are less than the full height of the wall. Nail one to the door side of the left-hand stud previously installed and the other to the door side of the right-hand stud. This gives you a rough opening 32½ in. wide.

Cut another 2x4 into two 35¾-in. lengths; place one on the other and nail them together; then nail them across the upper ends of the cripple studs to form the header.

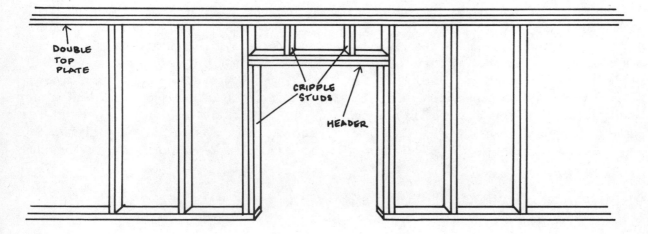

DOUBLE TOP PLATE

CRIPPLE STUDS

HEADER

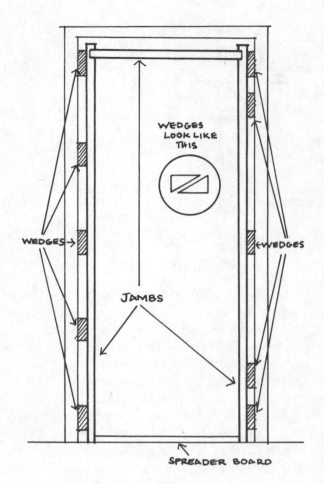

WEDGES
LOOK LIKE
THIS

WEDGES→

←WEDGES

JAMBS

SPREADER BOARD

Cut two short lengths of 2x4 to fit between the top of the header and the top-plate and nail them into place. These are also called cripple studs. They should be placed so they divide the space above the rough opening into three equal spaces.

When you cut out the soleplate between the first pair of cripple studs, you have completed the rough opening and you are ready to turn from the door and complete the construction and surfacing of the rest of the wall. Then back to the door.

Door jambs for doors of any size can be ordered ready for installation from a lumberyard. Made of 1-in. pine, they should be $\frac{1}{16}$ in. wider than the wall thickness. Insert the short head jamb into the notches cut in the side jambs and nail the three pieces together. Then set the frame in the center of the rough open-

ing, and, using a carpenter's level, make sure the head jamb is level. It may be necessary to take a little off the bottom of one of the side jambs to level the head jamb. Make sure also that the side jambs project the same distance to the front and back of the wall and that they do not slant forward or backward.

Taking pains to square the ends, cut a 6-in. board to fit exactly between the side jambs just below the head jamb. Place this on the floor between the side jambs.

Determine which way the door will swing and measure the thickness of the door (usually 1$\frac{3}{8}$ in. for interior doors) plus $\frac{1}{16}$ in. from the front edge of the jamb to which the door will be hinged. Draw a faint pencil line from top to bottom at this point. Do the same thing on the latch jamb. The lines mark the positions of the stops that will be applied later.

Cut several cedar shingles into narrow strips to serve as wedges and insert two of these between the hinge jamb and the adjacent cripple stud at the level of the head jamb. Drive the wedges from opposite directions so that they overlap and make a block of the same thickness at both edges of the jamb. Then drive two more wedges in the same way behind the latch jamb.

Repeat the procedure at the bottom of the door opening. Then, with a carpenter's level or plumb line, check whether the hinge jamb is plumb. If not, adjust the wedges at the bottom of the opening. Then drive a finishing nail through the jamb into the cripple stud at top and bottom; but let the heads protrude enough so they can be pulled if this becomes necessary.

Plumb the latch jamb and nail it in place.

Now insert additional double wedges behind both side jambs. On the hinge jamb, install one double wedge half-way up the door opening; a second wedge 11 in. up from the floor; and a third wedge 7 in. down from the top jamb. On the latch jamb, install one double wedge 3 ft. up from the floor (the location of the latch); another about 18 in. below this; and a third about 22 in. above. When installing these wedges, make certain that they fill the gaps between jambs and cripple studs exactly, otherwise the jambs will be crooked when nailed. Secure the jambs to the cripple studs with two finishing nails driven through each of the eight double wedges. Countersink the nail heads when you are satisfied that the jambs are straight and true.

The doorway is now trimmed on both sides with simple boards or milled lumber. The material is called trim or, more properly, casings.

The edges of the casings are placed $\frac{5}{16}$ in. back from the jamb faces. The upper corners of the casings may be mitered to 45° angles, or the side casings may be cut off square at the top of the door opening and the head casing butted to them. Nail the casings to the jambs and also through the wall surface into the studs.

After the casings are completed, cut the stops to the height of the side jambs and the width of the head jamb. Nail them along the pencil lines on the jambs. Drive the nails in only part way.

The actual hanging of a door is a slow, exacting operation. You need two sawhorses to rest the door on when sawing, and a portable vise which can be clamped to one of the sawhorses to hold the door straight up and down when you plane the edges. Lacking a vise, you should make a T-shaped door jack of boards to hold the door.

How much fitting of the door you must do depends on how carefully you have completed the door opening. The perfect fit calls for $\frac{1}{16}$-in. space between each side edge and the adjacent jamb and between the top edge and head jamb. At the bottom, the door should be cut so it clears the floor or carpet by about $\frac{3}{8}$ in.

First place the door flat on the sawhorses and saw the projecting lugs off the top and bottom edges. Then set the door in the door opening and note whether the hinge edge must be planed to comform with the hinge jamb.

If the door is a little too wide for the opening, draw a line along the latch edge; set the door on the floor and clamp it upright; plane down the edge. To permit the door to close without binding against the jamb, the latch

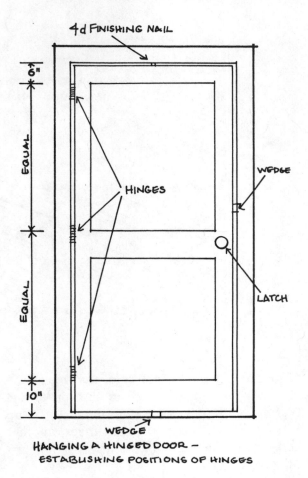

HANGING A HINGED DOOR — ESTABLISHING POSITIONS OF HINGES

edge must be beveled very slightly toward the back of the door.

Set the door in the opening once more and drive a wedge underneath to force it up against the top jamb. Draw a line on the door parallel with the jamb. This is called scribing. Then plane the top of the door to this line.

If you know the floor is level, you can cut off the bottom of the door at this time; but it is safer to wait until the door is hung so you can swing it and determine whether the bottom has to be cut off more than anticipated or has to be cut on an angle to clear a hump in the floor.

Set the door in the opening again and force it against the hinge jamb with a wedge inserted along the latch jamb. Put a 2-in. common nail on top of the door and force the door up against this with a wedge under the door. Mark the hinge locations on both the door and the jamb

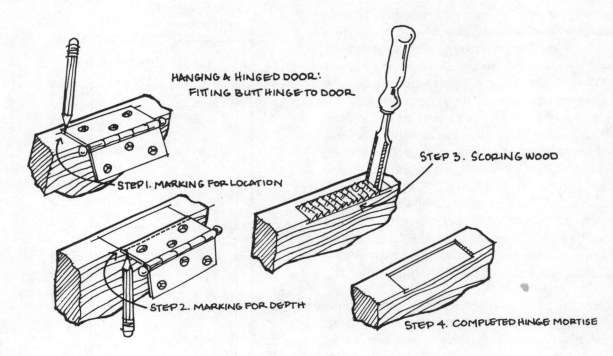

HANGING A HINGED DOOR:
FITTING BUTT HINGE TO DOOR

STEP 1. MARKING FOR LOCATION

STEP 2. MARKING FOR DEPTH

STEP 3. SCORING WOOD

STEP 4. COMPLETED HINGE MORTISE

with a sharp pencil. As a rule, the top of the top hinge is 7 in. down from the top of the door; the bottom of the bottom hinge 11 in. up from the floor. However, if the hinges on other doors in the room are placed at other heights, follow suit here.

The hinges for interior doors are swaged butts with loose pins. Use hinges 3½ in. long on doors up to 32 in. wide; 4-in. hinges on wider doors. The best way to mark the hinge mortises on the edge of the door and the jamb is with an inexpensive little tool called a butt marker. You just hold it against the wood and rap it with a hammer. Another, more expensive tool used for the same purpose is a butt gauge. But you can also mark the mortises with a pencil and square. In this case, remember that the open edge of each hinge leaf is set in ¼ in. from the back of the door and is set in from the stop on the jamb the same distance.

To make the mortises, also known as gains, cut along the lines with a sharp knife and chisel. Then, with the chisel, make a series of closely spaced crosswise cuts from one end of the mortise to the other. Scrape and cut out the chips, smooth the bottom of the mortise, and

set in the hinge to test the depth and evenness of the mortise. The hinge leaves should be flush with the surrounding wood.

After removing the pins, screw the hinge leaves into the four mortises. Be sure to install them so the pins will be at the top. If you don't drive the screws down tight at this time, it is easier to fit the leaves on the door into those on the jamb when you hang the door. Proceed to tighten the screws and check whether the clearance on both sides of the door is even. If the crack at the hinge jamb is too wide, deepen the mortises in the jamb slightly. On the other hand, if the door binds against the jamb, insert strips of cardboard in the mortises.

After determining the proper spacing between the bottom of the door and the floor, take the door down and cut it. Then install the latch. The easiest type is a tubular unit. Full directions for making the installation come with it. All you have to do is bore a large hole through the face of the door for the knobs, a smaller one into the edge for the tongue. Slip the pieces into place and bolt them together. Then complete the job by cutting a mortise in the jamb and screwing on the strikeplate.

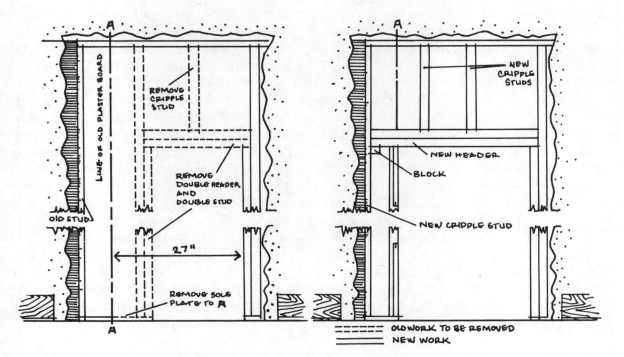

Now reset the stops as necessary so that the door is snug against them when closed.

Hanging a new door in an existing wall. Unless it is imperative to do otherwise, hang the door next to a stud and save yourself a little work. If you are installing a 24-in. door, measure 30⅜ in. to the left or right of the stud. This should bring you to the second stud from the starting point. If you are installing a wider door, which is probably the case, measure 46⅜ in. to the third stud. Carefully cut out the wall surfaces between the studs all the way up to the ceiling and remove the two intermediate studs.

Nail cripple studs 6 ft. 8⅛ in. long to the studs on either side of the opening. Then lay a double header across them and install short cripple studs between this and the top-plate.

Measure the width of the door plus 2½ in. from the first cripple stud and install a third cripple stud between the soleplate and the header. Then cut out the soleplate between these two cripple studs and your rough opening is completed.

The fitting and hanging of the door proceed as above.

Widening an existing doorway. This is done in the same way that you install a new door in an existing wall.

Making a doorway narrower. This can be done by moving both side jambs closer together or by leaving one side jamb in place and moving the other toward it. Since the latter procedure requires less work, I'll opt for that; but the technique is the same in both cases.

Remove the trim, head jamb and latch jamb. From the hinge jamb, measure the width of the new door plus 1¾ in. and mark the floor and header at this point. Then cut a 2x4 to serve as the soleplate between the old plate and this mark and nail it to the floor.

Cut a cripple stud to fit between the new plate and the header on the latch side of the door and nail it in place. Then cut the old head jamb to the width of the new door plus the depth of the mortises in the side jambs and fit it into the side jambs. Continue from here as when hanging a door in a new wall.

Installing and moving windows. Despite the fact that many windows come completely assembled except for the interior trim, installation is not for the amateur—especially in an existing wall. There simply are too many problems in waterproofing and replacement of the exterior siding. In addition, you must cope with varying wall constructions and thicknesses, not to mention varying window constructions.

I admit that if you are the least bit venturesome, you will be challenged by this negative attitude. Making a rough opening for a window is no more difficult than making one for a door. You need only a double header beneath, a double header above and double studs (cripple or otherwise) on both sides. And finishing the inside wall around the window presents no difficulties either—it's the exterior work which is troublesome.

Furring out walls. Furring out means to build out from an existing surface. When we're dealing with walls, it means to apply wood furring strips to the surface of an existing wall in order to provide a nailing base for a new surface.

The walls which are most commonly furred out are those in basements and others made of masonry. The purpose is to simplify the attachment of a new surface and it is also done, especially in basements, to provide an air space between damp masonry and the surface.

Other walls are furred out when they are so skew-gee that it is the only way you can make them square and vertical. And still others may be furred out when they are in such bad repair that you cannot apply a new surface directly to them and when you do not choose to knock them out completely.

Furring is done with rough 1x3-in. boards. If they will be exposed to dampness, they should be treated with wood preservative after they are cut to size and before they are put in place.

The strips are installed either vertically or horizontally. Vertical installation is made if the wall is to be covered with large panels such as gypsum board or plywood. The first step is to install a horizontal strip at the top of the wall (this corresponds to a top-plate). A horizontal strip at the base of the wall is also required if there isn't a baseboard; but if you have a baseboard, it may be omitted. Then install vertical strips from floor to ceiling on 16-in.

centers. On a stud wall, place the strips over the studs. This arrangement assures that all four edges of the gypsum board, or whatever, panels will rest on furring strips and won't give if you push against them.

The usual reason for installing horizontal furring is because you are going to cover the wall with vertical boards which are rigid enough not to require nailing along the sides. However, if the studs in a wall are not spaced on 16-in. centers, you might well use horizontal furring for applying large panels. In both cases you should install strips at the top and bottom of the wall. For vertical board paneling, install three additional strips in between; for large panels, install four strips in between. In a large-panel installation you also need vertical strips under the edges of each panel.

When furring out a stud wall, the strips are nailed into the studs and plates. Special anchors are required on masonry walls. The most popular, because they go in fastest and have exceptional holding power, are heat-treated steel studs or pins. These are driven through the furring strips into the masonry either with a pistol-shaped tool using gunpowder or with a stud driver actuated by hammer blows.

Another type of anchor is a large, flat, perforated steel plate with a nail in the center. The plate is glued to the wall with silicone-rubber adhesive. The furring strip is then hammered down lightly over the nails to mark their locations. Drill holes through the strip; reset the strip over the nails; and clinch the nails.

Applying trim. Trim comes under the general heading of woodwork, although door casings and jambs are sometimes fabricated in one-piece units of steel (they are not very attractive). The pieces of trim most often used in association with walls are: baseboards with shoe moldings and sometimes base-cap moldings; door casings; the casings, aprons and sills (also called stools) around windows; chair rails; picture or cornice moldings; and panel moldings. Most of these pieces serve functional as well as aesthetic purposes.

Door and window trim covers the open joints

between the frames and the surrounding wall surfaces. When constructing a new wall, therefore, you must complete the wall surface before applying the trim. If you are resurfacing a wall with a thick material such as gypsum board or plywood, you should remove the trim before applying the new surface.

Baseboards conceal the bottoms of walls, thus making it unnecessary to finish the walls carefully at this point. They also protect the wall surfaces against scuffing and banging. The joints between the baseboards and the floor are covered with shoe moldings (also known as base shoes). These are usually small quarter rounds but may be of more elaborate design. They are held in place with finishing nails driven diagonally into the subfloor through the joint between the baseboards and the floor.

Base-cap moldings are nailed along the top edges of baseboards for decorative purposes only. Because of this and because they add to the cost of building, they are rarely used in today's homes. If you desire a baseboard that is a little more attractive than an ordinary, square-edged board, you can buy several designs with specially milled top edges.

Baseboards, shoes and cap moldings are the last or almost the last things installed when a wall is built or rebuilt. They are always installed after the door casings.

Chair rails have also gone out of style. But in dining rooms, where all the chairs have backs of the same height and some of the chairs are placed against the wall, they help to protect the wall surfaces. They can also be a delightful decorative feature. Installation is made directly to the finished walls at a height of about 30 to 48 in. Use finishing nails long enough to penetrate well into the studs.

Picture moldings and cornice moldings are used alternately at the tops of walls. The former are actually installed about ½ in. below the ceilings, so that S-shaped hooks can be slipped over them to hang pictures and mirrors on long wires. They thus become dust-catchers *par excellence*, which is one reason not to use them. The other reason not to use them is that today pictures and the like are usually hung on hooks driven directly into wall surfaces. One advantage of picture moldings, however, is that they conceal poorly made joints between walls and ceilings. But cornice moldings do this even better, because they form an angle across the joints. In addition, they are more attractive and do not catch dust.

Panel moldings in modern construction are used mainly to cover vertical joints between large panels of plywood, hardboard and so on. For the most part these are small and of rather plain design. More elaborate moldings are occasionally applied right on painted walls to divide them into decorative panels.

All trim is applied with finishing nails; and the heads are countersunk and then covered with spackle (if the trim is painted) or with plastic wood (if the wood is given a natural finish).

At corners, wide pieces of trim such as casings are joined either with simple butt joints or 45° miter joints. Both are easy to make, but you should use a miter box for the latter. The alternative is to draw the angle with a combination square or try-and-miter square.

Baseboards are joined by setting one all the way into a corner and then butting the other against it. In the event that the second board does not rest snugly against the first because the wall behind the first is irregular or slanting, the end of the second must be scribed. To do this, set it on the floor and push it up against the first board as far as possible; open a pair of dividers or a compass about 1 in.; hold one leg against the first board and the point of the other against the second board; slide the leg down the first board. This marks a parallel line on the second board. Saw along this line.

Moldings are joined in corners either by miter or coped joints. The miter joints, which must be made with a miter box to assure accuracy, are preferred at outside corners because they conceal the end grain of the moldings. They may also be used at inside corners; but coped joints are better because, if the wood shrinks, the cracks are less noticeable. As

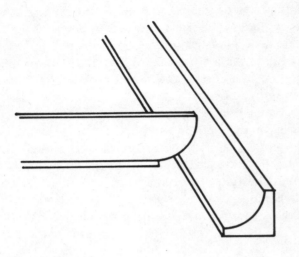

shown in the above drawing, a coped joint is actually a butt joint; but the butted end is shaped to fit the face of the molding against which it rests.

Joining of short pieces of molding in a straight line should be avoided, if possible, because the joints are difficult to conceal, no matter how carefully you fill them. If you can't help yourself, however, never simply butt a square end to a square end. Cut the ends at 45° angles, overlap them and hold them together with a brad.

Soundproofing walls. In most houses built since World War II, sound travels from room to room and even from one end of the house to the other as if the walls and ceilings were made of cheesecloth. Why has the problem become so serious? Simply because thick plaster walls have generally given way to thin gypsum board walls. Wall density, in short, is one of the keys to the quiet house.

This is not generally understood, for the simple reason that manufacturers of acoustical tiles tend to imply in their advertising that if you want peace and quiet, all you have to do is cover your ceilings and perhaps upper walls with their products. That just is not true. Acoustical tiles are valuable for soaking up and reducing the noise within a room. But they have

very little effect on the noise traveling to and from neighboring rooms.

In the chapters dealing with specific wall-surfacing materials, suggestions are made for improving sound control if it is likely to be an annoying problem. Here we are concerned only with gypsum board and plaster, the two most common surfacing materials; and the answer in both cases is not to skimp on the thickness applied. For instance, 3/8-in. or 1/2-in. gypsum boards on both sides of a wall are woefully inadequate. For good results, use 3/4-in. plaster. And for better results, use 1/2-in. gypsum backer board or sound-deadening fiberboard covered with 1/2-in. plaster or 1/2-in. or 5/8-in. gypsum board.

Best results are achieved in a new partition by framing it with 2x3-in. studs staggered so that they touch only one wall surface and cannot transmit sound from one side of the wall to the other. Then cover both sides of the framework with the two layers of material recommended above.

In the case of an old partition surfaced with 3/8-in. or 1/2-in. gypsum board, the easiest way to improve sound control is to apply another layer of gypsum board directly on top. But best results are gained by leaving the partition as is and erecting a second framework of plates and studs against one side. These need be only a nominal 2 in. thick. Place the studs so they are not directly behind those in the old partition. Then cover the new framework with one or, better, two 1/2-in. layers of gypsum board.

Regardless of the way a wall is built, one other step is necessary if a vertical copper drain-pipe from an upstairs toilet is hidden in the wall. Unlike the cast-iron drains of the past, copper drains are made of very thin metal—when a toilet is flushed, the water rushing through them sounds like Niagara Falls. To prevent this, the pipe should be slanted as much as possible to slow the flow and should be wrapped either in Armstrong Armaflex or in several thicknesses of asphalt building paper which is then overwrapped with fiberglass insulation.

4

Hanging Things on Walls

In recent years I have conducted several home-repair courses; and in every class, the subject of hanging pictures, mirrors, shelves, draperies and so forth on walls has aroused more questions than anything else. I am not surprised. One of the main purposes of walls is to hold things so you can look at them or use them, and it has been that way for eons. Early man painted pictures directly on the walls of his cave until he discovered that it was easier to paint out in the sunlight on a dried lamb skin and then hang the pictures inside. But that's where he ran into trouble because, if you think it's hard to hang something on weak plaster, you ought to try it on sandstone.

Obviously, we are much better off today than the caveman. Even so, we have our problems, because there are so many variables to contend with . . .

- the construction of the wall (this involves the materials in the wall, how the wall is assembled and whether it is anchored to the ceiling);
- the physical condition of the wall (a wall with a sound surface is easier to hang something on than one with a weak, crumbling surface; but if the framework under the weak-surfaced wall is sturdy, you can hang anything on it you like—you just do it in a different way);

- the weight of the object being hung;
- the shape of the object being hung (for instance, if it hangs flat against the wall, its pressure is exerted entirely downward, but if it projects out from the wall, as a shelf does, it pulls outward as well as downward);
- what if any weight or pressure is exerted on the object (for instance, most bathroom fittings such as soap dishes, toilet-paper holders and grab bars are leaned on or pushed by people);
- the permanence of the object upon the wall (actually very few things are left permanently on walls; the great majority—including many things that appear permanent—are taken down some time after they are hung; and this can make a difference in the way they are hung).

Yes, there are complications in hanging things on walls; but there are so many devices with which to do the job that you won't have to scratch your head too hard.

Nails and screws. I have hung many a picture, and the like, from ordinary nails and screws when I didn't happen to have a more suitable hanger. But this is not the main purpose of these common fasteners, which is to fasten things tight to a wall. And to do that they must be able to grip the wall. This they can do if you drive them into a stud or other wood-framing member. But if whatever you are hanging is not over a stud, nails and screws should be used only on wood paneling, plywood and particleboard more than ½ in. thick and on ¾-in. plaster.

Special hardened steel masonry nails can often be hammered directly into concrete, concrete and cinder blocks, bricks and the mortar joints between bricks and stones. The best type to use is a stout round nail with spiral grooves that give it excellent holding power. Flat, tapered, cut nails resembling those used in wood flooring are less good because they do not penetrate or hold so well.

Pegs. Cut from wood dowels to any length you like, pegs are sometimes used on wood-paneled walls to hold guns, hats and wet cloth-ing. To install them, just drill holes the same size as the pegs, coat the ends with glue and force them into place.

Picture hooks. These familiar hangers can be used on any wall into which the nails can be driven; but they are very unreliable on surfaces less than ½ in. thick unless the nails are driven into studs. The weight a hook will support is printed on the package. The smallest size supports 10 lbs., the largest, 100 lbs. For objects heavier than this, use two hooks spaced a foot or more apart. It's also wise to use two hooks for lighter objects if the wall surface is of dubious strength.

A simple trick to keep plaster walls from chipping when hanging a picture is to paste a little piece of masking tape to the plaster and drive the nail through this. Cellophane tape can also be used, but it makes a stain and is difficult to remove the next time you paint the wall.

Picture hooks that are riveted to gummed tapes are also available; but they are suitable only for small pictures and I have had no experience which makes me trust them even for these.

Wall hooks. Wall hooks resemble flat metal washers with a rounded hook at the bottom. They serve the same purpose as picture hooks but are only for very heavy objects, such as over-sized mirrors, because they are secured to walls with screws, nails or toggle bolts up to ¼-in. diameter.

Toggle bolts. Toggle bolts were the first gadgets invented for fastening objects—especially heavy objects and those subjected to external pressure—to hollow walls made of

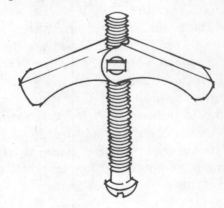

concrete blocks, cinder blocks and structural tiles and also to stud walls surfaced with materials which do not support other types of hanger. They consist of a long (up to 6 in.), slender bolt with a screw head, and a nut which is pushed into the wall cavity and then drawn up tight against the inside surface. In most toggle bolts the nut has two wings which fold back flat against the nut and then spring open once inside the wall. These are called spring-wing toggle bolts. Less common is the gravity toggle bolt with a one-piece nut which is pivoted so that it falls open by gravity.

To use either kind of toggle bolt, you must first drill through the wall surface a hole large enough to receive the nut. Herein lies one of the drawbacks of the gadget, because the hole is so large (⅜ in. for the smallest bolt) that: (1) It is sometimes visible after the object is hung; and (2) the slender bolt is hard to center firmly in the hole. Be that as it may, once the hole is made, remove the nut from the bolt and slip the bolt through the object you are hanging. Replace the nut and push it through the wall on the end of the bolt. Then pull the wings back tight against the wall and tighten the bolt. The pressure exerted on the face of the wall by the bolt head and the object under it, and on the back of the wall by the nut, is sufficient to support surprisingly heavy objects even on soft insulating board.

The bolt can be removed at any time; but when this is done, the nut falls to the bottom of the wall cavity and must be replaced.

Hollow-wall screw anchors. Also called Molly screws, these are slender bolts that are driven into cylindrical sleeves which expand and grip the inside surfaces of hollow walls.

Although the maximum length of hollow-wall screw anchors is just over 3 in., the devices can usually be substituted for toggle bolts (and vice versa). They have an advantage over toggle bolts in that they require a slightly smaller hole, completely conceal the hole and are centered in it. In addition, if you withdraw the bolt, the cylindrical sleeve remains in place. On the other hand, to use an anchor in a wall

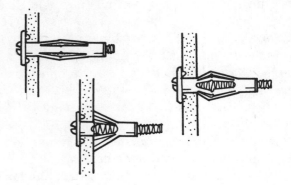

surfaced with ceramic tile or other very hard material, you must file off two sharp lugs designed to bite into the wall and keep the anchor from turning when you drive in the bolt.

To use most hollow-wall screw anchors, you must drill a hole through the wall. (One model, however, comes with a hard, sharp point, so you can drive it through gypsum board, plaster or insulating board with a hammer.) Withdraw the bolt from the sleeve, insert it through the object you are hanging and replace the sleeve. Then push the entire anchor through the wall and tighten the bolt with a screwdriver until the anchor is secure. During the tightening operation, if you find the sleeve turns with the bolt, ask your hardware dealer to give you a little wrench specially made to hold the sleeve.

Plastic, jute-fiber and lead anchors. These are excellent devices for solid masonry walls, and can also be used in hollow walls with thick surfaces—particularly plaster, ceramic tile, glass and plastics—if you don't elect to use toggle bolts or hollow-wall screw anchors. Plastic and jute-fiber plugs are especially suitable for installation in hollow walls and for supporting objects of medium weight. The larger lead anchors are mainly used in masonry and for heavy objects. But all work in the same way.

Drill a hole in the wall the same diameter as the anchor and slightly deeper than its length. In masonry, use a carbide-tipped bit in an electric drill or make the hole by hand with a star drill and hammer. In ceramic tile and glass, use an ordinary high-speed steel bit in an electric drill. Tap the anchor into the hole, flush with the wall surface. Insert a wood screw through the object you are hanging and drive it into the anchor, thus forcing the sides to expand tight against the hole. The screw must be of the gauge specified for the anchor you are using and it must, of course, be long enough to pass through the object being hung all the way to the tip of the anchor. (In other words, buy anchor and screw together.)

Nylon anchors. Nylon anchors are similar to the preceding but can be used not only in solid walls but also in very thin surfaces such as hardboard or ¼-in. plywood. The anchors expand when you hammer special screwlike pins into them.

Most nylon anchors have heads that project slightly above a wall surface, but one type can be set flush if you bevel the edges of the hole.

Expansion bolts. These are one-piece steel anchors for use in solid masonry. Shaped like a man with bowed legs, they are designed so that when you hammer them into a drilled hole of the prescribed diameter, the legs press so firmly against the sides of the hole that withdrawal verges on the impossible.

The bolts are made with different styles of head. For instance, one is similar to a flat screw head; another is threaded so you can screw on a nut.

Adhesives. The use of adhesive to attach furring strips to masonry walls is described in Chapter 3. Adhesives are also used to attach coat hooks and bathroom fittings to ceramic tile and other smooth walls you don't want to drill into. In these cases, the adhesive is supplied with the hooks and so on, and you simply squeeze it on the backs of the hooks and press them into place. The bond is surprisingly good.

If you want to fasten other things to walls with adhesives, there is no reason why you shouldn't. Use epoxy glue for the strongest possible bond of any material to any other material, or use contact cement for a slightly less permanent bond but one which is a lot easier to make because you don't have to hold the object being hung until the glue sets. I am,

however, hard put to think of many situations where adhesives are preferable to more conventional fasteners and hangers. And one thing definitely wrong with them is that you cannot remove the hung object without wrecking the wall.

Angle irons and shelf brackets. These simple L-shaped devices may be used to hang single shelves and other projecting objects. Installed with screws, they can be anchored directly—without other means of support—only to walls of wood or thick plywood or particleboard. On most other walls, the screws must be driven into the studs. And on masonry walls, secure anchorage is possible only by driving the screws into lead plugs.

Slotted shelf standards. These are long, straight, slender pieces of aluminum that are U-shaped in cross section and perforated from end to end with slots into which thin hanger brackets are hooked. Developed since World War II, the standards are widely used to cover sections of walls with cantilevered shelves for books, ornaments, phonograph records and the like.

Installation of slotted standards requires no skill, but it does require care, especially if you put up a lot of shelves and load them with weighty objects. More than one shelf-building project has ended in a thundering crash of books, shelves, metal strips and even large chunks of the wall itself.

The first step is to decide how many shelves you are putting in and how much space is needed between them. Then, with a hacksaw, cut the standards about 1 ft. longer than the planned distance between the top and bottom shelves, and draw a level line on the wall for the tops of the standards.

The number of standards needed depends on the length of the shelves. Shelves over about 5 ft. long can be allowed to overhang the end brackets as much as 12 in.; but on shorter shelves the overhang should be about half this, so there will be little chance of the shelves tipping if you happen to put a heavy weight on the overhangs.

But the main thing which determines the number of shelves is the spacing between them. Up to 24 in. is occasionally permissible; but a uniform 16-in. spacing makes a much stronger installation and is in many cases mandatory.

On walls surfaced with 1-in. boards or ¾-in. plywood, you can attach the standards anywhere you like. This is also true on masonry walls into which you drive lead anchors. But on all other walls the standards should be placed directly over the studs and screwed into them.

Before installing each standard, make sure that you have the top end up. I have a not-so-handy friend who neglected to do this, and it took him an hour after completing the shelves to figure out why he couldn't get them level.

Holding the first standard against the wall just at the top line, drive a screw through the top screwhole. Then plumb the standard with a plumb line or carpenter's level and insert a screw through the bottom hole. Install screws through all the holes in between. Then go on to the other standards.

When the standards are up, insert the shelf brackets in the slots and tap them down firmly so they cannot accidentally come loose, and lay the shelves across them.

A special kind of slotted standard which needs only one screw at the top to hold it secure is bent outward at the bottom and rests on the floor.

Pegboard. You may never have used pegboard, but it has been so well publicized that you undoubtedly know it well. It is ⅛- or ¼-in. hardboard perforated horizontally and vertically at 1-in. intervals. The holes hold a variety of hooks, brackets and the like for hanging tools and just about anything else you can think of. One piece of board is capable of supporting hundreds of pounds.

Pegboard is sometimes nailed or screwed directly to studs and used as a finish wall surface. *(Follow installation directions in Chapter 13.)* But it is usually applied in sections over an existing wall. In this case, it must be mounted at least ½ in. out from the wall, so the hooks can be inserted. For very small pieces of pegboard, this spacing is easily done with lengths of hollow metal tubing. Drive screws through these into the studs; or if the wall is surfaced with wood or plywood ¾ in. thick, the screws can be driven into this anywhere.

For larger sections (as well as small sections), mount the pegboard on wood furring strips securely anchored to the wall. If the articles to be hung on the pegboard are light, the furring strips need be no more than ½ in. thick; but if the load is heavy, use ¾- or 1-in. furring strips.

How to hang specific objects on walls. **Unframed mirrors.** If a mirror has holes drilled in the corners, it is hung by placing small metal

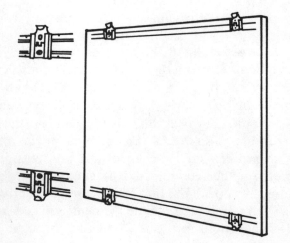

rosettes over the holes and driving screws through them into the wall.

Undrilled mirrors are sometimes stuck to a wall, if it is smooth and level, with silicone-rubber adhesive. This is spread in thick ribbons over 25 percent of the mirror back, and the mirror is then held in place until the adhesive sets. For security, the mirror should also have clips around the edges. Unfortunately, the installation is permanent.

The easiest and commonest way to hang mirrors is to clamp them to the wall with small mirror clips or two metal straps. The latter make a neater installation because they are almost completely hidden. You simply cut them to the width of the mirror and screw them to the wall (and into the studs if the mirror is large). Then attach permanent clips to the bottom strap, set the mirror in these and press adjustable clips on the top strap down over the top edge of the mirror.

Installation with mirror clips is simpler, regardless of the size of the mirror. Most clips are made of transparent white plastic with a ¼-in.-deep rabbet in the top to slip over the edge of the mirror, and a screw hole. The number of clips required depends on the size of the mirror and on how securely the clips can be screwed to the wall. There are no rules. To be on the safe side, I recommend one clip per stud across the bottom of the mirror if the wall surface will not hold screws. The equivalent spacing is advisable on wood-paneled walls and others that will take screws. Use half as many clips across the top of the mirror. One clip on either side is enough, except for tall mirrors.

Install the bottom clips first; make sure they are solid; set in the mirror and have a helper hold it while you install the top clips.

Kitchen cabinets. I am not going to go into the whole installation procedure. I just want to make one point: Kitchen cabinets should be hung with long wood screws—*not* with nails. The reason: You can't take down cabinets that are nailed up without damaging them so they cannot be used again—either in the kitchen or in the basement or garage.

The screws must be driven well into the studs. On masonry walls, drive screws into lead anchors; or hang the cabinets with expansion bolts with nuts on the exposed ends.

Bathroom cabinets. Hang surface-mounted cabinets like kitchen cabinets. If a recessed cabinet is small enough to fit in a stud space, simply cut a hole in the wall surface, nail a 2x4 cross-block between the studs at the bottom of the hole, set the cabinet in on this and screw it to the studs.

To recess a larger cabinet requires so much work that I question whether it's worthwhile unless you are ripping out the entire wall surface anyway. In that event, if you are installing a cabinet in a nonbearing partition, determine the position of the bottom of the cabinet (not the mirror), measure down from this 1⅝ in. and cut through the stud in the center of the space selected for the cabinet. Measure up from this point the height of the cabinet plus 4 in., cut the stud again and remove the piece. Frame the opening at top and bottom with 2x4 headers nailed to the studs on either side. Then mark the exact location of the cabinet and nail cripple studs between the headers. The space between the cripple studs should be about ¼ in. wider than the width of the cabinet. After surfacing the wall, set the cabinet into the opening and screw it to the cripple studs.

If the installation is made in a bearing partition, the headers should be doubled; cripple studs should be placed under the bottom header at both ends; and the cabinet opening should be framed with double cripple studs on both sides.

Fluorescent lights. Fluorescent lights are usually hung on walls in wood valances, brackets or coves. The long metal fixture, or channel, into which the tube is plugged is heavy; and although the wood shielding is comparatively light, it projects out from the wall so far that it exerts considerable downward and outward pull. Another complication in mounting a fixture stems from the fact that, in order to spread the light, the tube should be centered at least 4½ in. out from the wall; and if the light is

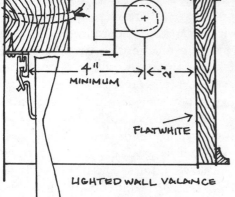

SHEILDING IN LINE WITH TOP OF CHANNEL, 12" BELOW CEILING, AND BEVEL TOP INSIDE EDGE 45°

4" MINIMUM

FLATWHITE

LIGHTED WALL VALANCE

over a draperied window, the tube should be centered at least 4 in. out from the drapery track.

To make the installation, cut a 1x3-in. board to the length of the fluorescent fixture, or to the length of the shielding board if that is longer. Nail this through the wall into the studs or fasten it with screws driven into lead anchors in a masonry wall. (The thickness of the board must be increased if the light is centered more than 4½ in. out from the wall.) Screw the fixture to the board.

The shielding board should be made with returns at the ends. These hide the ends of the fluorescent tube and also help to hold the shielding board on the wall. Actual attachment is done, however, with angle irons. If the light is no more than 6 ft. long, screw one angle iron to the inside surface of each return near the top. They should be in horizontal position. Then fasten the angle irons to the wall with screws driven into the studs or into lead anchors on masonry walls. Or use toggle bolts if the angle irons are attached over a hollow space.

On longer shielding boards, additional angle irons should be installed between the ends at 3- or 4-ft. intervals. Screw the angle irons vertically to the back of the shielding board and to the top of the board supporting the fixture.

Decorative fluorescent fixtures of the kind used in bathrooms around the medicine cabinet are hung directly on walls, with screws driven into the studs.

Incandescent lights. These must be connected directly to octagonal steel electrical boxes anchored inside the walls. To install a box, cut away part of the wall surface to expose two adjacent studs. A metal hanger available from an electrical store is then nailed to the studs and the box bolted to it. The alternative is to nail a board to the sides of the studs and screw the box to this. In all cases, the box is mounted so the rim is flush with the finished wall surface.

Outlets and switches. In a new wall, rectangular or square outlet and switch boxes are nailed to the sides of studs with the rims flush with the wall surface. Boxes made with attached nailing flanges are the easiest to put in.

In old walls, use boxes without nailing flanges. If possible, locate them so you can nail them to the sides of studs. This is not easy, as the boxes have small projecting ears for which shallow holes must be made in the studs and as the nails must be inserted at an awkward angle. However, the job can be done and produces the solidest possible anchorage.

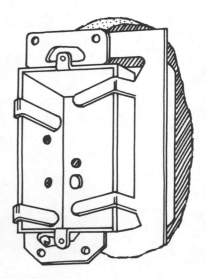

If a box is installed between studs in a wall that does not take or hold nails or screws, it is held in place—after you cut a hole for it—with metal box supports. These are thin, flat pieces of metal shaped like a T, but with two legs. They are installed with the legs in horizontal position; the crossbar upright. Slip the crossbar through the hole, pull it back against the inside-wall surface along one side of the hole and fold the legs back at right angles against the wall surface. Install the other support in the same way on the other side of the hole.

After connecting the box to the cable in the wall, push it into the hole until the small screw flanges at top and bottom are snug against the wall surface. Then bend the legs of the box supports around the edges of the box and press them flat against the inside surfaces. The box is now secure, although it will probably move a little when you plug in a lamp cord or flick a switch.

Draperies. Hanging drapery hardware is not difficult. I am simply suggesting how you can make life a little easier for yourself when you hang a drapery which extends beyond the sides of a window frame. Sometimes the brackets supporting the rod lie directly over studs; and in that lucky situation, you can hold them in place with screws driven into the studs. In many cases, however, the brackets are attached to the walls between studs; and that means you must install them with toggle bolts or hollow-wall screw anchors. This is a nuisance.

To simplify matters when you build a new wall or do extensive remodeling of an old one, install 2x4 blocking between the studs where the curtain-rod brackets will be attached. Then you can drive screws through the brackets into these.

5

Paint

Paint is the easiest and cheapest way to decorate walls. It is usually the fastest. And sometimes it is the only reasonable solution to a problem. Consider . . .

Ease. Anyone can paint a wall. No experience is required to produce a very acceptable job. After they were married, all three of my daughters eventually reported: "We painted the living room [or maybe it was the bedroom or kitchen]. It was easy! And you know, the room looks lovely." Well, naturally.

Cost. A gallon of superior interior paint costs about $10 and covers roughly 450 sq. ft. To put two coats on the walls in a 14x20-ft. living room requires approximately 2 gals. The woodwork requires an additional ½ gal. Total cost

for materials: about $27. (That's $2 more than you figured, because I am buying the trim paint by the qt.) This figures out to 5¢ a sq. ft.

Of course, you have some additional investment in painting equipment and supplies: Three brushes (one for latex wall paint; two for alkyd trim enamel)—$15; roller, roller cover and tray—$4.50; a gallon of thinner for soaking trim brushes—75¢ a quart of brush cleaner for the trim brushes—$1.25; stepladder—$12. But you can use most of these things time and again. I am still using one paint brush I bought 25 *years ago*.

Speed. If that 14x20 ft. living room doesn't require a great deal of washing, sanding and patching, you can probably finish it off in two days. That's speed you can't match with any other material. On the other hand, paint loses its advantage to wallpaper and vinyl wall coverings if you have to increase the number of coats to get acceptable coverage, or if you have an excessive amount of preparation.

Only solution. On woodwork, paint or stain (which comes under the heading of paint) are the only materials you can use. This is also true in other situations. For instance, I mentioned in the opening chapter that the first thing Elizabeth and I did in our present house was to paint a room that took three coats. We thought we'd never finish. But we had no alternative. One wall was paneled in oak which had been stained, I feared, with creosote; so it needed a coat of stain-killer before painting. Two walls were covered with plaster too rough even for heavy vinyl wall covering. The fourth wall was covered with grass cloth which we wanted to remove; but it was firmly stuck to gypsum board, and I was certain I couldn't get it off without pulling the paper covering off the gypsum and thus weakening the wall. So we had to coat it with paint and more paint. The stuff was like a sponge. I think it actually required four coats in all.

Kinds of paint, stain and clear coatings. You really need only three: alkyd enamel, latex paint and varnish. But there are others. Here is the complete rundown, in alphabetical order:

Alkyd enamel. This has almost replaced interior oil paint because it has little odor and dries faster. Easy to apply with brush, roller or spray gun, it is tough and washable. And it produces a very attractive flat, semigloss or gloss finish.

Alkyd enamel is the best finish for wood, plywood, hardboard, particle board and insulating board. I also prefer it on gypsum board and plaster walls in kitchens and bathrooms. Always use a semigloss or gloss in these rooms and also use them on all woodwork everywhere, because they are much more washable than a flat enamel.

On unfinished wall surfaces, apply an enamel undercoater first, sand lightly when dry, and apply one or two coats of enamel. On painted surfaces, use an enamel undercoater if you are changing the color of the wall, and follow with enamel. If you are not changing color, use enamel only.

Bleach. Bleach is used on wood and plywood to make the natural color of the wood lighter or to soften or eradicate stains that have been applied to it, either purposely or accidentally. Oxalic acid is the best general-purpose bleach for most common stains, but stronger commercial bleaches are sometimes necessary for tougher ones.

Before using a bleach, strip all finish from the wood or plywood and sand it thoroughly. Mix ½ cup oxalic acid crystals (from the drugstore) in a quart of hot water in a glass container. Brush or sponge it on liberally while it is hot and let it dry. Then remove the crystals and repeat the process until the wood is the desired tone. Then neutralize the surface with 1 part of household ammonia in 10 parts of water, allow to dry thoroughly and sand smooth once again. The wood or plywood may then be covered with a clear protective finish, or you can proceed with a special finish such as limed-oak or heather-mahogany.

Block filler. This is a thick primer, usually made of latex, which is used to fill the voids in concrete and cinder blocks and other porous masonry walls. It not only reduces the number of finish coats you must apply but also makes for a smoother final finish. Apply it with a brush or roller.

Casein paint. You can just about forget this. A water-thinned coating, it has been outmoded by latex paint. It is sometimes used on acoustical tiles, however, because it clogs the pores less than do other paints.

Chlorinated rubber paint. This is similar to a latex paint, but is thinned with a solvent rather than with water. Its primary use is outdoors. But it is probably the best finish for asbestos-cement board. When applied to this, the board should first be coated with an alkyd primer.

Epoxy paint. If you are looking for an extremely tough, durable finish with exceptional resistance to abrasion and scrubbing, use epoxy. It can be applied to any material which isn't porous, but its special function in the wall department is to change the color of ceramic and metal tile, plastics, fiberglass and glass.

Epoxy is a two-part paint, meaning that it comes in two containers. The ingredients must be mixed together just before you use them and they do not keep more than a few hours. So you have to work fast with a brush, roller or spray gun.

Epoxy paint can be applied only to unfinished surfaces or to itself. Two coats are usually needed, but one may be enough. Because the fumes are toxic, the room in which you are working must be very well ventilated.

Fire-retardant paint. Called an intumescent coating, this paint foams up when exposed to fire and helps to insulate the wall material beneath. It produces a flat, not-too-attractive finish, but you might use it anyway to increase fire safety in rooms occupied by babies, the elderly or invalids.

Latex paint. This is everybody's favorite because it dries rapidly—sometimes so rapidly that you can apply a second coat within an hour—and because all cleanup work is done with water. Furthermore, the paint is nearly odorless, produces an attractive, durable finish and can be touched up without showing patched spots. Most finishes are flat, but semigloss and gloss are available to a limited extent. Application is made with a brush, roller or spray gun.

After it has been allowed to dry for several weeks, latex is very washable; but I don't think it is quite the equal of alkyd, which is why I don't like it on kitchen and bathroom walls. But on gypsum board, plaster and masonry walls in all other rooms you cannot beat it. One of its unique advantages is that it can be applied to plaster and masonry as soon as they have hardened—while the alkalis are still active. Don't use it on wood or materials derived from wood, however. Although some types are advocated for this purpose, they are considerably short of perfection.

On new walls, start with a latex primer; then apply one or two coats of latex paint. On old walls, skip the primer. Because latex usually gives good coverage, one coat is often enough on redos.

Multicolor paint. This is a latex paint which contains several colors to produce a two-tone look that has the extra advantage of covering up flaws in a wall. It must usually be applied with a sprayer.

Oil paint and enamel. Now that alkyds are available, these have nothing to recommend them. But they are still to be found. Their main use is on wood and plywood.

Oil stain. Oil stains are applied to wood, plywood and particleboard. There are two types: clear and opaque. The clear is a penetrating material that changes the color of the surface but lets the grain, texture and imperfections show through. On the other hand, opaque stain—a semipenetrating material—not only changes the surface color but also obscures the grain, texture and imperfections to some extent—though not so completely as paint.

Clear stain is used on bare wood or the like, or wood that has been previously treated with a clear stain. It is particularly effective and long-lasting on rough surfaces. Apply it with a brush or, on a smooth surface, with a rag. Work it in rapidly and thoroughly; let it penetrate for a few minutes; then wipe off the excess with clean rags. You can apply a second coat, if needed, within 30 minutes, or you can wait longer. Allow the final coat to dry 48 hours before applying a protective finish of varnish, lacquer or wax.

Opaque stain goes over a clean or previously stained surface. It can also be used on a painted surface if most of the paint has been removed. You can even change the color of a painted or stained surface as long as you don't try to go from very dark to very light. Brush the stain in well and let it dry before applying a second coat.

Portland cement paint. This can be used on all masonry walls that have not been finished or that were previously finished with cement paint. It is especially suited to damp basement walls.

The paint comes as a dry powder which is mixed with water and applied to a wall with a stiff bristle brush. First spray the wall lightly with water. After the paint sets, spray frequently with water for 48 hours. A second coat —needed on new work—is applied in the same way. One coat is enough on old work.

A special type of cement paint, usually identified as a cement-base coating or sealant because of its thickness, is used to waterproof masonry walls while decorating them. It is applied like ordinary Portland cement paint to a damp surface but does not need to be fogged with water while hardening, except in very hot weather. If a second coat is necessary, apply it within 24 hours of the first.

Sanded paint. Sanded paint is a latex containing sand or a sandlike material named Perltex. Because it produces a sandpaperlike texture when dry, it is a favorite of developers who want to conceal bad taping on gypsum board walls. It can also be used on plaster. But it doesn't hide imperfections as well as you want it to and, in my experience, it flakes off badly. In short, I don't think much of it.

You can produce a sand finish with any paint by mixing in washed builder's sand or Perltex. Apply with a brush or roller. For a pronounced grainy effect, go over it immediately with a whisk broom or other stiff brush.

Sealer. A sealer is a white or clear finish that penetrates and seals the pores of the material to which it is applied, thus minimizing staining and soiling. It leaves a not-too-obvious, slightly glossy finish.

Sealers are made for wood and masonry. Use them on walls that are subject to soiling but which should appear in the most natural possible state. Apply two coats with a brush on new work; one on old work.

Phenolic resin primer-sealer is made solely for use on softwood plywood to even out the grain so it doesn't show through the final finish as wild, wavy stripes. The sealer is sold as a clear liquid and with white pigment. Use the former on plywood to be stained; the latter on plywood to be painted. One coat does the trick. Sand smooth before applying the final finish.

Stain-killer. Use this as a primer, not a final finish. A white-pigmented shellac, it has two unique advantages: (1) Brushed on wood, it seals in the resin in knots and keeps them from bleeding through a finish paint and making brown stains on the surface. Since the pine and other softwoods sold today are so full of knots, this is an almost essential material if you intend to paint the wood. It is also used on wood to which a creosote stain has been applied. (2) Because stain-killer is made and thinned with alcohol, it can be applied in extremely cold weather. When you're building a house or making an addition, this permits you to seal all interior woodwork as soon as it is installed—long before your heating system is working.

Stain-killer dries in about 30 minutes. As soon as you sand it lightly, you can apply any type of finish paint.

Stain wax. This mixture of stain and wax is used on wood, plywood and particleboard to give an easy, quick finish. It is best suited to walls not subject to soiling and abrasion. Simply brush or wipe it on with a clean rag, let it penetrate briefly and then even it out with a dry rag. Apply one or two coats, as necessary.

Textured paint. This is a thick latex or oil-base paint used on plaster and gypsum board walls to cover up flaws or simply because you like a textured finish. Some brands are made in white only, but can be tinted a light shade (a laborious job). Others come in a few light pastel shades. If you want a dark color, the best way to achieve it is to apply a coat of ordinary paint over the textured paint.

Textured paint is put on with a brush over a small area. Then, while it is still wet, you can texture it any way you like with a whisk broom, comb, sponge, crumpled newspaper or rollers that produce special patterns. Practice the technique you intend to use before you go to work on a wall.

One drawback of textured paints is that they

cover only about a quarter of the area covered by ordinary paints. Another drawback is that, once a wall is textured, it is hard to make it smooth again. Sanding is tedious even with an electric disk sander; use of paint remover is worse. One company makes a so-called strippable paint which can be taken off with a wallpaper steamer; but if you have ever used this device, you may not think the brand represents much of an improvement over others.

Varnish. The principal use for this clear finish is on wood, plywood, particleboard and unfinished hardboard. These are subject to soiling and therefore need to be washed occasionally. In other words, it is used mainly on doors and windows and the trim around them; on baseboards and chair rails; and on paneling that is exposed to grease and hands. It is also used in damp areas to seal out moisture and prevent swelling and warping to some extent. But to be effective, it must be applied to all exposed *and* hidden surfaces and edges.

All varnish has a slightly yellowish cast and deepens the color of the bare or stained surface to which it is applied. For wall decoration, use an interior varnish; or if you need an exceptionally durable finish, use polyurethane varnish. You have a choice of high-gloss, semigloss or flat.

Surfaces to be finished should be sanded very smooth and dusted thoroughly. Always apply varnish in a warm, dust-free atmosphere. Do not stir it before use, because this creates bubbles that are transferred to the surface. Work with a well-filled brush (which should be used for nothing except varnish) and don't apply too much pressure. Flow the varnish on with the grain; brush lightly across the grain; then brush lightly with the grain.

You can also apply varnish with a lint-free cloth. Simply get a good amount on the cloth and wipe it on the surface, gently, with the grain.

One coat is usually all you need on wall paneling, but two coats are recommended as a starter on doors, windows, baseboards and chair rails. Go over the first coat with fine sandpaper or steel wool before applying the second. If the finish surface is objectionably glossy, rubbing with very fine steel wool will correct matters. You can then give the finish a gentle glow by waxing it.

One serious problem with varnish is that you cannot touch it up invisibly when it becomes scarred.

Varnish stain. A mixture of varnish and stain, this is used to change the color and simultaneously protect the surface of wood, plywood or particleboard. Two coats are brushed on to give a semitransparent effect which, alas, is rather unattractive and not at all durable. So don't use varnish stain unless you are in an awful rush and care little about the results.

Water-clear lacquer. This is the most colorless protective finish available. Use it to protect the surface of wood, plywood, particleboard or unfinished hardboard without changing its appearance.

Surfaces to be finished must be bare and satin-smooth. Apply the lacquer with a spray gun or aerosol can in very thin coats. It can also be brushed on, but running and sagging are hard to control. Apply two or three coats. A new coat can be put on as soon as the preceding coat has dried (a rapid process) and is steel-wooled. Rub the final coat down with very fine steel wool.

Estimating paint requirements. There is no sense in buying more paint than you need for a project, because you can't be sure you will want the same color or even the same finish the next time you redecorate. Furthermore, a lot of partially filled paint cans take up storage space you may not have to spare.

On the other hand, it is better to overestimate the paint you will need than to underestimate it, because it is a nuisance to run out before you finish a job. More important, if you have the paint especially mixed and you run out, you may discover that the paint dealer is unable to match it exactly. This is a sound reason for finding and sticking with a dealer who is a good paint mixer.

To estimate the amount of paint needed to

finish the walls in a room, measure the height of the walls and their total length, and multiply the figures. Then subtract the area of the windows and doors if you are not painting them just like the walls. This gives you the net area of the wall surfaces proper.

The size of the area a quart or gallon of paint will cover varies with the brand and type of finish. It also varies with the surface you are painting: paint goes further on a hard or smooth surface than on a rough or porous one. In many cases, the label on the paint tells you what coverage you may expect. If it doesn't, ask the dealer.

The amount of paint you need buy is the net area of the wall surfaces, times the number of coats you will need, divided by the coverage of the paint. Example: If the net wall area of a room is 960 sq. ft., and you are using a paint that normally covers 450 sq. ft. per gal. you need 2 gals. by close figuring. But to be on the safe side—particularly with paint mixed to a special color—you should buy at least an extra quart.

The paint required for doors, windows and trim is harder to estimate. As a rough rule of thumb, figure your needs at 25 percent of what you need for the walls. For a better estimate, figure each average window at 15 sq. ft., and each average door at 21 sq. ft. (don't forget that the door may have to be painted on both sides, adding up to 42 sq. ft.); and add all doors and windows together. For the baseboards and other moldings, translate the figure for the total length of the walls into square feet (that is, if the walls are 40 ft. long, the baseboards and moldings have an area of 40 sq. ft.).

For the tightest possible estimate, measure the exact sizes of doors and windows with surrounding trim, and of baseboards and moldings, and add the figures together.

Preparing walls for painting. This takes time. Trying to cut corners doesn't help much, if at all; and ultimately it makes extra work.

If you are redoing all four walls in a room —which is usually the case—the first step is to strip the room of all easily removed rugs, furni-ture, pictures, picture hooks, mirrors and so on. Leave only the heavy or awkward pieces and the large rugs. Cluster these in the middle of the room and cover them with tarpaulins, sheets—anything that will keep off dust.

Make whatever repairs the walls require according to directions for the materials they are made of.

Wash kitchen walls with detergent solution or trisodium phosphate (sold under such names as Spic 'N Span and Soilax) and rinse thoroughly—despite manufacturers' assertions that rinsing is unnecessary. Wash walls in other rooms, if they are soiled and marked up. And always wash doors, windows and baseboards, because they are dirt catchers. On baseboards, use a kitchen-wax remover or benzine to wash off floor wax.

If walls are mildewed, wash them with ⅔ cup trisodium phosphate, ⅓ cup household detergent, 1 quart laundry bleach and 3 quarts warm water. Rinse well.

With a sharp knife or scraper, scrape old paint drips down flush with the surrounding surfaces and sand smooth.

Old paint on walls and woodwork that is scratched, chipped or loose must be scraped off and sanded smooth. Badly chipped paint and under-surfaces, if sound, are most easily leveled by spreading gypsum board cement over them in a thin layer with a 4-in. or wider flexible scraper. Sand when dry.

Paint on woodwork is sometimes so badly scarred that complete removal is called for. This is particularly true in old houses with woodwork that has been painted and repainted so often—with many incompatible paints— that the finish has become so thick and brittle that it chips off in big flakes, leaving deep scars. Use a paste-type remover on small or intricate areas, an electric paint remover on large areas.

Sanded and textured finishes are smoothed with an electric sander, but it is slow going. A disk sander has the most aggressive action; but after the walls are smooth, you must go over them again with a reciprocating sander, or by hand, to remove the scratches left by the disk.

Painting over wallpaper and similar wall coverings is inadvisable except when you suspect that they were applied to gypsum board that had not first been primed. In that event, if you tried to remove the wallpaper, you would remove the paper covering on the gypsum board, too. So the only alternative is to go over the wallpaper carefully, cleaning off dirt and stains and sticking down all loose spots. Sand down lapped edges with fine sandpaper so they will be less noticeable. Then apply two or three coats of alkyd or latex paint.

For how to remove wallpaper, see Chapter 7.

The two final steps in preparing walls for painting are to take off all hardware, except door hinges and the internal works of locks and latches, and to run a vacuum cleaner over the floor and the top edges of the baseboards.

Painting tools. Paint is applied with a brush, roller or spray gun.

A brush is the all-purpose applicator you cannot do without. It is used to apply any finish, anywhere. It is the most economical of paint. It produces the smoothest finish (unless you are expert with a sprayer). But, it is slow, because it doesn't hold much paint.

The types of brush used in wall projects are wide (4 to 5 in.) wall brushes, 1- to 3-in. trim brushes and ½- to 1½-in. sash brushes, also called sash tools. I use different brushes for alkyd enamel and latex paint, although this is not essential. But you should definitely use different brushes for clear finishes, so there won't be any pigment in the bristles that might discolor the finish.

I happen to favor brushes with hog bristles over those with synthetic bristles—but that is a debatable preference. The important thing is to buy good brushes. Good brushes are expensive—that's the easiest way to identify them. They flow the paint on better and more smoothly, they hold their bristles and they last for years. You may dislike the idea of spending, say, $10 to $15 for a wall brush, but you will never regret it.

When painting, dip the brush bristles only halfway into the paint and remove the excess by slapping gently against the inside of the can or under the rim—but never wipe the bristles off on top of the rim, because this interferes with resealing the can when you are through painting. It also leads to drips down the outside of the can. Holding the handle any way you like, draw the brush wide side forward across the surface. (The only times a brush is drawn thin edge forward is when you "cut in" along a ceiling line, door frame and the like, and when you paint window mullions.) It's best to work *with* the grain, as this saves a bit of time by reducing brush strokes; but if the surface is rough, you will cover it better by applying the paint across or at an angle to the grain and then smoothing if off *with* the grain. For the smoothest possible finish, apply paint *with* the grain; brush across it lightly; then brush up and down lightly. On walls without grain, the final strokes are usually vertical; but if the wall is grooved or textured horizontally or at an angle, the brush strokes follow these lines.

Clean brushes at the end of the work day by sloshing them up and down in a can of the appropriate thinner; but wash brushes used in latex paint in a sink under a running stream of water. Work the paint out of the upper ends of the bristles with your fingers or a steel comb. Then shake out the thinner and place the brushes on newspapers until the next day. On the other hand, if your work is finished or will be interrupted for several days, give the clean brushes a final wash in a strong household detergent solution, rinse, dry them on newspapers and store them flat.

Painting with rollers is a great deal faster than painting with a brush, and that's why most people, including professionals, use them on walls and ceilings. I also highly recommend using them in conjunction with a brush on doors, and on all wide trim. In this case, I spread the paint on all the flat surfaces with a roller, and then go back over it with a brush to smooth it out and to fill in bare spots.

The other advantage of rollers—which is

partly a result of their speed—is that they are less tiring than both brushes and sprayers. Even after a whole day's work, there is little ache in your wrist (unless you were doing ceilings).

But rollers have disadvantages, too. They use up paint faster than brushes, and they leave a slightly bumpy texture. You can't work a big roller up tight to a door frame, baseboard, corner and the like; and the small rollers made for such cutting-in operations are not ideal either. Finally, on walls that are uneven, it is difficult to fill in the valleys; but you don't always notice this until the paint is dry. Then you may find that the paint in the valleys is thinner than that on the high spots and you need to go over them again.

The standard roller for wall work is either 7 or 9 in. long. I use this size on doors and trim, although some people prefer a 3-in. roller for such work. There are also very small rollers and specially shaped rollers for cutting-in. A short extension handle attached to a large roller allows you to paint the upper part of walls from the floor, but it does not eliminate the necessity of getting up on a stepladder to cut-in along the ceiling line.

Roller covers should be selected for the type of paint you are using and the surface you are covering. Today they are all clearly labeled for "smooth surfaces—latex paint" and the like. Buy top-quality rollers for latex paint, because the paint is easily washed out so the rollers can be used again and again. I use cheap rollers for alkyd enamels because the enamel is difficult to wash out and I therefore discard the rollers after each job. To be sure, cheap rollers sometimes come apart at the seams, but they last through most projects.

When painting a wall surface with a roller, paint around the edges first with a small cutting-in roller or brush. I am a brush man because I can control it better and get into the corners better; but when the job is done, a narrow strip of brush marks which does not match the rolled-on paint is visible at the corners—provided you look for it.

Fill the paint tray a half to two-thirds full of paint; roll the roller down into it; and then roll it up and down the upper part of the tray to even out the load and remove the excess. Place the roller against the wall and roll one stroke upward and one stroke downward to prevent dripping; then roll any which way you like; but go back over the area all in one direction (usually up and down). Take care to eliminate any little ridges that may be left by the ends of the roller.

To blend new paint into that previously applied (this is particularly important with fast-drying latex), start in an unpainted area and work into the close-by painted area. At the top and bottom of a wall, in corners and alongside door and window frames, roll slowly along the corner line as close as possible to it. Don't exert too much pressure, as this may leave a ridge.

To clean a roller used in latex paint, put it in its tray into a sink or bathtub and run water into the tray while rolling the roller back and forth until the water is clear. Damp-dry the roller on newspapers and hang it, with the cover in vertical position, to dry. Don't lay it flat, because, if any pigment remains in the nap, it will migrate to the underside of the cover and set in a hard line.

Rollers used in alkyd enamel should be run over newspapers to remove as much pigment as possible. Then place them in the roller tray; pour in thinner to half the depth of the roller; run the roller up and down the tray to wet it all over; and then just leave it in the deep end of the tray. Even the top of the roller will remain damp and soft for several days; and if you make a point of turning it over every two or three days, you can store it this way for several weeks. But complete cleaning is a waste of time.

Spraying is another speedy way to paint wall surfaces—and also woodwork, if the same paint is used. In fact, actual painting time with a sprayer is faster than with a roller. Long ago, before rollers were invented, I once spray-painted four very large rooms in one day (and had a numb trigger finger for a week thereafter). But spraying requires much more thorough preparation than rolling or brushing, because all surfaces not to be painted must be masked to keep the fine mist from drifting onto them. Consequently, I no longer spray-paint house interiors.

But if you want a perfectly flat paint surface without texture, spraying is the way to get it.

When talking about spray-painting, I am not thinking of aerosol cans or vacuum-cleaner spray guns. Aerosols are fine for fairly small jobs, but they're costly. Vacuum-cleaner sprayers are an atrocity, because they produce miserable work. Spraying should be done with a good paint-spray outfit with a compressor. For wall work you need either a pressure-feed gun or an all-purpose gun—both with nozzles giving a wide, round pattern. Either rent or buy.

After stripping the room to be painted and covering surfaces you wish to protect, you should take several other preliminary steps: Make sure the room is well ventilated but breezeless. Have a fire extinguisher handy. Strain the paint through several layers of cheesecloth into the sprayer. Put on hat, gloves and respirator. And practice with the sprayer on newspapers until you get it adjusted properly.

Hold the spray gun level, perpendicular to the wall and 6 to 8 in. from it, and move the gun back and forth always parallel to the wall, never in an arc. Start at one end of a wall with a vertical band from floor to ceiling. Then paint in horizontal strokes about 3 ft. wide from the top of the wall to the bottom. Each band of paint should overlap the preceding band 50 percent. The edges of each completely painted section should overlap the edges of the preceding section about 4 in.

The big trick in spraying is to avoid *over-spraying*. The technique is called "triggering." Start moving the gun before pulling the trigger. Pull the trigger just before reaching the area to be painted. Release the trigger just before completing the stroke.

When painting an inside corner, paint each side of the corner in a separate stroke; but on an outside corner, hold the gun at a 45° angle, so that you can spray both sides at the same time.

Clean the spray equipment immediately after your job is done. Follow the directions for the gun you buy or get them from the rental agency. Use the proper solvent and plenty of it. It must come out clear before you can consider the gun clean and ready to use again.

Applying paint to walls. Before getting down to business, cover the floor. A heavy painter's canvas is the best cover. But old mattress pads are excellent too—and cost nothing. You can also do well with newspapers, if you don't mind the way they slide around. But stay away from plastic paint cloths. Paint splatters just lie on the surface; you pick them up on the soles of your shoes and track the paint all over the house.

Make sure you have everything you need for the job: stepladder, brushes, roller, a piece of sandpaper in case you come on a rough spot and lots and lots of rags.

If you don't think your hand is steady, apply masking tape to the floor alongside the shoe moldings and wherever else you must paint to a sharp line. This is cheap, brown paper-adhesive tape that is easy to stick down in a straight or not-straight line and that pulls up without leaving a trace of itself.

Read the directions on the paint can carefully and take in and follow what they say. One thing most important to note is whether a minimum or maximum room temperature is called for. Some paints dry too fast at high temperatures; almost all dry slowly at low temperatures. You can also expect slow drying in damp or humid weather.

If you have just bought the paint, you should have had it shaken up on the paint dealer's vibrator before you brought it home; then it should not need further mixing. But if you've had it for more than a couple of days, give it a stir with a clean stick of wood. If hard stirring is required and the can is full, pour some of the paint into another clean can and stir the two cans separately before mixing them and stirring a little more. This saves paint and mess. Note that in pouring out of a paint can you should always tip the big-name-side down so that *it* gets obliterated rather than the valuable instructions on the back label when you tip the can back up.

Clear finishes, such as varnish and sealer, should not be stirred before use.

If a skin has formed on paint, sealer or varnish in an old can, cut around the edges with a sharp knife, grasp the center of the skin in your fingers and try to lift it out in one piece. Should the skin break or should the paint contain other lumps and particles, stir thoroughly and then strain the paint through cheesecloth or screen wire into another can. Have someone hold the strainer while you pour; otherwise it may fall into the new can.

If the wall you are painting has ever been mildewed, add a mildewcide to the paint. This is a liquid that comes in a small bottle. Special ready-mixed mildew-retardant paints are also available.

On walls or woodwork that have been patched with spackle or other filler, spot-prime all patches larger than a pencil and allow to dry before painting the entire surface, otherwise the patches will show through the paint. To save time, use latex primer or latex paint as a spot-primer under all finish paints, including alkyd and oil.

You should also prime knots in pine and other softwoods regardless of whether the wood is bare or has been previously painted. Use a stain-killer or ordinary shellac.

The proper order for doing over an entire room is to paint the ceiling first; then the walls; then the doors, windows and trim; and last of all the baseboards. However, if you use the same pain on walls and woodwork, there's no reason why you can't do them at the same time, completely finishing one wall before starting on another. On doors, do the edges first; then the panels or louvers; then the rails and stiles; then the jambs and casings. On windows, do the mullions first; then the surrounding sash frames; then the jambs and casings.

Paint walls in strips from the ceiling to the baseboard. As a rule, a 3-ft.-wide strip is about right because you can stand in one place until it is finished and you can complete it before the paint has dried very much. This is important because the second strip blends better into the first if the first is still wet.

Keep an eye out for sags and drips and brush or roll them out as you see them. Then go back in a few minutes and check whether they have reappeared. Finally, when the wall is completed, inspect it once more for sags, drips, skipped and thin spots, lumps, insects and the like.

Let the walls dry before painting the woodwork (unless the same paint is used on everything).

At the end of a project, before storing a paint can, write on the top with a china-marking pencil the room in which the paint was used and the date. Also indicate the type of finish, if the label has been obscured.

Maintaining and repairing paint on walls. Maintenance consists mainly of wiping off dirt, pencil marks, ink and the like with a damp cloth or sponge. Sometimes you also need a little detergent, household ammonia or the white liquid wax that is made primarily for cleaning and polishing kitchen appliances. The last is effective on several stains that other solvents do not faze: lipstick, crayon marks and rubber-heel marks.

Kitchen walls need fairly frequent spot-washing with detergent solution to clean greasy areas near the range and ventilating fan; and they really need to be thoroughly washed every year or two, depending on how much you fry foods.

Repairs are called for only when the paint is chipped or scratched. I recommend the easy way on small scars: just take a little art-brush and dab on the appropriate finish. Large, deep scars, however, should be filled with spackle or gypsum board cement and sanded smooth before painting. This may not obliterate them, but they will be less noticeable than if you simply paint them.

6

Several Paintlike Products

In one case, "paintlike" may be stretching a point. In the other cases, you will say, "Well, if they aren't paint, what are they?"

Bear with me. Whatever these materials are or resemble, they're intriguing. And the chances are that you don't know much about them—because they are new, or relatively so.

Roll-on fabric. The producer * of this wonderfully crazy material says it has been "popular for 20 years in Japan, where millions of packages are sold each month." I'll take his word for it. Now it's available in Canada. As of this writing, only in Canada. But you can buy it in the U.S. by mail.

* Dream Wall Sales, Ltd., 1397 Commercial Dr., Vancouver, B.C.

When I first heard about it, I immediately sent off for information and got back a package of samples plus minor pieces of literature. There are eight patterns, most of them in several colors. Some were too jazzy for my taste; but both my wife and I were excited by all of them. Description is difficult. The material is a mixture of fabric fibers such as rayon, cotton, nylon and silk; metalliclike glitter in threads and chips; and a glue powder. When mixed with water and applied to a wall, this turns into a thick, rough covering that looks like brocade, grass cloth, marble or pure-white sand littered with bits of white feathers. I immediately hit on the one I liken to grass cloth for my office; then I discovered it would cost more than $2 a sq. ft., which is too rich for my country working quarters. But there are other patterns which cost only a quarter as much.

In addition to being a good-looking conversation piece, roll-on fabric's big advantage is that it conceals imperfections in the wall to which it is applied. Furthermore, I can imagine that if you put it on plaster, and the plaster then cracked and opened a crack in the fabric, you still wouldn't see the crack.

Wearability and cleaning, however, are things to worry about a little. The material is easy to gouge, and it's a dust catcher. On the other hand, the medium and dark colors don't show dirt and stains badly.

Applying roll-on fabric. Roll-on fabric is packaged in bags which cover 25 to 35 sq. ft. To estimate how many you need, measure the height of the wall above the baseboard and the length in feet. Multiply the figures. Then measure all windows and doors, including casings, and subtract from the wall area. Divide by 30, and if there's a fraction left over, order to the next higher whole number.

For maximum washability, a glue additive should be mixed with the fiber. Order one-half pint for each bag of mixture. (Note, however, that the additive is not essential.)

The walls to be covered must be clean and free of loose paint, wallpaper and the like. Fill large holes and indentations, but don't bother with little ones. Unfinished plaster, gypsum board, wood, plywood and hardboard should be covered with an oil-base primer. Walls painted with latex should also be primed, since latex paints often "bleed" through the fabric. Similarly, walls painted with gloss or semigloss enamel should be primed unless glue additive is used with the fabric. In all cases, the primer should be approximately the same color as the fabric. This helps to save fabric, since it must be applied more thickly if the wall is much darker or lighter.

It is best not to use the fabric on fiberboard or acoustical tiles.

To prepare the fabric for application, mix 1 bag with 5 qt. of water in a large plastic bucket. Work it with your hands, but wear rubber gloves if you have sensitive skin. Make sure all particles are thoroughly wet. Break up lumps. If you are using the glue additive, mix it in now. Then let the material soak for an hour.

Just before starting application, mix another bag in a second bucket. Since it takes about an hour to apply a bag, the next bag will be ready for use when its predecessor is on the wall.

Apply the fabric to the wall handful by handful; and roll each handful out with a short-napped paint roller which has been wet in water. Make the coating as thin as possible, but obviously not so thin that you can see the base. At corners and in other tight spots, smooth it out with a putty knife or wall scraper. After covering about 6 sq. ft., hold a lamp close to one edge and inspect the covering from the other edge. The light shows up thick spots that you can't see head-on. If at any time the fabric clings to the roller, scrape it off with your fingers, rinse the roller in warm water and squeeze out the excess.

Complete one wall before going on to another. The material must be allowed to dry for two or three days. Don't try to force the process with heaters or fans. Just keep the temperature in the room at about 70°F. and provide some ventilation.

If you must interrupt application overnight while you still have a batch of wet fabric, seal it in a plastic bag.

Maintaining and repairing roll-on fabric. Vacuum regularly to remove dust. The suction tool should have a very soft bristle or a smooth plastic or metal mouth. Even so, try not to rub the wall.

Mild stains can be removed with a sponge or soft cloth dampened in water; but don't rub too hard.

Keep a little of the material for repairs; and if the wall is gouged, mix it with water and roll it on the damaged area.

Glaze coatings. Glaze coatings are totally unlike roll-on fabric. Made with epoxy, polyester or acrylic resins, they are hard, dense, damage- and stain-resistant and about as cleanable as anything I know. It's easy to understand why they are often called tilelike coatings. You have seen them, perhaps without knowing it, in schools, factories, hospitals—wherever an attractive covering of exceptional durability is required. But they also have a place in many homes. For instance, one of my friends, an architect, used one of the simpler coatings to "paint" the concrete block walls in the family room on the lowest level of his hillside home. "Why?" I wanted to know. "Because it's practical," he answered. Takes wear; easy to wash; ought to last as long as the house itself.

Some of the fancier, textured coatings made with colored pebbles or marble chips are useful, too. Perhaps not on large wall areas, but for purely ornamental use in smallish panels.

If I seem to be suggesting that the glaze coatings comprise a mixed bag of wall coverings, you're exactly right. There are transparent coatings; smooth-colored coatings; colored coatings with veiling, fleck or spatter finishes; textured coatings; and coatings containing sand, pebbles and so on.

Most are difficult to apply—so difficult, in fact, that many manufacturers sell only to professional applicators. But some firms condone do-it-yourself application—if you can buy the coatings. Usually you won't find them in local stores and must buy direct from the factory.

The final problem is the cost, which runs much, much higher than the cost of the best paint. One major manufacturer gave me the following figures for the materials required in a very small job: sealer (1 gal.)—$6; block filler (1 gal.)—$5.25; glaze (sold only in 2-gal., two-part kits)—$35; reducer (1 gal.)—$3.50.

Applying glaze coatings. Because of the variations in products, I'll give only a couple of for-instances. The coatings in both cases were those of the Glazed Cement Corp.*

* 460 Straight St., Patterson, N.J. 07501

One was a cinch. It's a handsome, rough-textured coating that can be applied to any strong, rigid, clean surface such as masonry, plaster or plywood. All you have to do is mix together the two parts of the epoxy matrix and spread it on the wall with wall-scraper. The thickness of the layer depends on the aggregate you use. If it is sand, for instance, the matrix need not be much more than thumbnail thick. If you use crushed stone, on the other hand, the matrix should be $\frac{1}{16}$ to $\frac{3}{32}$ in. thick.

The aggregate is embedded in the matrix immediately. If you're working on a wall, about the only thing you can do is to press it into the matrix, handful by handful. If you're working on a plywood panel, however, you can lay the panel on sawhorses and simply scatter the aggregate over it. The final step in either case is to press the aggregate firmly into the adhesive with a board.

Once the matrix has set for 24 hours or more, you can consider the wall complete. If you prefer, however, cover it with an acrylic glaze which adds strength and improves cleaning. This is best applied with a spray gun but can be rolled on with a thick-napped roller.

Application of the second glaze coating was more complicated and there's no point in giving a blow-by-blow account of it. The coating produces a tough, colored surface with a spatter or veiling effect and a semirough texture. It is suitable for application to plywood, hardboard, metal or any other strong backing to which Portland cement will not adhere.

The first step is to apply an acrylic sealer and let it dry thoroughly. Next you spray on a thick block filler to produce a texture. Next comes a color coat, applied by sprayer or roller. Then you spray on a decorative coat. Finally comes the protective glaze, which may be made of polyester plus epoxy, urethane, vinyl or acrylic. Application of the glaze is usually made with a sprayer, but acrylic can also be brushed or rolled on.

All of which is a lot of work. But I felt justified by the end result.

7

Wallpaper

I learned to wallpaper by reading. That was many years ago, when there wasn't much published on the subject, so there were many techniques left to the imagination. Today, published material is plentiful; and this particular chapter is the most complete discussion yet. So you should become an expert paperhanger in short order.

But there is still much to be learned by watching an experienced paperhanger at work.

I remember when the *Ladies' Home Journal* helped us to remodel our kitchen. Like so many magazine projects, this one got started late and we had little time to finish a very extensive overhauling so the editors could meet their photography deadline in mid-December. The day before the shooting, we had a 12-in. snowfall. But the editors, decorators and photographer arrived undaunted. They were laden with props, including armloads of forsythia which had been specially forced to provide the appropriate springlike setting for the article due to run in the April issue.

The paperhanger we had hired also arrived that day. He didn't have a great deal to do and it wasn't complicated; but I guess he was flustered by all the people running around, and his work space was certainly circumscribed by the traffic. Whatever the reason, his work was pretty awful. The paper was full of blisters and tears; and when a big hole appeared, he just covered it with a patch. "Everything'll look all right when the paste dries," he kept assuring us. And sure enough, it did—if you didn't look closely.

What I learned from that experience is that you shouldn't hang wallpaper under pressure or with a lot of people—even well-intentioned people—looking on.

This lesson was reinforced by the only other paperhanger I ever employed—this one, only a couple of years ago, when I was tied up writing a couple of books. By contrast with the kitchen job, this was a difficult installation in our central hall and stairway. There was tricky trimming to be done around moldings; the walls curved and rose to a height of two stories over the stairs. But Mr. Maynard took everything in stride. He was careful to the point of being painfully slow. Or so it seemed. Actually he hung six double rolls in two days, which is good going when you're up against the problems he faced. And when he was through, there wasn't a flaw to be found. What's more, he hadn't wasted a single strip.

When you're painting walls you can go fast, because if you make mistakes you can go back and correct them easily. But the reverse is true when you hang wallpaper.

This is not to say that paperhanging is really slow work. Once he set up his paste table, Charlie Hull—the young fellow I mentioned in Chapter 1 who bought a Royal Barry Wills-type house with dark wood-paneled walls—papered the four walls of his 12x30-ft. living room in two days plus six evenings. That doesn't break any records, but it's rather remarkable when you consider (1) that Charlie had never hung wallpaper before, and (2) that he is a perfectionist. There isn't a bubble, tear or lapped seam in the whole room.

As opposed to painting, wallpapering is fast (though not necessarily faster) in the following situations: (1) If the wall is already covered with a sound layer of paper. (2) If a great deal of work is needed to provide a proper base for paint. (3) If you need more than two coats of paint to get complete coverage on a wall. Otherwise, painting comes out ahead on the racetrack.

Paint is also the winner from the cost standpoint. A single roll of unpasted wallpaper, covering approximately 36 sq. ft., costs anywhere from $1 to $20 (prepasted paper goes as high as $12). So to paper a room with 960 sq. ft. of wall surface would cost from $27 to $535. (That figures out to from less than 3¢ to more than 50¢ per sq. ft.) Admittedly, the first figure is not far out of line with the cost of paint; but dollar-a-roll wallpaper isn't anything you will get very excited about.

Is wallpaper more durable than paint? Some of the plastic-coated papers have an edge, but not a big edge. On the other hand, many papers are very undurable.

Then why does anyone use wallpaper in preference to paint except in the few cases when it is easier to install? Because it's beautiful. You have an infinitely greater choice of colors, patterns and textures in wallpaper than in any paint or any other single type of wall material. In fact, the choice is so great even in a single small paint-and-wallpaper store that it's often hard to decide which pattern to buy.

Types of wallpaper. Wallpaper used to be a rather simple subject. No more. There are many types and varieties.

Machine-printed wallpapers. These are the commonest wallpapers, rolling off high-speed presses by the millions of feet. But this doesn't mean there's anything wrong with them. They are good-looking, durable, easy to hang; and one roll matches the next roll exactly.

Hand-printed wallpapers. These are produced by the silk-screen process, one roll at a time. They are the most expensive, beautiful and luxurious papers, and also the most fragile and difficult to hang. They are usually used only in living rooms, dining rooms and other highly decorated areas. They should definitely not be used where they are exposed to soiling and wear.

There are plenty of ready-made hand-printed papers to choose from. But if you want a given design printed in special colors, you can usually arrange for it.

Pretrimmed wallpapers. Most machine prints are now sold with the selvages cut off, though some come untrimmed. But hand-printed papers usually come untrimmed.

The disadvantage of pretrimmed papers is that occasionally the cutting machine strays off the track a hair and you wind up with a wavy or broken edge that doesn't match the adjacent strip precisely. But this doesn't happen often enough to convince me I should use untrimmed papers except when buying hand prints. Not having to trim the selvages from wallpaper represents a considerable saving of time and patience.

Prepasted wallpapers. These are machine-printed papers which are coated with adhesive at the factory. All you have to do is wet them with water and paste them to the wall. This sounds like a great labor saving, and I have some friends who swear that it is. I don't agree. If you follow the manufacturer's instructions for wetting the adhesive (by rolling a strip of paper through a cardboard box full of water), you wind up in a mess; and for various reasons, the paper is hard to position and smooth down on the wall.

If I buy prepasted wallpaper—which I sometimes do—it's because I like the pattern and because the paper is going to be hung over a porous surface or old wallpaper (both especially good bases for this kind of paper). But I don't handle it according to directions. More on this later.

Washable wallpapers. These are wallpapers that have been surface-coated with a clear plastic, so you can clean them with a damp rag or even mild detergent solution without damaging the color or the paper. Most washable papers are machine prints, but a few hand prints are also washable or semiwashable.

The main use for washable wallpapers, of course, is in kitchens, bathrooms, laundries and on any wall subject to considerable soiling and staining. But in selecting wallpapers for such areas, remember that there are differences in the degree of washability of all the papers labeled washable. In cases where you need nearly complete washability, ask the wallpaper dealer to let you test the patterns of your choice by dropping water on them. Papers which absorb the water are less washable than those that do not.

Strippable wallpapers. Strippable papers are washable machine prints made in such a way that, once you pull an edge loose, you can rip the entire strip off the wall in one piece. These papers are therefore valuable mainly to people who redecorate frequently, because there is almost no work involved in removing the paper from a wall. But another less obvious advantage of strippable papers is that they are very difficult to tear accidentally during hanging operations, and they are easy to repair if they come loose from a wall later on.

On the other hand, strippable papers are usually rather stiff—they do not stretch as other papers do—and this makes them hard to hang on uneven walls. Butting the edges of adjacent strips is especially difficult.

Flocked wallpapers. Flocked wallpapers are hand prints with flocking applied to the surface to resemble a thick velvet. Aside from their decorative value, they are useful for hiding imperfections in walls. But they are tricky to handle.

Sand-finished wallpapers. Another type of hand print, these have a sandpaperlike surface. Like the foregoing, they are hard to hang, but hide imperfections in walls.

Estimating how much wallpaper you need. You are bound to have some waste when you hang wallpaper. There are several reasons: (1) You waste some paper trimming it to fit the walls. (2) You often waste some more paper matching the patterns on the strips. (3) You may waste still more paper because the pattern you selected is manufactured and sold only in double or triple rolls when you actually needed a single roll.

Because of the waste resulting from trimming and matching, wallpaper requirements are usually based on the assumption that a single roll will cover 30 sq. ft. of wall surface, even through the roll actually contains 36 sq. ft. and even though its width varies from 18 to 28 in. (after removal of the selvages).

It follows from this that the easy way to estimate how much wallpaper you need is to measure the height of the walls to be covered and their total length, and multiply the two figures. From the answer subtract the total area of all windows and doors, including trim. Then divide by 30 to determine how many single rolls you must buy.

I emphasize that this is the *easy, usual* way of buying wallpaper. You can avoid some of the waste which may result from this process in two ways:

1. Take note of the wallpaper pattern. Most papers are designed so that, in order to match two adjacent strips on a wall, you must raise the second strip several inches (in a few cases, as much as 20 in.) to match the first strip. This brings about a loss of paper and is the main reason for the assumption that a single roll covers only 30 sq. ft.

Other papers, however, are designed so you can match strips on a wall with very little if any loss of paper. And if this happens to be the type of pattern you choose, you can figure on a single roll covering more than 30 sq. ft.—perhaps as much as 34 sq. ft.

2. Don't buy a wallpaper pattern sold only in double or triple rolls, unless the actual number of single rolls required is evenly divisible by two or three. Example: If you need 10 single rolls, a paper sold in double rolls is a good buy; but if you choose a pattern that comes only in triple rolls, you'll have two-thirds of a triple roll left over.

Equipment needed. The amount you must invest in tools and equipment is comparatively modest. Here are the items required:

12-in. smoothing brush.
1-in. seam roller.
8-in. paste brush.
6-ft. or, better, 8-ft. folding rule for all measuring operations. A flexible steel tape can be substituted but is not as handy.

6-ft. straight-edge. The best type is made specifically for paperhanging and is made either of solid metal or of wood edged with metal; but this is essential only if you are putting up untrimmed wallpaper. If you're using pre-trimmed paper, a straight pine board will do just as well.

Pair of large shears—preferably 12-in. shears.

Box of single-edge razor blades. A box containing 100 blades is available from the wallpaper dealer and is the best buy, because you use up blades rapidly.

4-ft. spirit level to make sure wallpaper strips are vertical. A less expensive and just about as good alternative is a plumb bob on an 8-ft. cotton cord, plus a piece of blue chalk.

4-in. or 6-in. flexible wall scraper.

Pencils.

Screwdriver for removing electrical fixtures.

Wallpaper scraper of the Strip-zum type. This consists of a sharp, thin, rectangular blade 4 in. long attached at about a 75° angle to the end of a rigid metal handle.

3x6-ft. paste table. Make this of wide boards set on top of two sawhorses. It's easy to put up, take down and store. And you can use the horses for other household jobs.

Stepladder. In certain situations you may need a second stepladder plus a 12-in.-wide, 2-in.-thick plank about 10 ft. long to build a trestle for working on high walls.

Drop cloths.

Paste bucket. Use an ordinary 10-qt. or larger pail and tie a string across the top to rest your paste brush on.

Water bucket.

Sponge.

Clean rags.

Preparing to hang paper. First strip the room of all but the largest furnishings. See Chapter 5. Remove switch and outlet plates and heating registers but leave the light fixtures till later. Mirrors hung with clips or channels should be taken down also. Mark the locations of the screws by inserting tacks, head first, in the holes. The points should protrude only ¼ in.

or so. They will poke through the paper when you hang it over them.

Wallpaper can be hung on any sound, solid surface; but I don't recommend it on fiberboard, wood or plywood because the expansion and contraction of these materials rip the paper; and you are not likely to use it on tile, plastics or glass. That leaves plaster, gypsum board, hardboard and particleboard, all of which form a good base for wallpaper, although the first two are the ones most commonly encountered.

New plaster should usually be allowed to cure for two months before it is papered; but you may start papering earlier if you make a test for free lime (hot spots). Have a druggist dissolve 1 gram of phenolpthalein powder in 15 cc. of alcohol. Swab this on the wall in a number of spots. If the plaster turns pink or red anywhere, coat the entire wall with a solution of 4 lb. of zinc sulfate dissolved in 1 gal. of hot water.

New gypsum board must always be painted with one coat of latex primer; otherwise you will never be able to remove the wallpaper without also removing the paper covering on the board.

Fill holes and cracks in existing walls with spackle or patching plaster and sand smooth. If nails in a gypsum board wall have popped, hammer them down and drive in a new annular-ring nail close by each of them. Cover the heads with gypsum board joint compound. If plaster walls are badly cracked and weak, don't count on wallpaper to reinforce them and conceal the damage. Knock them out and apply a new wall surface instead.

Smooth walls with a sanded or textured finish with a disk-type electric sander. If this doesn't work, cover the surface with gypsum board joint compound and sand smooth when dry. The alternative is to hang a very heavy, strongly textured wallpaper or other wallcovering. A second alternative is to cover the wall with lining paper.

Wash off every trace of calcimine with warm water and steel wool. Take the shine off glossy paint and varnish with sandpaper and/or washing soda. Wash mildewed walls with ⅔ cup of trisodium phosphate, ⅓ cup of household detergent, 1 qt. of laundry bleach and 3 qt. of warm water. Rinse well. Use the same solution, or simply detergent, to remove grease. Take off crayon and lipstick with white appliance wax.

For best results, old wallpaper should be removed—especially if there is more than one layer. Even though the paper seems tight and smooth, the paste on the new paper often penetrates it and loosens the paste underneath. This causes blisters. Of course, if you're willing to take a chance, just make sure all loose edges are pasted down, and sand the joints smooth if they are lapped.

But the new strip-off wallpaper scrapers make complete removal easy—even when there are several layers of paper. All you have to do is work the blade in under the paper and push. The paper usually comes off down to the base in a long strip. If it doesn't, wet it with a sponge or garden sprayer. If the moisture isn't absorbed because the surface has been made washable with plastic or varnish, sand it with coarse sandpaper and then apply water.

Should the wallpaper defy all these efforts, the only thing you can do is to rent a steamer. This consists of a tank of boiling water and a large perforated metal plate, connected to the tank by a hose, from which steam emerges. Holding the plate against the wallpaper loosens the paste so you can scrape it off easily and rapidly.

One thing to remember whenever you wet or steam wallpaper is to cover the floor with drop cloths and keep the strips of paper picked up; otherwise they will stick to the floor and your shoes.

When a wall is finally bare, go over it with a sponge and scraper to remove dirt and any remaining particles of paste and paper.

Vinyl wall coverings, burlap and other fabrics are removed in the same way; but they usually require less effort because they are stronger and rip off in larger pieces.

Sizing walls and hanging lining paper. "Size" is a glue that seals wall surfaces and makes new paste adhere better. It also helps you to slide the new paper around on the wall and position it accurately.

Size today is frequently mixed with wheat paste at the factory. Thus you size the wall at the same time you hang each strip of paper. But the old-fashioned size which is applied in a separate operation is a bit more reliable. This is mixed with water according to the directions on the package; applied with a wallpaper paste brush; and allowed to dry (it takes about two hours) before you start hanging paper.

All walls except those which are covered with old wallpaper, lining paper or muslin should be sized before you hang wallpaper with wheat paste. Note, however, that if you use an adhesive other than wheat paste, you should size the walls only if the directions on the paste package call for it.

Lining paper is a pale, brownish-white paper with a dull, porous texture. It is generally not used under machine-printed wallpapers except when the wall has a rough texture. But it is almost always used under hand prints and scenic wallpapers.

Lining paper is applied like finish paper (*follow the directions below*) but with somewhat less care. Using a carpenter's square to square the ends, cut each strip ¼ in. short of the distance from the baseboard to the ceiling. Then it will be unnecessary to trim the strips after they are hung.

Start the first strip next to a door jamb, but about ⅛ in. away from it, centering it between the baseboard and ceiling. A slight gap is maintained around the outer edges of all strips so that the finish paper will overlap and adhere to the wall proper. Then hang all floor-to-ceiling strips all the way around the room. The joints between strips should be butted, but don't worry if they are not perfectly butted. They must not be lapped, however, because the ridges will show through the finish paper.

Plumbing the strips is unnecessary because it doesn't matter if they are not absolutely vertical. In corners, however, you must take pains not to let the paper wrinkle or bend around the corners. To avoid these problems, paste whole strips around corners and then slit them from top to bottom and smooth them on to the walls.

After the long strips are hung, fill in the gaps over doors and over and under windows. Cut the paper carefully to fit, and paste it up horizontally rather than vertically.

Mixing wallpaper paste. Wheat paste (with or without size) is the standard adhesive for wallpaper but white cellulose paste may be recommended by your dealer when you hang a paper that is extremely subject to staining.

Mix fresh wheat paste each day in a clean pail. Start by slowly adding 1 lb. of dry paste powder to 5 qt. of cold or warm water. Mix thoroughly to remove all lumps. The paste should be about the consistency of a good split-pea or potato soup. If it is too thick, add water. This can be done any time during the day, indeed it is often necessary because paste tends to thicken with the passage of time.

Examining the wallpaper. When you order wallpaper, the rolls you receive from the factory via the dealer are usually of the same "run." In other words, they were printed during the same press run. But every once in a while the rolls that come through are from two or even three different runs; and if that is the case, the colors may not be a perfect match.

To guard against this, the first thing you should do before starting to hang any wallpaper is to look at the back of each roll to determine whether the run numbers printed there are all the same. If they are, you have nothing to worry about. However, if some of the run numbers are missing, or if you find that they are not the same on all rolls, you should unroll the rolls about 3 ft. and compare the colors. This is called "shading." Again, if the colors match, you are ready to get on with the job; but if they don't, you should take the whole batch back to the dealer and tell him either to replace it entirely or to find substitutes for the out-of-step rolls. The alternative—which is poor—is to use one run number on one wall and the other run number on another wall; but don't use them side by side on the same wall.

Hand-printed wallpapers should be checked in the same way. Many of these do not carry run numbers, however. Consequently, you must shade them carefully. Slight differences in color are common; and there isn't much you can do about them because new rolls from the factory would probably show differences, too. In other words, assign the closest matches to the same wall and be happy.

One other point you should check before hanging nonwashable wallpaper is whether it is colorfast. Just swab water on a scrap and note what happens. If the colors fade or run, it's a warning not to get any more paste on the surface of the paper than you can possibly help, because you won't be able to wash it off without affecting the appearance of the paper.

Sizing up the job. Now it's time to pause and take a close look at the room you are going to paper.

The first thing to decide is where you are going to start. This depends partly on the pattern and partly on the design of the room. If the paper is a solid, or has a small overall repeat pattern, you can start the first strip almost anywhere. The best place is usually alongside a door or window or in a corner. But if the paper has a very strong pattern with definite features that catch the eye, these should be positioned where they contribute most to the appearance of the room. This means, as a rule, that they should be centered on the most prominent wall. This may be directly over the fireplace; on the wall opposite the sofa; on the wall between large outside doors or wherever.

The second thing you should decide is where you are going to finish hanging the wallpaper. The reason for this is that when you paper the four walls of a room, you can be pretty certain that your last two strips will not come together in a perfect match. This is because the total length of the walls of a room can rarely be divided precisely by the trimmed width of a wallpaper.

Unfortunately, there is no perfect solution to the problem. The best you can do is to hang the paper in such a way that the mismatch occurs where it is least noticeable. This may be in a corner or over a door or window.

The third thing to decide is how the pattern should be positioned vertically. Again, if you are working with a plain paper or one with a small repeat design, the positioning below the ceiling doesn't matter. But if the paper has a bold pattern, the main element of the pattern should be placed a couple of inches below the ceiling so that the whole effect is visible.

Finally, using a carpenter's level, you should draw a level line all the way around the room, a few inches below the ceiling. This will help you to determine whether the ceiling is level. If it is, you can hang the wallpaper from it. But if it isn't, you should use the line to control the vertical placement of the paper. This is particularly important if you have selected a "straight pattern"—a pattern exactly the same on one side of the strip as the other—and if the design is repeated at intervals of, say, 6 to 12 in. If patterns of this type are hung from a sloping ceiling, there is a tendency to change the height of each strip a fraction of an inch, with the result that the final strips come together at completely different levels.

Cutting and pasting wallpaper. Cutting and pasting are simplified considerably if you first take the curl out of the paper. Holding a roll pattern-side up, let about 3 ft. droop down over the front edge of the paste table. Grasp the bottom edge with one hand and the roll with the other hand and saw up and down over the table edge a couple of times.

When you have straightened 8 to 10 ft. of paper, roll it out lengthwise on the paste table and locate the point at which it will touch the ceiling. The top of the paper should be to your left—now and always. Measure down from this point the height of the wall (to the top of the baseboard); add 2 or 3 in.; lay a straight-edge across it at right angles and cut off the strip with a razor blade or simply tear it off.

All wallpaper strips—whether they extend from the ceiling to the baseboard, the ceiling to the top of a door casing or the baseboard to the apron of a window—should be a total of about 4 to 6 in. longer than the actual space to be papered. This allows 2 or 3 in. of overlap at the top of the strip; the same amount at the bottom. Because of the way most wallpapers are patterned, the strips often exceed the "actual-space-plus-4- to 6-in." rule. When this happens, it is advisable to cut or tear off the excess paper, because it interferes with hanging.

After the first strip is cut to length, take the curl out of the next section of the roll and spread the paper alongside the first strip. If you are planning to hang paper from the left to the right, the roll should now be to the right side of the first strip. If you are hanging from right to left, push the first strip to the back of the paste table and place the roll on the left side of the strip. Match the pattern of the second-strip-to-be very carefully to the first. As a rule this is a simple task; but sometimes it is quite tricky. Then make a pencil mark on the second strip directly across from the cut bottom edge of the first strip. The second strip will be cut off at this mark.

Before cutting or tearing the second strip, note how much excess paper there is at the top of the strip. Wallpapers with straight patterns generally have little excess and sometimes have none at all. But "drop pattern" papers may have considerable. In this type of paper, the design at one edge differs from that at the opposite edge; consequently, as I said earlier, in order to make two adjacent strips match, you must sometimes raise the second strip as much as 20 in., thus wasting paper. You can reduce this waste, however, by cutting the first, third, fifth and all other odd-numbered strips out of one roll of paper, and cutting the second, fourth, sixth and all subsequent even-numbered strips out of a different roll. To save confusion, mark the odd-numbered strips on the back near the top edge, A; the even-numbered strips, B.

After cutting your second strip, match a third strip to the second, a fourth to the third and so on. Professionals sometimes tear strips from two or three rolls at one time before they start pasting; but I don't recommend that you follow suit until you have gained experience. Five or six strips at a time is enough. Stack them from the table up in the order that you cut them.

Strips to be hung around doors and windows are matched to one another and to adjacent full-length strips in the same way. But of course you don't cut the strips any longer than the space to be filled.

Having matched and cut several strips, turn the pile over so the first strip is on top, with the back facing up. The top edge of all the strips should still be at the left edge of the paste table. Align the front edge of the first strip with the front edge of the table, the top edge with the left edge of the table and push the strips underneath back a few inches toward the back of the table.

The object in pasting wallpaper is to cover every square inch of the back surface without getting any on the front. The paste should be even and not too thick. Fill your paste brush well and run it down the center of the strip from the left end of the table almost to the right. Then brush the paste out at right angles. Be sure to cover the edges of the strip completely. If some of the paste brushes out on the back of the strip underneath, that's the way it's supposed to be. But try not to get any of the paste on the front edge of the table. If you find this difficult—perhaps because the paper slides around—lift the front edge with your left hand and apply paste with your right. Avoid pasting parallel to the edges, as some of the paste usually creeps underneath.

When you have pasted the upper 6 ft. of the strip, take the top corners in your hands and make a 3-ft. fold from left to right. Align the edges of the fold carefully with the edges of the paper underneath, and smooth the fold down tight. No real pressure is necessary. Don't crease the folded edge too hard, but smooth the fold out so that there are no bubbles.

Now push the second strip underneath toward the back of the paste table another few inches so the paste on it will not transfer to the

first strip. Pull the first strip to your left until the bottom edge is aligned with the right edge of the table. Align the front edge with the front edge of the table. Then apply paste to the un-pasted portion of the strip, fold it to the left and smooth it down. The bottom edge should just meet the top edge.

Most wallpapers can be hung as soon as they are pasted, but some soak up paste very slowly. These should be set aside while you paste two or three additional strips. If during this period you find that the paste along the edges of the strips that are soaking dries out some, roll each strip after it is pasted and folded into a loose roll and put it in a large plastic garbage bag so it won't be exposed to air.

Trimming untrimmed paper. This is a rather difficult job, which is why you'll be better off using pre-trimmed wallpapers, at least until you have grown accustomed to paperhanging.

As soon as the pasted strip has been folded at both ends, line the front edge up with the front edge of the table. Decide how far in you should trim to get a good match with the adjacent strip. Then lay your metal or metal-edged straight-edge (don't use an ordinary straight board for this kind of work) up and down the paper at this point. With a rule, measure from the table edge to the straight edge at the left end of the strip; then measure in the same distance at the right end of the strip. (In other words, don't depend on your eye to lay the straight-edge parallel with the table edge.) Holding the straight-edge firmly so it doesn't move, slice the paper from one end to the other with one long, even stroke of a razor blade. The blade must be held straight up and down or you will bevel the edge of the paper and it will show up as a white line on the wall.

Now turn the strip around and, if the folded edges are not perfectly aligned, realign them. Then line them up with the table edge and repeat the procedure.

Hanging the first strip of paper. The normal temptation of the beginning paperhanger is to assume that the corner, door or window with which he plans to line up his first strip is vertical. Rest assured that it very probably is not. If wallpaper is to look well, it must always be hung straight up and down; and that means you must use a carpenter's spirit level or a plumb line to establish the verticality of the first strip and various other strips as your work proceeds.

If you use a carpenter's level it must be a 4-footer, so you can establish a long straight line. Since this tool is an expensive item I don't have much use for, I prefer a plumb line with a proper plumb bob—not just a nail or other weight—at the bottom end. At the top, tie the line to a nail.

If you're starting from a door or window, measure from the edge of the casing the width of the wallpaper minus 1 in. If you're starting

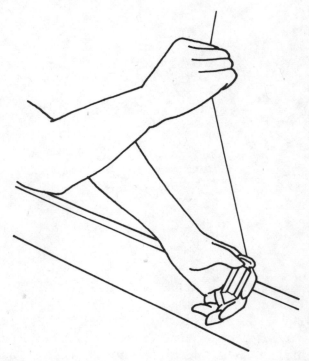

from a corner, measure from the corner the width of the wallpaper plus 1 in. (The reasons for these measurements will become apparent when we get to hanging wallpaper around doors and windows and in corners.) If you're centering the first strip of wallpaper on a wall, find the exact center of the wall and measure half of the width of the wallpaper to either side.

In all three cases, mark the point of measurement about a foot down from the ceiling and tap in the nail on the plumb line. You can now do either of two things to mark a vertical line on the wall. (1) Rub blue chalk from one end of the plumb line to the other. Then, when the line stops swinging, press the bob against the wall with one hand and pull the center of the line—like a bow string—straight out from the wall about 6 in. with your other hand. Then let the line snap against the wall. (2) Do not coat the plumb line with chalk. After it stops swinging, make from three to five pencil marks about a foot apart up and down the wall directly behind the line.

Of the two procedures, the first is considered correct. But I adopted the second years ago for several reasons: If you butt wallpaper to the chalk line on the wall, the chalk may rub off on the paper, leaving a stain on nonwashable paper. You sometimes erase the line when you are shifting the paper around on the wall. And if you are not careful to pull the plumb line out perpendicular to the wall, it does not snap back in a straight line.

But decide for yourself.

Carry the first wallpaper strip (and those following) from the paste table to the wall, over

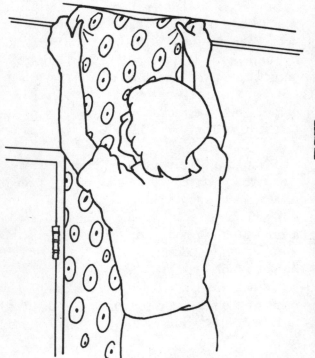

your arm, like a coat. At the wall, stand straight in front of the strip's position. With your free hand, grasp one of the top corners of the strip and pull the long fold open part way. Then take the other corner in your other hand, hold the strip out in front of you and let the long fold open slowly. If you see it opening with a rush, stick out a foot to catch it.

Align the edge of the strip along the chalk line (or line of pencil marks) and hold it at the height selected for the pattern. Then press it to the wall at the ceiling line and smooth it down with a hand, enough to hold it briefly in place. Then run your smoothing brush up and down the paper to stick it securely. If the edge lies tight against the chalk line, good; continue smoothing. But if the paper hangs crooked, pull it up part way and move it toward or away from the chalk line, as necessary. Frequently a strip is so far off vertical, or so full of wrinkles or bubbles as a result of positioning and repositioning, that you must pull it entirely from the wall and start all over again.

When you finally have the upper part of the paper aligned with the chalk line and pretty well smoothed down, open the bottom fold and smooth it on the wall with a vertical stroke of your smoothing brush. Then smooth the entire sheet with crosswise brush strokes. If there are air bubbles or wrinkles that do not brush out readily (never use pressure on them), pull the strip up from the bottom as far as necessary and smooth it down again. (Note that wrinkles are most likely to appear in paper that is very wet, but that they usually disappear when the paper dries. However, there's no point in risking this.)

When the strip is properly positioned and smoothed, brush the top tight into the corner of the ceiling and the bottom tight down against the baseboard. Draw your shears lightly along the corner creases to make fairly sharp lines. Then cut along the creases with shears or a razor blade. Shears are more accurate, especially if the corners between wall and ceiling and wall and baseboard are not tight and smooth. A razor blade is faster, once you get the hang of it.

If you use shears, pull the wallpaper down from the ceiling (or up from the baseboard) a few inches and cut along the creased line carefully. If you use a razor blade, the safest procedure is to press the edge of a wide wall-scraper blade into the corner. The blade and scraper handle should be parallel with the wall. Then cut the wallpaper by running the razor blade along the edge of the scraper blade. With experience, you will probably find you can do without the wall scraper and simply run the razor blade along the crease. But you can be sure of a smooth, straight cut only if the corner is perfectly shaped. If it is uneven or has lumps or open cracks, watch out!

(*Note*: The ease with which you can cut pasted wallpaper on a wall with either shears or razor blades depends on the condition of the cutting edges. Your shears must be sharp to start with. Wipe them off frequently with a damp rag, to keep paste from gumming them up. Razor blades do not stay sharp very long. If you want to pinch pennies, you can touch up the edges after every one or two cuts with emery cloth or a sharpening stone. But it's easier to be extravagant and toss out a blade as soon as it displays any reluctance about its job.)

After trimming the first strip at top and bottom, smooth the ends down once more with your smoothing brush. Then wash off the paste on the ceiling and baseboard with a clean, damp cloth. Don't scrub, but be thorough. If any paste is left, it will show up within a few weeks as a brown smear and it may remove the ceiling or baseboard paint.

Hanging succeeding strips. These go up like the first strip although there are several additional steps to take.

1. Carefully match the pattern of the strip you are hanging to the strip already on the wall. Unfortunately, because something went awry in the printing plant or because the paste has stretched one of the strips, you may find that the match is not perfect at all points. This can't be corrected. But you should try to adjust the new strip so that the mismatch occurs near the bottom of the wall, where it will not be very noticeable.

2. Make the joint by butting the edge of the new strip to the previous strip. A butt joint is much less noticeable—in fact, it may be almost invisible—than a lapped joint; it is easier to make; and if you want to repaper over the

paper, you won't have to worry about the joint showing through.

Hang the new strip as close as possible to the previous strip and then slide it up tight against it. Use your smoothing brush as much as possible to push the paper; your hands may be dirty or sweaty. And work from the middle of the strip, not just along the edge. The reasons: You're less likely to tear the paper. For another thing, wallpaper when wet has a certain amount of give; and if you stretch the edge only, the seam may open up when the paper contracts in drying.

Don't be discouraged if, despite repeated efforts to butt joints perfectly, you wind up with a slight overlap or slight gap at some point. This happens because the wall is not level, and there isn't much you can do about it. However, it is possible to eliminate a lap by holding a metal straight-edge or framing square over it and slicing down through the two layers of paper with a razor blade. The straight-edge must, of course, be exactly lined up with the butt joint above and below the lap. The paper will cut better if you first allow it to dry a little.

3. As soon as you have hung and trimmed a new strip at top and bottom, wipe the edges with a damp cloth to remove paste and dirt. Then gently wash the entire strip.

4. About 10 to 15 minutes after completing a joint, roll it from top to bottom with a seam roller. By this time, the paste has dried slightly; nevertheless, you should not exert too much pressure lest some of the paste squeezes out or the roller makes a glossy stripe on the paper.

If the edges of adjacent strips do not butt tightly, roll not only the joint but also the paper within 3 in. of it on either side.

(Note that embossed papers should not be rolled. Special care must be taken in rolling flocked and sand-textured papers.)

5. Check every fourth or fifth strip with your plumb line or spirit level to make sure they are vertical. If you notice that the ceiling line seems to be cutting down further into the paper or moving up from it, it is probably because the

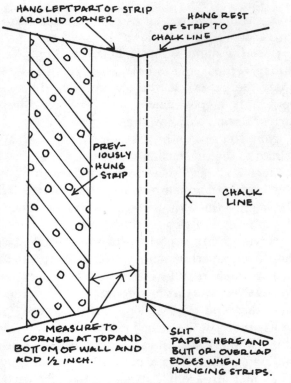

HANG LEFT PART OF STRIP AROUND CORNER

HANG REST OF STRIP TO CHALK LINE

PREVIOUSLY HUNG STRIP

CHALK LINE

MEASURE TO CORNER AT TOP AND BOTTOM OF WALL AND ADD ½ INCH.

SLIT PAPER HERE AND BUTT OR OVERLAP EDGES WHEN HANGING STRIPS.

WALLPAPERING AROUND A CORNER

ceiling is uneven or not level. But it may also be because you are hanging each strip at a slightly different height. Check this with a spirit level. Any adjustments called for should be made gradually unless the mismatches are minor. If they are major, you would do well to take off the most recently hung strips while the paste is still soft, and rehang them.

Special paperhanging techniques. Rounding a corner. Corners, door frames, window frames and similar interruptions in walls present various problems for the paperhanger if he tries to paper around them or beyond them with a full-width strip. Half the paper may develop ineradicable wrinkles. Gaps may appear at top or bottom. And the strip is almost always difficult to hang because a wide flap dangles in your face. Such things may be hard to comprehend in the reading; but they become clear in the doing.

The first step in papering around a corner, whether it be an inside or outside corner, is to measure from the edge of the last strip hung

to the corner. Make the measurement at the ceiling and also at the baseboard; and add ¾ to 1 in. to the higher figure.

After pasting and folding a full-size strip of paper and aligning the edges, transfer this measurement to it. Make sure you measure from the proper edge; it's easy to get confused. Lay your straight-edge the length of the folded strip, parallel with the edges, and cut along it with a razor blade.

To illustrate: Assume you are hanging wallpaper which is 21 in. wide. You are working from left to right. The strip just before the corner measures 6¼ in. from the corner at the ceiling, 7 in. at the baseboard. You should therefore cut the corner strip lengthwise into two pieces—the left side, 8 in. wide; the right side, 13 in. wide.

Butt the edge of the 8-in. strip to the previous strip, smooth it to the wall, work it firmly into the corner crease and smooth the flap down on the second wall. Since it is only 1 in. wide, the flap should not have any obvious wrinkles; but it may not hang straight if the corner is out of plumb. Check it with your plumb line or spirit level.

If the flap is straight, measure 13 in. from the edge to the right and strike a plumb line. If the flap is not straight, measure 13 in. to the right from the edge where it slants in closest to the corner. Then hang the 13-in. strip to the plumb line. Hopefully, it will butt the edge of the flap; but it may overlap the edge if the flap is on a slant. However, the lap is not very obvious, because it is in the corner and because —in the case of an inside corner—the paper is lapped toward the corner so the shadowline is invisible. On outside corners, if the partial strips must be overlapped, the lap should be made away from the light or from the point from which you usually view the corner. You may have to try it both ways to see which conceals the lap better.

Hanging paper toward a door. At the top and bottom of the door frame, measure the distance to the strip you have just hung. If the wider

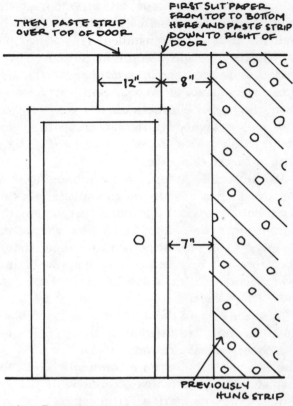

THEN PASTE STRIP OVER TOP OF DOOR

FIRST SLIT PAPER FROM TOP TO BOTTOM HERE AND PASTE STRIP DOWN TO RIGHT OF DOOR

←—— 12" ——→←— 8" —→

←— 7" —→

PREVIOUSLY HUNG STRIP

WALLPAPERING AROUND A DOOR.

measurement is no more than 3 in. less than the full width of the wallpaper, hang the full strip in the usual way; but don't try to smooth it down directly above the door until you have smoothed it up against the side casing. Then snip it horizontally at the top of the head casing, so that it will lie flat on the wall above.

If the distance from the last strip to the door frame is more than 3 in. less than the full width of the wallpaper, add ¾ to 1 in. to the wider measurement. (Add the smaller amount if the space at the baseboard is the wider; add 1 in. if the space at the top of the door frame is the wider.) Transfer this measurement to the pasted and folded strip and cut the strip lengthwise.

Butt the measured strip to the previous strip and smooth it to the wall and tight against the casing; snip at the top of the door and brush the flap down over the door. Cut the remaining partial strip into a short length, paste it over the door and trim it to the ceiling and top of the

door casing. (Note that in hanging short strips above doors and windows, it is easy to hang them on a slight slant because you don't have a long vertical line to butt the edge against. So study the pattern at the ceiling line and make certain it is positioned like previously hung strips. Use a rule as well as your eye.)

Now go back to the first part of the strip and trim it to the side casing of the door. Use a wide scraper and razor blade as when trimming at the baseboard or ceiling. Hold the scraper blade flat against the wall, with the front edge against the casing, and cut along the edge.

Having hung a partial strip above the door, continue papering across the wall above the door with short full-width strips.

Papering away from a door. As you approach the other end of the door frame, reverse the procedure just described. First measure from the last short strip hung the full width of the wallpaper and strike a plumb line on the wall. Then measure from the short strip to the corner of the door frame, subtract 1 in. and cut a full-length floor-to-ceiling strip lengthwise to this measurement.

Shorten the first piece to fit over the door and hang it. Then hang the second piece to the plumb line, trim it at the top of the door frame and butt the flap to the first piece. Finish by trimming the second piece to the side casing.

Hanging paper around a window. This is similar to papering around a door but is a bit more difficult, because you must trim the long strips beside the casing at both top and bottom and also around the sill. The best procedure is to get the strip butted to the previous strip (or plumb line) and smoothed to the wall. Then work down, snipping and fitting the strip over the top of the window; then snipping and fitting around the sill; and, finally, snipping and fitting around the apron.

The other problem is to position the short strips above and below the window so that, when you are papering away from the window, they make an exact pattern match with the final long strip. Since the space below the window is less visible than that above, any discrepancies should occur at that point. But you can avoid a mismatch there if you don't trim the short strip at the bottom until the final long strip is in place and the short strip is adjusted up and down to conform with it.

Hanging wallpaper around an electric switch or outlet. The cover plate should have been removed before you started your project.

Hang the paper right over the metal box as if it didn't exist. Then, carefully trim a hole around the edges of the box. Use a razor blade or sharp knife and take care not to let it touch the terminals. (I was jolted once when I worked too fast.) Finally, smooth the paper to the wall tight around the box and replace the cover plate.

Hanging wallpaper around a light fixture. Turn off the light and take down the fixture just before hanging paper behind it. Let it hang by its cord unless it is extremely heavy; in which case, someone must hold it. Position the paper and smooth it on the wall down as far as the light wires. With shears, cut straight in from the nearest side to the wires and cut out some of the paper directly over the electric box. Fit the wires through the slit and smooth down the paper, butting the slit edges carefully. Replace the fixture after the strip is hung.

Hanging wallpaper behind radiators and toilet tanks. You will be better off if you remove radiators; but if you can't, no matter. (Toilet tanks are too difficult to remove even to contemplate it.) Simply smooth the paper strip down as far as possible with your smoothing brush. Then reach behind the radiator, open the bottom fold and pull the paper down. Finally, smooth it by holding a yardstick horizontally and drawing it down flat against the wall.

If you can't reach the strip to open the fold, open it slightly before dropping it behind the radiator, insert a yardstick through the partial opening and work the end of the paper down to the baseboard. Then run the yardstick over the surface of the strip to smooth it.

Hanging wallpaper around bathroom cabinets. Don't! Both surface-mounted and recessed cabinets are easily taken down by removing the screws holding them. Hang paper over the wall where they were installed. Then cut it out for a recessed cabinet and replace the cabinet.

Hanging wallpaper in a dormer. There's no way you can do this so you can get a good—let alone perfect—pattern match at all points. So use a wallpaper with a confused or all-over design which more or less hides the mismatching.

If the dormer wall is in the same plane as the adjacent knee walls (a knee wall is a short vertical wall below a slanting wall), the strips hung on it are matched to those on the knee walls as if you were papering a normal straight wall. Then paper the two triangular walls inside the dormer separately, making little attempt to match them with the other walls.

On the other hand, if the dormer is a deep walk-in design, treat the entire thing separately from the main walls.

Hanging wallpaper on a slanting wall. To do this with comparative ease on a long slanting wall, you need a spirit level to establish a vertical line on the wall for the first paper strip. You obviously can't do this with a plumb line. However, if a slanting wall is short—only 2 or 3 ft., say—you can use a plumb line to establish a vertical line on the knee wall. Then hang the strip on the knee wall before finishing the job on the slanting wall.

But I don't want to oversimplify the work. The corner between the knee and slanting walls is frequently not horizontal. As a result, the paper on one wall may slant while on the other wall it is straight. When this happens, the only thing you can do is to slit the paper across, slide the portion on the bottom wall up slightly and lap the top portion over it in the corner.

Hanging wallpaper on a stairway. Unless the pattern requires special placement, hang the longest strip (or strips) first. Enlist a helper to open and lower the strips slowly, so they don't tear. The whole job takes time, because the long strips are hard to handle and because you are teetering on a ladder or trestle; but the technique is no different from that used in papering an ordinary wall.

Prepasted wallpaper. If you insist, go ahead and follow the manufacturer's directions for hanging prepasted paper. *I'll* stick with my method.

Cut and hang the strips as you do unpasted paper. The only thing you do differently is to apply water to the back rather than paste. Don't brush this on carefully; in fact, slosh it on. You need plenty to get the factory-applied paste soft and sticky. After folding each strip, let it soak while you wet a couple more strips.

Hand-printed wallpaper. It's advisable to hang these papers over lining paper. True, you can get away without this. But it makes for a smoother, more attractive finish wall. It absorbs some of the paste on the wallpaper and thus helps to keep you from getting paste on the surface of the wallpaper. It also, in some cases, helps to assure that the wallpaper will not come loose at the seams.

Hand prints are handled in the way described above. Trimming of the selvages is almost always necessary. Roll the joints with as little pressure as possible. If the pattern you use seems to soak up paste better in the undecorated areas than on the designs, roll the pasted, folded and trimmed strips loosely and put them into a plastic bag for 15 or 20 minutes to let the designs take up the paste.

Glossy papers have a strong tendency to curl along the edges if they are pasted in the conventional manner. To prevent this, sponge water on the back and let it soak in until the strip is limp and lies flat. Then apply paste and proceed with folding, trimming and hanging.

Flocked wallpaper. Hang this over lining paper. Use a slightly heavier paste than usual. If there is a great deal of loose flock on the surface, vacuum it off before you paste the strips.

Don't be too rough with your smoothing brush when you flatten the strips on the wall. You might prefer to use a soft paint roller. Press down the edges of the strips by tapping with the smoothing brush. You should not use an ordinary seam roller. However, if you have trouble with the seams, you can go over them with a roller covered with a piece of flocked paper. To attach this to the roller, use a double-faced adhesive tape.

The most important precaution in hanging flocked paper is to keep it free of paste and to prevent loose flock from clinging to rough ceiling surfaces and crevices in baseboards. The best way to accomplish this is to stick a 3-in.-wide strip of masking tape to the ceiling at the top of the wall. The baseboard can be covered in the same way; or you can simply hang a strip of wrapping paper over it with narrow masking tape. This makes it unnecessary to wash the ceiling or baseboard and thus transfer some of the paste to the paper. It also prevents the flock from getting on these surfaces.

If paste should get on flocked paper, blot and wash it as best you can; then go over the entire strip with a sponge wrung out in clean —always clean—water. When the surface is dry, if the flock is matted, go over it lightly with a soft-bristle brush.

Sand-finished wallpaper. Cover the wall with lining paper. Because sand-finished paper often cracks when creased, the edges cannot be trimmed in the usual way. Do it before applying paste. Turn each strip pattern-side up, align it with the front edge of the paste table and cut along a straight-edge laid parallel with the edge. Then proceed with pasting and folding. But don't press the folds tight; roll the strip loosely and put it in a plastic bag to soak for a while.

Keep paste off the surface as much as possible by the methods described for flocked paper, and roll the seams very lightly if at all.

If strips must be lapped, scrape or sand the roughness from the bottom strip, to reduce the thickness of the joint. Breaks in the finish are almost impossible to avoid but can be touched up with alkyd paint containing a little sand.

Scenic wallpaper. Scenics are expensive, hand-printed papers sold in sets consisting of a number of strips of patterned paper and three strips of "matching ground" (a solid paper colored like the background of the patterned paper). All the strips are 28 in. wide after trimming and 10 to 12 ft. long. When ordering, note the total width of the set; and if it is less than the wall to be covered, order additional ground papers. To assure a perfect match with the ground papers in the set, the additional strips must be specially printed. Do not settle for the "companion papers" which are available, because these may not be exactly the same color as the ground papers in the set. Companion papers may, however, be used on adjoining walls.

Additional patterned papers may also be ordered in some cases. These should be hung in the order recommended by the manufacturer. For example, if the standard set comes with five patterned strips numbered 1, 2, 3, 4, 5 and you order two extra strips—3 and 4—the manufacturer may tell you to arrange the strips 3,4,5,1,2,3,4.

A scenic paper must be hung over lining paper. The patterned part is usually centered on the wall. If wider than the wall, it may as a rule be trimmed at both ends; but a few designs lend themselves to trimming at one end only.

Directions accompanying the paper suggest the best height for the design and also the amount of unprinted paper below the design. For example, the directions may say: "Highest point of design, 65 in. Height of ground below design, 35 in." However, if a wall is not a standard 8 ft. high, you may raise the design on high walls, lower it a trifle on short walls. But don't do this without first holding the strips against the wall.

Scenic papers as well as other valuable hand prints are sometimes hung over muslin or unbleached cotton instead of lining paper if the homeowner wants to preserve them when he moves to another house. You can buy either material in widths and lengths sufficient to cover almost any wall in one piece.

Spread the fabric on the floor and cut out a piece somewhat larger than the wall. Allow 1 in. per yard for shrinkage plus about 2 in. for trimming at top and bottom and the ends. Apply wheat paste in an even coat and brush it well into the weave; then fold the cloth paste-surface to paste-surface and let it soak for about 20 minutes.

Have an assistant help you hang the material. Start from the upper right or left corner and smooth it on the wall from top to bottom and side to side. Cover right over any door or window in the wall, and then trim out around it with a razor blade and wide wall scraper. Finally, trim the edges and let the cloth dry completely before starting to hang wallpaper.

Maintaining and repairing wallpaper. Dust wallpaper occasionally or, better yet, go over it with a vacuum cleaner. A vacuum is essential on flocked paper.

To remove soil, mild stains and mildew from washable paper, sponge with a little warm water or, if this doesn't work, with mild detergent solution. Use a "dough" cleaner for dirt on nonwashable paper. You must go over the entire wall with this, not just the dirty areas, otherwise the effect will be uneven. Grease stains on nonwashable paper are removed with a special aerosol cleaner which is sprayed on, allowed to dry and dusted off. Mildew must be dusted or vacuumed off when it is dry.

Nonwashable paper can be soil-proofed by rolling on one or two coats of a prepared transparent wallpaper coating. Test this on a large scrap before applying to the entire wall.

Stick down edges that come loose with wallpaper paste. Apply this with a small brush or an artist's metal spatula. A paste put up in tubes for repair work is available.

Objectionable blisters can be removed by slicing through them with a razor blade and applying paste underneath.

If wallpaper has a hole, rip or stain, tear—never cut—a patch out of a matching piece. (Never throw out wallpaper left over from a paperhanging project until you repaper the walls.) Then paste it down. A torn patch is much less noticeable than a cut one.

8

Other Flexible Wall Coverings

Every time I turn around I hear of someone decorating walls with a new kind of flexible covering. Just the other day it was leather. I've thought of using leather on walls. I have a feeling I've seen it illustrated in magazines. But I've never been able to pinpoint an actual installation until now. One of my daughters has seen it and says it is handsome. I am certain it is. Also durable.

If you think how many flexible materials are made, the range of decorating possibilities available to you begins to open wider and wider. The only real problem is to figure out what adhesive will do the best job. I tried covering a wall with the four-color illustrations from one of my gardening books a few years ago, and it didn't work out at all well. Because the paper was glossy, I was sure wallpaper paste wouldn't be right, so I used rubber cement. But no—the blistering was terrible.

The wall coverings described in this chapter have much in common. Most are installed like wallpaper, so if you want a clear understanding of the process, you must first read Chapter 7. Most are, at best, only semidurable. And most are in the higher price brackets.

The last problem—if you want to call it a problem—is aggravated by two inescapable facts:

1. If the covering or pattern you want is

available only on special order—meaning that it must be produced for you alone—you will probably have to buy a minimum order of, say, half a dozen or a dozen rolls, even though you don't need anywhere near that many.

2. Many of these wall coverings are sold only in lengths more or less exactly divisible by 8 (the height of the average interior wall). This causes no hardship if you need only full-length, 8-ft. strips. But what if your walls are broken up by a number of windows and doors? In this case, instead of getting three full-length strips out of, say, a 24-ft. roll, you may get only two full-length strips, plus a short piece to fit over a door.

"But, no," you protest. "I'll still have 5 or 6 ft. left to cut into short pieces for another door or maybe two doors."

True, but I haven't told you quite the whole story: Because many of these special wall coverings are hand-produced, the colors are very often not identical from roll to roll. So the 5 or 6 ft. of material left over from that first roll may not be usable when you get to a second door, because it doesn't match the material hung on the wall between doors.

But let's not dwell on such unhappy thoughts. These are beautiful—often exotic—wall coverings; and anyone who uses them does so in the knowledge that supreme beauty is rarely attained without some pain.

Vinyl wall covering. Next to wallpaper, vinyls are far and away the most popular flexible wall coverings. Once made only in very plain patterns, they are now available in a great many decorative designs. There are also wet-look and flocked vinyls.

As opposed to a few wall coverings which are labeled vinyls but which are really nothing more than plastic-coated wallpapers, the true vinyl wall coverings are made either with a paper or cloth backing and come in a considerable range of weights (thicknesses). The heavy- and middleweights, which are classified by the industry as Type C and Type B, are rarely hung in homes, because they are much more durable than necessary. The heavyweights, for instance,

are made to withstand abrasion by stretchers, hand trucks and the like; the middleweights, to withstand wear by hordes of people moving through school and hotel corridors.

For the home, the Type A lightweights are just right. They are stain-resistant, not merely washable but scrubbable and they can withstand most ordinary wear. This makes them ideal for children's rooms, family rooms and halls—as well as kitchens, where frequent washing may be a necessity.

Both machine prints and hand prints are available. The former are usually pretrimmed; the latter usually are not. Widths range from roughly 20 to 27 in. Rolls contain about 36 sq. ft. Prices range from a little more than the cheapest wallpaper to a little less than the most expensive. Installation is almost identical in technique and difficulty.

Hanging vinyl wall covering. Wash, patch and prepare the walls in the same way as with wallpaper. It's strongly advisable to remove old wallpaper—essential if you have an old vinyl covering—since paste does not adhere to it well. Cloth-backed vinyl, like strippable wallpaper, rips off in large pieces down to the base. Paper-backed vinyls are removed by scuffing up and pulling off the vinyl film. The paper backing that remains serves as a first-class base for all new flexible coverings if you apply size to make it less fuzzy.

Use the type of size specified by the wall-covering maker—if he specifies any at all. Concrete, concrete blocks, cinder blocks and asbestos cement boards must first be covered with acrylic latex paint to seal in the alkalis they may contain. If a wall surface has a fine, even sand texture, a fairly thick vinyl can be hung directly over it. But anything rougher than this must be smoothed by sanding. The alternative is to apply gypsum board joint compound in a thin layer and sand it.

Three precautionary steps to take before starting to hang a vinyl wall covering are: (1) Turn up the heat in the room to 60°F. or more. (2) Make sure you have the adhesive recommended by the covering manufacturer. (3)

Make sure also to ascertain whether all strips should be hung top up or whether every other strip should be reversed (the first top up, the second top down, the third top up, and so on). Reversing used to be required for all vinyls, but today many are hung in the standard way.

Cut and match the strips as you do with wallpaper. If you have purchased an untrimmed pattern, remove the selvages now by laying the strips face up and cutting along a straight-edge.

Vinyl adhesives are thick, sticky mastics designed to dry in the absence of air (the wall coverings are nonporous). If you start with a powder, mix it exactly to the manufacturer's directions. If you use a premixed adhesive (which obviously saves work), do not dilute it unless it is extremely difficult to work with; and in that case, add water up to no more than 10 percent of the volume of the adhesive. Apply the adhesive to the back of the wall covering in an even coat, either with a wallpaper paste brush or a paint roller with a medium nap. The latter applies a more even coating, and is easier to use, because the slippery face of the paper makes it hard to hold in place while brushing out paste.

After pasting a strip, fold top and bottom to meet at the center and smooth down the folds, but don't crease them hard. A sharp crease is difficult to rub out when the vinyl is on the wall. Then roll the strip loosely and set it aside, preferably in a plastic bag, while you paste two or three additional strips.

Hang the strips like wallpaper. Trim them at top and bottom and along the edges (as necessary) with a razor blade and wide wall scraper. The razor cuts vinyl more smoothly than shears, although you still need the latter for some cutting.

I have found that you can carry vinyl further around a corner than wallpaper without creating wrinkles on the second wall, but I must confess I don't know how far you can go. That obviously depends on the contours of the corner. In any case, if you are hanging into a corner and find the strip will lap 6 in. or less

on the next wall, try it with a full strip first. If it wrinkles or if the edge on the second wall is out of plumb, you can always slit it close to the corner and hang in the normal wallpapering fashion.

The most important step in hanging vinyl wall covering is to remove all air pockets. If you're working with a very lightweight material, this can be done with the usual wallpaper smoothing brush; but on heavier material, you may find it desirable to trim the brush bristles to 1-in. length. And you may occasionally need a broad knife. This is, in effect, a wide scraper made of plastic. But you can use a steel scraper if you carefully round the edge and corners. Or you can even use a short piece of ⅛-in. hardboard with a smooth edge.

Go over each strip several times as you hang it to work out blisters. If necessary, don't hesitate to pull the strip off the wall back to the bubble and start over again. Blisters left under vinyl usually are permanent.

About 15 or 20 minutes after the strip has set, when you go back to roll the seams, look for blisters once again. Hold a strong light close to the wall on the right and left sides of the strip to show them up. This is especially important with cloth-backed vinyls because blisters usually do not appear under these until they have been on the wall awhile.

If you should find a blister after the adhesive has set too much to permit pulling off the strip, puncture it with a large needle or a razor blade. Then smooth it down. Blisters appearing several days after the wall is completed are opened in the same way. Then squirt a few drops of water into them with a hypodermic needle or tiny oil can and smooth down.

Flocked vinyl coverings must be hung with the same care as flocked wallpapers. Wet-look vinyls with a very glossy surface like old-fashioned oil cloth are hung like ordinary vinyls, but it is imperative that the wall surface to which they are pasted be absolutely smooth. Even the tiniest bump shows through. Remove lumps and brush bristles from the adhesive, too.

Maintaining and repairing vinyl wall coverings. Wash with a cloth wrung out in mild detergent solution to remove soil and most stains.

If strips come loose at the edges, try to scrape off the old adhesive and apply new with a dull knife or artist's spatula. You should use special vinyl adhesive, but if it isn't available, white wood glue will do.

If a hole develops, tear a patch to match and apply it with vinyl adhesive or white glue.

Grass cloth and similar fabric wall coverings. This group of wall coverings is charming for the textures it affords. They range from open linenlike weaves to rather coarse weaves suggestive of straw table mats. The colors are muted and almost invariably fade if exposed to sun.

All the coverings are laminated to paper backings. Some of the facing materials are synthetics; others—mostly imports from the Orient—are made of natural fibers. The former are uniform in color as well as texture. The latter need to be unrolled a number of feet and overlapped on a table, so you can shade them.

Grass cloth is available for as little as 18¢ a sq. ft., but most patterns are considerably higher. They are sold in double rolls 3 ft. wide and 24 ft. long. Fortunately, there is enough lengthwise stretch in them when they are wet to permit you to get three full strips out of each roll.

Hanging grass cloth and the like. First cover the walls with lining paper. (This soaks up some of the paste applied to the wall coverings.)

The synthetics are usually started in a corner. But because of the differences in color between rolls of natural-fiber wall coverings, you should usually start the first strip in the center of an unbroken wall and work to the corners on either side. Or you should start in the center between doors, or between windows, or between doors (or windows) and corners. Note, however, that this arrangement may look wrong —especially on an unbroken wall—if the strips at the ends of the space are much narrower than those in between. (Example: If there are three 35-in. strips in the middle, flanked by 10-in. strips at either end, the effect is disturbing.) To correct for this, you should reduce the width of the middle strips and increase that of the end strips. (Example: You might rearrange the preceding wall with strips 22, 27, 27, 27, 22 in. wide.) But obviously this wastes expensive material, so study each wall carefully before getting to work. Tacking strips to a wall for examination is a very good idea.

After cutting strips to the required length, roll each one out along the edge of the paste table to make sure the edges are straight. Very often they are not; in which case you should trim them back a fraction of an inch to a straight line. If you fail to do this, you won't be able to cut the edges straight after pasting. Conversely, if you fail to trim the edges after pasting (*see next paragraph*), paste will crawl around the edges and stain the surface of the covering.

Brush on paste of medium thickness; fold the strips, and trim the edges again (or for the first time). The final strips should be close to 35 in. wide. Hang them at once: The paste is absorbed very quickly, and if you let it soak too long, the coverings may delaminate.

The edges of adjacent strips should be butted. However, since this type of covering has no sideways stretch, you can't push the edges close together. You should instead stretch the strip downward. This eliminates slight overlaps. Similarly, it forces a new strip which has been bent away from the preceding strip to bend back toward it.

Another trick you should learn, if you find a little gap between the edges of two otherwise well-hung strips, is to squeeze the edges beside the gap up and down, thus forcing them together. This leaves a wrinkle in the paper; but it can be removed by slitting horizontally and pasting one edge over the other so you can't see the lap. (In other words, if the slit is below normal eye level, lay the top edge down over the bottom.)

A question that puzzles people hanging grass

cloth and similar wall coverings for the first time is what to do when the wall is crooked and a strip goes out of plumb. Obviously, you shouldn't butt the next strip; and if you lapped it over the edge of the crooked strip, it would create a thick, all-too-obvious seam. The easiest solution is to strike a plumb line along the crooked edge and then trim off the edge with a razor blade and straight-edge.

Rolling seams should be avoided, especially on coarse materials, because it compresses the fibers and leaves a visible strip. Just tap the seams down well with your smoothing brush.

If grass cloth is sufficiently flexible to permit right-angle bending of a strip from top to bottom, hang the material around corners like wallpaper. But if sharp bending is difficult, butt the strips on either side of a corner right in the corner.

Keep paste off the surface of the coverings by the methods described for hanging flocked wallpaper. If you do get sloppy with the paste, blot it up with a soft dry rag. If water is required, use a barely damp sponge.

Maintaining and repairing grass cloth and the like. The material is hard to clean. Try water on a well-wrung-out sponge first. Then a mild detergent. Then dry-cleaning fluid or a spray-on dry-cleaning powder. For repairs, see vinyl wall covering.

Burlap. This once coarse, utilitarian material has become popular as a wall covering because of its texture and durability. It is available in many colors and even in some printed patterns. And if you're looking for a water-resistant burlap, a vinyl-coated type is also made.

Burlap wall coverings come with or without a paper backing. Use the "with" type only—it's easier to handle. You have a choice of 36- and 45-in. widths; but as with other coverings, all single rolls cover approximately 36 sq. ft. They cost about 25¢ per sq. ft.

Hanging burlap. Apply burlap over lining paper. Start in a corner and work around the room. Every other strip should be hung upside down. Use powdered vinyl adhesive and mix it with water according to the maker's directions.

Apply it with a short-napped paint roller. After rolling on one coat, let it set about a minute and roll on a second coat. Then fold the strip like wallpaper and remove ½ to 1 in. along each edge with a razor blade. Because burlap is tough and ravels easily, don't try to get much mileage out of any one blade.

Instead of a wallpaper smoothing brush, use a plastic broad knife or the equivalent to flatten the burlap on the wall. Don't rush the job. Butt the edge of the strip you are hanging to the preceding strip for about 2 ft. down from the ceiling, and smooth the strip carefully. Then work on the next 2 ft., and so on to the bottom. Smooth the burlap horizontally and vertically, but do *not* smooth the edges lest you distort or ravel the threads. The edges should instead be pressed down by hand or with a flat seam roller.

At corners, and whenever hanging a new strip beside one with a slanting edge, follow the procedure for hanging grass cloth. Take pains not to get paste on the surface of the material. You can keep it clean by trimming at the top and bottom like flocked wallpaper. Blisters which appear after the paste sets are slit with a razor blade and pressed down. If necessary, inject a little water to soften the paste.

Should any threads ravel at the edges, spread a very thin coat of white wood glue underneath and press them down.

Maintaining and repairing burlap. Vacuum regularly. But removal of embedded dirt and stains is almost hopeless. Use dry-cleaning fluid or a spray-on dry-cleaning powder, and hope for the best. Paste down loose edges with white wood glue.

Felt. The felt used for covering walls is a preshrunk, mothproofed, flameproofed wool felt laminated to a paper backing. (Unbacked felt is available, but don't play with it.) It comes in many beautiful colors and with a smooth or textured surface. The material is 54 in. wide, put up in long rolls and sold by the yard. The cost per sq. ft. is about $1.70.

Felt is a warm-looking material that actually has some insulating qualities. It also helps to reduce noise in rooms. But while it can be vac-uumed, it is not easy to keep clean; and stains are stubborn. A few colors are prone to fading.

Hanging felt. Hang felt over lining paper. All strips are hung with the same end up. Arrows are printed on the back to keep you straight.

Because of the width and weight of the ma-terial, get someone to help you install it. You should also add to the width of your paste ta-ble, otherwise you must work on the floor. Use wheat paste.

The principal installation problem—and a very difficult one—is to keep paste off the sur-face, because water used to remove it shrinks the wool and also changes the color slightly. The best solution worked out by professionals sounds more troublesome than it actually is.

To protect the material along the top and bottom edges, apply masking tape to the ceil-ing and baseboard, as for flocked wallpaper.

To protect the side edges, cut heavy-gauge polyethylene sheets, like those used in vapor barriers in houses, into straight strips 3 in. wide and slightly longer than the felt strips.

Start hanging felt from a corner. (For sake of clarity, let's say you are working from left to right.) Let the felt lap around the corner about 1 in. Strike a plumb line on the wall to the right of the corner at a point equal to the felt less 1 in.

After applying paste to the upper part of the felt strip, center one of the plastic ribbons over the edge which will align with the plumb line and stick it down along the edge. Then paste the rest of the felt and stick down the rest of the plastic strip. Hang the felt to the plumb line on the wall. Smooth it with a plastic broad knife or a very clean, soft, smoothing brush. Trim it at top and bottom with a razor blade and wide wall scraper. Then check the 1-in. lap to the left of the corner with a plumb line and cut it to a true vertical with a razor blade and straight-edge.

Measure the width of the felt minus 2 in. to the right of the first strip and strike another plumb line. Then paste the second strip of felt and stick plastic strips along *both* edges. Hang

the strip to the new plumb line; smooth it on the wall, letting the left edge lap over the right edge of the first strip; and trim at top and bottom.

Center your plumb line over the lapped edges and make a few light pencil marks di-rectly behind it. Aligning a straight-edge with the marks, cut through the two layers of felt and plastic from top to bottom with a razor blade. Remove any plastic which remains un-der either strip of felt. Then smooth the edges of the felt down from top to bottom and, after the paste has set for 10 minutes, roll them lightly. This should give you a perfect butt joint without any paste on the surface.

When hanging the last strip of felt, omit the plastic strip from the edge that will butt the 1-in. lap in the starting corner and make this joint very carefully. Then double-cut the other edge and preceding strip.

If paste should get on the surface, brush over it with a damp cloth in the direction of the finish.

Maintaining and repairing felt. Never scrub felt or use a lot of water on it. Remove soil and stains with any good granular rug cleaner.

If edges come loose, reglue with wheat paste.

If felt is badly damaged or stained, hold a scrap over the area and cut a square through both layers at once with a razor blade. Then scrape off the damaged felt and set in the patch with wheat paste. It won't look right, but it will be an improvement.

Shiki silk. This laminated, 36-in. wall cover-ing resembles grass cloth inasmuch as it has a definite horizontal weave and color shading; but its texture is much more delicate. The color is usually solid but patterns with hand-printed designs are available. The price runs about $2 per sq. ft.

Hanging shiki silk. Hang shiki silk over lin-ing paper with stainless cellulose paste. Shade the rolls carefully before cutting. The strips have a very irritating way of curling at the ends. To prevent this while pasting, weight the ends down under sticks of wood. A more reli-able solution is to screw two spring-type clips to a 3-ft. piece of wood, clip these to the end of the paper and let the wood hang over the table edge.

Do not pile the strips one atop the other when pasting. Instead, lay the back edge of the strip you are pasting over a piece of lining paper and use this to keep the tabletop clean. Apply the paste evenly and not too heavily with a short-napped paint roller. Then fold, trim off the edges and hang the strip as quickly as possible, before the paste dries or soaks deeply into the paper backing.

Silk coverings don't have much stretch, so it may be hard to butt the edges on an uneven wall. If necessary, slit the paper horizontally for a few inches to bring an edge into line with a previous strip. Overlap the slit edges so they won't be visible.

As with grass cloth, you must keep paste off the silk. If any spots of it appear, remove them with a dry rag, sponge with a very little water and blot dry.

On hand-printed silks, the actual design is usually considerably narrower than the paper backing; and the backing often has crooked edges. Before pasting the paper, therefore, you should trim back the edges slightly to a straight edge. Then apply paste, fold the strip and trim the edges again to the design.

Maintaining and repairing shiki silk. Follow directions—such as they are—for grass cloth.

Cork wall covering. This wall covering is made of feather-thin slices of cork glued to a paper backing. The latter—which shows through cracks in the cork and the narrow spaces between the cork slices—is frequently a shiny red, orange, gold or black. Some of the more expensive coverings are decorated with hand-printed designs.

The rich, warm appearance of the covering is so unusual that you may well want to feature it on a single wall of a room. I doubt if you would use it on all walls except in a very small room. But, whatever you do, bear in mind that it is fragile and stainable, and should not be exposed to oily hands or wear.

Cork coverings come in 30- and 36-in. widths

and in 24-, 36- and 45-ft. lengths. They cost upward of 30¢ a sq. ft.

Hanging cork wall covering. Line the walls. Use an adhesive made of four parts wheat paste and one part prepared vinyl adhesive. After pasting and folding a strip, roll it loosely and put it in a plastic bag while pasting, folding and rolling the next strip. Then apply a second thin layer of paste to the first strip, fold it, trim the edges and hang it.

Although cork coverings may at first glance appear to have a definite pattern, they in fact do not. Adjacent strips are butted together at random. Do the job carefully, and roll the joints at once to assure that they stick tight. Any paste that oozes out can be sponged off with water.

Maintaining and repairing cork wall covering. Sponge with a very little water to remove soil, but don't count on success. Paste down loose edges with wheat paste.

Metal-foil wall coverings. There are ordinary wallpapers coated with metallic particles and there are exotic wall coverings made by laminating ever-so-thin sheets of metal to paper or cloth. I'm talking about the latter here. You can tell them from metallic wallpapers because they tear like kitchen aluminum foil; and if you work hard at it, you can rip the foil from the backing.

Most of the metal foils have an overall plain or random design, but some of the newer patterns have hand-printed or flocked designs. There are also coverings with raised patterns, giving a three-dimensional effect. The coverings come in widths and in rolls covering 36 sq. ft. They cost 30¢ to $1 a sq. ft.

Hanging metal foils. Cloth-backed foils are usually pretrimmed and can be applied directly to clean, smooth, sound wall surfaces. Paper-backed foils, on the other hand, should be applied over lining paper and edge-trimmed before pasting. The trimming procedure is unusual.

If a foil strip is longer than 6 ft., roll it out pattern side up on the paste table and lay a long, clean board from end to end over the back half to hold the strip flat. Determine how much is to be trimmed from the front edge, and measure at the top of the strip and at a point 3 ft. down. Place your straight-edge on these marks and cut along it with a razor blade for the 3 ft. Then measure and trim another 3 ft.; and so on until the entire strip is trimmed.

If a strip is less than 6 ft. long, measure in the same distance at the ends and halfway between. Then weight down the back half of the strip; lay a straight-edge along the three marks; and cut from end to end in one stroke. If you can't line the straight-edge up with all three marks, remove the weight and straight-edge and let the back edge of the strip roll toward you. Then line the straight-edge up with the marks and slice off the selvage. (Yes, surprisingly, the straight-edge will now line up with the marks.) Repeat along the other side.

To hang foils which have a white paper backing, vinyl adhesive is applied to the wall with a medium-napped paint roller and paint brush just ahead of each strip. The strip, which has been rolled loosely with the backing on the outside, is then rolled out over the adhesive against a plumb line or the edge of the preceding strip. After smoothing, trimming and sponging the foil with water to remove paste, cover the next section of wall with adhesive and hang a second strip. Butt the edges and, after the paste has set for a few minutes, press them down with a wallpaper seam roller. This should be used, with very little pressure, to prevent denting of the foil.

If you have trouble applying paste close against the previously hung strip, try the following: Cut a piece of cloth-backed vinyl wall covering to the height of the wall and cover the back with a thick layer of adhesive. Fold the strip like wallpaper and cut it into straight, inch-wide ribbons. Place these in a plastic bag until you need them. After each strip of foil has been hung on the wall and trimmed at top and bottom, butt one of the vinyl ribbons carefully to the edge, press it down, then pull it off and throw it away just before hanging the next

strip of foil. It will leave just the right amount of adhesive to anchor the edge of the foil.

Foils with brown paper backing are easier to hang. After cutting them into wall-length strips, sponge the backs with water. Work from the bottom up, wetting a section 8–10 in. wide across the foil. Then immediately roll that section of foil, back side in, into a loose roll and sponge another 8–10-in. section. When the entire strip is wet and rolled, place it in a plastic bag and wet two or three more strips in the same way.

They are then ready to be pasted like wallpaper, folded (but don't crease the ends) and hung at once. To keep adhesive off the paste table, spread a piece of lining paper under each foil strip.

Cloth-backed foils are handled like wallpaper. Use the adhesive recommended by the manufacturer.

No matter which type of foil you use, all those with solid or random patterns are hung by reversing every other strip.

Maintaining and repairing foils. Follow the directions for vinyl.

Silks, velvets, linens and other fine fabrics. There must be some significance in the fact that some of the most recently redecorated rooms in the White House have fabric-finished walls. The Red Room walls are covered with red twill satin with a scrolled frieze in gold. The Green Room walls are covered with a shimmering moire in moss green.

Interior decorators have always used beautiful fabrics for wall coverings; and today, the example they have set is beginning to rub off on just plain homeowners. Fabric-covered walls are not only attractive but also quite practical. You can keep them clean without too much effort. Abrasion resistance is good, although obviously other materials are better in this respect. You can change the positions of pictures, mirrors and the like without leaving visible nail holes.

Fabrics are sold in large bolts usually measuring 45 in. wide. You can buy exactly what you need and no more. In cost they are comparable with most of the other coverings discussed in this chapter. And they are no more difficult to hang. In some instances, in fact, they are easier.

Hanging fabrics. Installation is made in five ways, although the methods are not always interchangeable. In all cases, paint the woodwork first. Remove outlet and switch plates. Also take down light fixtures and remove them from their leads. Clean the floor very, very thoroughly.

LATH-AND-STAPLE METHOD. This is the traditional installation method—and not the best. It involves stretching the fabric on a wood framework nailed to the wall. This means that when you push the fabric, it bends inward and if you snag it with a fingernail or anything sharp, it may tear. On the other hand, no preparation of the wall surface is necessary. If it's covered with chipped paint or old wallpaper, if it's crisscrossed with cracks and full of gaping holes, no matter.

The framework should be made of smooth ¼-in.-thick lattice strips. Nail these end to end across the wall at the ceiling line and baseboard; all the way around door and window casings; and up and down the corners—one strip on one wall, a second strip on the adjacent wall. You must also tack strips around electric boxes.

Trim the selvages from the fabric; then cut the bolt into strips equal to the height of the wall plus 3 in. at the top and 3 in. at the bottom. You should also allow 3-in. extra width for any strip starting in a corner, and ½-in. extra width for sewing adjacent strips together. If the fabric is to be extended around a corner on to a second wall, add 6 in. to the width at that point to help you handle and fit it.

Before stitching the strips together, make sure the weave and nap, if any, are running in the same direction on all strips. Match the pattern as necessary. Then seam the edges on a sewing machine and press them flat.

Attach the fabric to the lattice strips with a staple gun. The staples should be positioned

¼ in. in from the edges of the fabric. Start attaching the fabric to the ceiling strip at the middle of the wall and work to the left corner. Then work to the right corner. The fabric should be taut, but don't stretch it out of shape.

Then attach the side edges to the corner strips temporarily with a few pushpins; and staple it securely to the baseboard strip, working from the center. Finally, staple the sides.

The fabric is stretched over doors, windows and electric boxes as if they weren't there. If the casings are not unusually thick, staple the fabric to the lattice strips around the casings and then cut the fabric slightly smaller than the openings. But if the casings, window sills and so on are thick, the fabric should be cut slightly smaller than the openings before it is stapled down.

When all staples are in, examine the fabric for smoothness and tightness. Then trim around all edges with a razor blade and a wide wall scraper.

The last step is to cover the staples with braid, ribbon, tape and so on. Use a standard fabric adhesive or a white wood glue, and hold the covering in place with pushpins until the adhesive dries.

Painted or stained wooden moldings can also be used to conceal the staples.

DOUBLE-FACED TAPE METHOD. In this installation, the fabric is held flat against the wall and is therefore somewhat more resistant to snagging and ripping. But the wall underneath must be clean, smooth and sound.

Remove the selvages and cut the fabric into strips the height of the wall plus 2 in. at the bottom. You may also allow 2 in. extra at the top and trim this off later; or you may cut the top perfectly square and butt it against the ceiling line.

Stick double-faced vinyl tape to the wall at the ceiling line and baseboard, around doors, windows and electric boxes, and in the corners (two strips per corner). Starting at a corner, mark the wall off into sections equal to the width of the fabric strips, strike a plumb line at each point and apply vertical strips of tape to secure the edges of the fabric.

Do not remove the protective covering from the tape until you actually hang the fabric strips. Then, on the vertical tapes, remove it only about 1 ft. at a time.

Hang the initial strip of fabric from the starting corner. Stick it to the ceiling tape first; then work down the wall, sticking it to the side tapes. Go slow and smooth the fabric carefully. Don't stretch it too much but see that it is taut.

Hang succeeding strips in the same way. Butt the edges. Trim the fabric around the tops of doors and windows as you come to them. When the entire wall is covered, trim around all edges.

ADHESIVE METHOD. This makes a more secure, abrasion-resistant installation. The wall, however, must be prepared very carefully—as for wallpaper or vinyl wall covering—to assure a perfectly smooth finish. And the actual installation must be made with great care to keep from getting paste on the fabric. I strongly advise finding someone to help.

Before hanging any fabric, mix powdered vinyl adhesive to the manufacturer's directions and paste a large scrap of fabric to the wall to see what happens.

Cover the wall first with lining paper. After removing the selvages, cut the fabric into strips to the height of the wall plus 2 in. at the bottom. You may also allow a few inches extra at the top or cut the fabric off square and butt it to the ceiling. If you allow extra at the top, stick masking tape around the edges of the ceiling, so you won't have to wash off paste.

Roll each strip, from the bottom up, on a broomstick so it is easier to handle. Make the roll tight and wrinkle-free.

Start the first strip at an end of the wall and let it lap around the corner a fraction of an inch. Establish a plumb line for the other edge, and from here on strike a plumb line for each new strip. One difference between fabric and wallpaper is that, while the fabric has much more stretch, it does not slide very easily on a wall; so you must watch both edges of a strip to make sure one is hung to the plumb line and the other butts against the preceding strip.

Apply adhesive to the wall for each strip as you get to it. Use a medium-napped paint roller and paint brush. Professional paperhangers cover the wall from top to bottom; but until you get used to working with fabric, it's a smart idea to apply paste gradually from the top down. Paste an area; smooth the fabric onto it; paste another area; and so on.

If you have trouble pasting close to the edges of strips already hung, use cloth-backed vinyl ribbons, as in hanging metal foils.

Butt fabric strips tightly into corners of the walls, ceiling, door casings and so on and butt the edges of adjoining strips. Smooth them down with a brush or broad knife. Try not to use a seam roller.

At doors and windows, stretch the fabric across the openings and glue it only around the casings. It is usually necessary to cut the fabric back to some extent so that it does not exert too much tension on the pasted areas.

Blisters which appear should be brushed well to force the air out through the pores of the fabric. If you find a blister after the paste is dry, press it down and roll it a bit with a damp sponge to soften both paste and fabric.

Let the paste and fabric dry well before trimming them at the ceiling and baseboard, around casings and the like. Fabric is hard to cut cleanly when wet.

PAPER-BACKED-FABRIC METHOD. Fabrics which are laminated to a paper backing are much easier to hang with adhesive than are unbacked fabrics because they soak up less moisture and adhesive, the added stiffness makes them easier to handle and the edges are less likely to ravel. The actual hanging procedure is like that for grass cloth.

SELF-ADHESIVE-FABRIC METHOD. These fabrics come with contact-type adhesive already applied to the back. After preparing the wall, striking plumb lines and cutting the fabric into strips, all you have to do is peel off the protective paper backing foot by foot as you hang each strip down the wall.

Cut the strips to fit around doors and windows before hanging them. Make the cuts as accurately as possible, but err on the generous side so the fabric will lap on to the casings rather than leave gaps around them. The lapped portions can be trimmed off with a razor blade.

Maintaining and repairing fabrics. Use dry-cleaning fluid or powder to remove dirt and stains.

Carpet. If you want to tie a room together (so to speak), extend the carpet right up the walls. The effect is soft and warm. The acoustics of a noisy room are improved. And the walls can absorb an extraordinary amount of abuse.

Use any carpet that suits your fancy. But it's best to stick with tightly constructed carpets with a jute or synthetic backing. Most commercial carpets fall into this category. On the other hand, if you are especially interested in reducing the noise within a room, select a carpet with a foam-rubber backing. This has 50 percent better acoustical qualities than ordinary carpets.

Carpeting a wall is a moderately difficult job which must be done by two persons. On paper, the cost runs from 75¢ per sq. ft. way up; but there is usually so much waste (since carpet is sold in 12- and 15-ft. widths) that you can be pretty sure of paying more than this.

Installing carpet. Walls should be plaster or gypsum board; smooth, sound (though cracks are permissible), clean and free of peeling paint and any other material such as wallpaper which might pull off.

Because of its weight, carpet is best rolled out on a wall horizontally—from one end of the wall to the other. This simplifies installation and eliminates joints. But it's possible to hang carpet in vertical strips like wallpaper.

Cut the carpet to the height of the wall and slightly longer than its length. Starting at one end of the wall, apply a 3-ft. strip of adhesive from the ceiling to the floor. Use waterproof latex adhesive only—not a water-soluble or alcohol-base material. Apply the adhesive with a notched spreader.

Roll the carpet into a tight roll; press the end against the end of the wall, and fasten it with several stay-tacks (double-headed tacks like those used in classrooms). Roll it firmly into the adhesive and smooth it down with a piece of 2x4. Fasten the top edge with two or three stay-tacks.

Then trowel on another 3-ft. strip of adhesive, roll the carpet into it; tack the top; and continue thus across the room. At the end of the wall, crease the carpet tight into the corner, and cut it from top to bottom with a razor-sharp utility knife. Overcut a fraction of an inch to ensure that the corner is completely filled. Tack the edge.

After 48 hours or a bit longer, pull the tacks. The carpet should stay put for as long as you are happy with it.

Maintaining carpet. Vacuum the carpet every month to remove dust. Most soil marks and stains can be removed with water. Treat bad stains like those on floor carpet. If the carpet ever needs thorough cleaning, use one of the shampoos used on floors or hire a professional carpet cleaner.

Leather. As a wall covering, leather is an out-and-out luxury. But you'll have to look far to find any other that is as handsome and as durable. It is not so easy to use, however, because it is available only in the irregular shapes taken from the animals. Consequently, you must plan the manner in which you use it.

Cowhides are the largest hides you can buy. A better-than-average size covers about 40 sq. ft. Out of this you could probably cut a single 5x5-ft. square plus a number of small squares, rectangles, triangles or whatever.

For the best effect with the least work, try to cover a wall with large squares only. But the economics of the installation may give you pause. In a medium, 5- to 7-oz. weight—the best for wall-covering purposes—cowhide costs about $2 a sq.ft. So it is very possible you may want to use the small pieces, too.

Hanging leather. The first step in the process is to draw a plan of the wall to scale. Then, working on the back of the leather, divide it into squares and rectangles, draw these to the same scale on paper and cut the paper into pieces. Place these on the drawing of the wall and move them around until you have the most effective design. Then make a tracing and number each piece on the plan and on the leather.

Although the leather pieces you cut from a hide bear no resemblance to vinyl wall covering, they are applied to walls in the same general way with the same adhesive.

When the wall is completed and the adhesive has had at least 24 hours to dry, finish the leather to give it maximum protection against soiling and wear. The natural color of the material is oak. You can change this by brushing or rubbing on dyes available from the leather supplier. For a final finish, use the wax or lacquer also available from the leather supplier.

Maintaining and repairing leather. Clean leather with saddle soap, a mild detergent solution or a spray-on leather conditioner. Stains are difficult but may yield if you brush on rubber cement and peel it off. If this doesn't work, try cleaning fluid.

To maintain a polish, use paste floor wax.

If pieces come loose from the wall, clean off the old adhesive and stick them down again with vinyl adhesive or rubber cement.

Solid cork. Cork is a high-fashion wall covering. Interior decorators are using it in all sorts of buildings and in all sorts of ways. And with reason: It is strangely handsome stuff which imparts a sense of great warmth to any room. At the same time, it tends to absorb and deaden sounds within the room. Its main drawbacks are its susceptibility to staining and to fading when exposed to the sun.

Cork is available in several forms* including the cork wall coverings previously discussed.

* Dodge Cork Co., Lancaster, Pa. 17604

One-foot-square tiles $\frac{3}{16}$ in. thick are made for flooring, but are just as useful and attractive as a wall covering. They come finished either with wax or urethane.

Heavy, rough-textured cork in various thicknesses up to 2 in. is available in 12x12-in. pieces all the way up to 24x36-in. pieces. These are particularly popular with decorators, who use them on walls in several thicknesses and sizes to produce a sort of random-block effect.

Bulletin-board cork is finely textured and ¼ in. thick. It is produced in rolls as much as 6 ft. wide and 90 ft. long. Cork which is dyed a color is laminated to burlap.

Cork has been rising rapidly in price because the supply cannot keep up with demand. The current price for natural bulletin-board material—the least expensive type—is about 40¢ a sq. ft.

Installation of all types is easy.

Installing solid cork. Because of its thickness and flexibility, cork does a good job of disguising imperfections in a subwall. You don't have to worry too much, therefore, about cracks, small holes and minor roughnesses. Just make sure the wall is level, clean and free of scaling paint or a flexible wall covering.

Installation is made with linoleum cement which is applied to the wall with a notched spreader held at a 45° angle. The beads of cement should be full; the valleys between almost bare. If you're setting tiles, place them precisely; don't slide or twist them. Roll out large sheets carefully. Smooth all pieces down firmly with a clean rag or clean gloves. Adhesive which gets on the surface can be washed off with water.

For how to lay out tiles, follow the directions for laying out ceramic tiles (*see Chapter 16*). The tiles at opposite ends of a wall should always be equal in width.

Bulletin-board sheets can be installed vertically or horizontally. If the cork is being used above a wainscot, horizontal installation is always best. Burlap-backed sheets and large sheets of natural cork should be fastened along the top edge with small finishing nails. This will hold them until the cement dries. The nails can then be pulled or countersunk.

Cork can be colored with wood stains. A protective finish is not essential but helps to preserve the looks of the material. Wallpaper lacquer applied in two coats gives an almost invisible finish with moderate protection. White shellac applied in several very thin coats is more apparent but also more protective. You can also treat cork with a paste floor wax.

Maintaining and repairing solid cork. Keep the walls vacuumed. If they become soiled, wash with a detergent solution and rinse well. Stains and burn marks can be removed only by sanding with fine sandpaper.

Bad dents and holes can be filled by grating a bottle cork into small slivers and mixing with white shellac. After smearing this into the holes, let it dry and sand smooth.

Laminated wood veneers. These are made of wafer-thin sheets of beautiful woods bonded to a fabric backing to produce a flexible material only .015 in. thick. The sheets are produced in widths of 10 to 24 in. and in lengths of up to 12 ft.

Matching veneers are used to produce a definite pattern effect, such as you can have with wallpaper. Unmatched veneers give the effect of a wall paneled with solid lumber. One U.S. manufacturer alone offers more than 80 different native and exotic foreign woods ranging from afromosia to zebrawood. The cost of the veneers depend mainly on the availability of the woods, and ranges from 80¢ per sq. ft. upwards. Installation, however, can be made by the homeowner and is only a little more difficult than the installation of wallpaper.

Where would you use laminated wood veneers in the home in preference to conventional plywood paneling? The answer is that you wouldn't except in special circumstances: (1) You want perfectly matched wood paneling on a very large wall. (2) You don't want any horizontal joints on an unusually high wall. (By special order you can have the veneers end-matched, so you can panel a wall over 12 ft. high.) (3) You want to panel a curved wall, pillars or other surface with unusual contours. (4) You want wood paneling in a building or community where conventional wood and plywood paneling is banned because of its combustibility. (Laminated wood veneers have a very low flame-spread rating and are even permitted without restrictions by New York City's tough building code.)

Installing laminated wood veneers. Special tools you will need include a stiff-bristled paint brush to apply adhesive, a plastic broad knife to smooth the material and an electric flatiron.

The veneers can be applied to any hard, smooth, completely dry surface. However, you must not try them over the inside surfaces of exterior masonry walls or walls below grade unless the walls are furred out. And if veneers are to be hung in an air-conditioned room on a wall separating the room from a nonair-conditioned space, the wall must be insulated and waterproofed.

Prepare the walls as for wallpaper. All old flexible wall coverings must be completely removed. Roughen slick surfaces. Prime porous plaster with several coats of white shellac.

The room temperature should be raised to 70°F., or higher, before work starts. Use the adhesive specified by the veneer manufacturer. It should have the consistency of heavy cream. If too stiff, warm it in hot water; if too thin, cool in cold water.

Paint a priming coat of the adhesive on the walls and sand lightly when dry.

Unmatched veneers can be hung in any order and either end up. Matched veneers, on the other hand, must be hung in the sequence numbered on the back by the manufacturer and always with the top end up. The reason for this is that there is a progressive change in the grain pattern on the strips; so the first strip does not match the last. Because of this, you must hang the strips only in one direction all the way around a room.

The strips come pretrimmed. Cut them to

the length needed as your project proceeds— only two or three at a time. They should be the height of the wall, plus about ¼ in. at both top and bottom, to allow for fitting.

Working at your paste table, apply adhesive to the back of each strip just before you hang it. Brush it out thoroughly from the center toward the edges. Don't leave a single lump.

Hang the first strip to a plumb line and plumb every few strips thereafter. Smooth it down with the broad knife, working only with the grain. Go over it several times. Don't use a seam roller. On uneven walls, the veneers can be stretched slightly; but take it easy and stretch the entire width of the strip—not just along the edges. Force the top and bottom into the corners formed by the ceiling and base-board, and trim with a razor blade drawn along the edge of a wide wall scraper.

Butt the edges of adjoining strips. If they overlap because the walls are not flat or because they hang on a slant in a corner, center your straight-edge over the lap and cut along it through both veneer layers with a razor blade. Be sure to hold the blade straight up and down. Then remove the slivers and smooth the veneers down.

Hang veneers around corners, doors and windows like wallpaper. At electric switches, cut a small hole for the switch handle, paste the strip down and cut it out around the box. Remove light fixtures, disconnect the wires and make a small hole for them in the veneer. Then trim out around the box when the veneer is smoothed down. Remove radiators completely: you can not bend the veneers down behind them.

Wipe off adhesive at once and scrub with a sponge dampened in water or alcohol. Remove dried adhesive with fine sandpaper. Blisters should be worked out during hanging of strips. But go back over the strips 24 hours later to make sure you did your work well. Hold a strong light close to the wall to highlight the blisters. To remove any that show up, wet a scrap of veneer in water and lay it, wood to wood, on the blister. Heat an electric iron to the temperature setting for linen and press hard on the scrap.

Let the adhesive set for at least 24 hours before finishing laminated wood veneers. Then go over the entire wall—with the grain—with fine sandpaper. You can apply almost any transparent finish except penetrating oils and oil stains. The best is lacquer, because if blisters should appear after it is applied, they can be heat-treated as above without causing deterioration of the lacquer. If any other finish is used, the only way to handle blisters is to squirt adhesive under them with a hypodermic needle.

Maintaining and repairing laminated wood veneers. Occasional cleaning with a barely damp sponge should be all the attention a wall requires. Most stains can be removed with white appliance wax.

If the edges of a strip come loose, try sticking them down with a hot iron. Otherwise, scrape off the adhesive as well as you can and stick the edges down with white wood glue.

A badly damaged area can be repaired— semisuccessfully—by holding a matching scrap over the area and cutting through the two layers with a sharp knife. For simplicity, cut a square or rectangle. Then scrape out the damaged veneer, remove old adhesive and set in the patch with white wood glue.

Gypsum-coated wall fabric. Although gypsum-coated wall fabric* is especially recommended for use on concrete block and other smooth masonry surfaces, it may also be applied to gypsum board, plaster, glass, wood and plastics. It's ideal for covering cracked and patched walls because its rough texture and $\frac{1}{16}$-in. thickness conceal all but the worst irregularities at a cost of about 50¢ a sq. ft.

Sold in rolls 4 ft. wide and 30 yd. long, the covering resembles a loose-woven burlap with color in the pores. The color is actually mixed into the gypsum, which impregnates the jute. Seven pastel shades are currently available.

* Flexi-Wall Div., Wall & Floor Treatments, Inc., 300 University Ridge, Greensville, S.C. 29601

Once applied to a wall, the fabric hardens to the consistency of conventional plaster. The result is a very durable, strong wall which is resistant to fire. The fabric's main drawback—which it shares with a good many other materials—is its susceptibility to staining by ink, shoe polish, and the like.

Installing gypsum-coated wall fabric. Work only in a normally warm room. The wall must be clean, hard, dry and structurally sound. Cut down high spots and fill wide low spots. It is usually unnecessary, however, to fill mortar joints in masonry walls provided you don't press the fabric too vigorously into them. If a wall is painted, it should be washed, but the paint need not be removed if sound.

The fabric is hung very much like any flexible wall covering. Roll it out on the work table back side up, and cut it 4 in. longer than the height of the wall. Apply the adhesive supplied by the manufacturer with a medium-nap roller. Then fold the ends to the middle of the strip; align the edges carefully; and trim the selvage edges on both sides with a straight board and razor blade. Because the gypsum dulls blades in short order, lay in a big supply and use a new blade for just about every cut that you are making.

Hang the fabric on the wall like wallpaper, reverse every other strip. Butt the seams tightly. Use a smoothing brush with bristles trimmed to about 1-in. length. Roll the seams with a wallpaper roller.

Cut the strips at top and bottom with a razor blade drawn along the edge of a wide wall scraper.

As soon as a strip is hung, wipe off excess adhesive.

Maintaining gypsum-coated wall fabric. As noted, stains are hard to remove; but ordinary soil can be washed off with a mild detergent solution. (A special clear coating can be applied at the factory to increase washability.)

If you want to paint the fabric at a later date, use latex or alkyd paint. Three coats may be required to give an even finish.

Bamboo. Use bamboo for an exotic, oriental look in rooms or areas where there is a lot of traffic or rough housing. This is very tough stuff.

The bamboo used is normally seen as a sun- or windscreen on terraces. It is sold in rolls consisting of very slender canes tied tightly together side by side. The rolls are 6 ft. wide and 15 ft. long and cost roughly $10 each (a little more than 10¢ a sq. ft.). Install the rolls vertically or horizontally with finishing nails driven through the larger canes. The completed installation can be sprayed with any clear finish or alkyd enamel.

Vacuum the wall regularly and wash with detergent solution to remove soil.

9

Gypsum Board

Gypsum board—also known as drywall and Sheetrock (a trade name)—is the No. 1 material for building new walls and completely rebuilding old. Nothing comes close to it. It has won its position not because it makes a better wall than anything else but because it is cheaper, goes up quickly, does not cause moisture problems like its main rival—plaster—requires little maintenance and produces a smooth, durable surface.

And to add to this list of advantages—it is a material any reasonably strong, able-bodied handyman can install.

Except for vinyl-surfaced gypsum panels, gypsum board is not a finish wall surface. It is, rather, a base for paint, wallpaper, other flexible wall coverings and tiles. Usually it is applied directly to studs and joists; but it is also used over furring strips on masonry walls and crumbling walls that you do not elect to rip out; and in some cases it is nailed right over old walls to provide a sound new surface.

The cost varies with the thickness of the board. If you use ½-in. board to cover one side of a wall, the cost of all materials required—including nails, joint-sealing compound and tape—will come to approximately 11¢ per sq. ft. To this you must, of course, add the cost of paint, wallpaper or whatever final finish you decide on.

Types of gypsum board. All gypsum boards are made of calcined gypsum mixed with water and other ingredients to form a smooth, dense, fire- and sound-resistant panel which is sandwiched between two layers of strong paper. The boards—panels is a more descriptive word—are 4 ft. wide and 6 to 16 ft. long. The standard thicknesses, which are not available in every type of board, are ¼ in. (used for resurfacing existing walls); ⅜ in. (used for multi-ply construction of walls and in single thicknesses for top-story ceilings); ½ in. (the thickness most often used for walls and ceilings); and ⅝ in. (used mainly to give greater fire resistance and noise control). The edges of the boards are generally squared, beveled or tapered.

Although the average handyman building a gypsum board wall seldom worries about the type of board he uses ("Send me four 4x8 sheets," he tells the lumberyard and takes whatever he gets), it's well at least to have some idea of what's available.

Standard boards are just that: the type most often installed in homes.

Superior-fire-rated boards have greater fire-resistance than standard boards, but they are usually available only in ½- and ⅝-in. thicknesses.

Special-edged boards are sold under various trademarks. These differ from standard boards in that their edges are tapered as well as beveled or rounded. The joints are filled initially with a special high-strength compound and then taped and plastered in the conventional way. The boards are used primarily when walls are framed badly or exposed to high humidity, conditions which may cause excessive warping.

Foil-back boards have aluminum foil laminated to the back surface to provide thermal insulation and act as a vapor barrier. Use them only on the inside surfaces of exterior walls.

Backer boards are low-cost panels used as the base layer in multi-ply walls.

Water-resistant backer boards serve as the base for tile walls in bathrooms and other high-moisture areas.

Vinyl-faced boards are used if you want a strong wall covered on the front with an attractive, durable integral finish. (*For how to install them, see page 95.*)

Estimating how much gypsum board you need. Measure the total length of the walls to be covered and multiply by the height. If you are figuring close, you then deduct the area of the windows and doors; but the saving is minimal and you may wind up using scraps of material to complete the walls. For these reasons, you may prefer to figure a room "solid."

The actual number of gypsum panels you should order is determined by dividing the total square footage of the walls by the area of a single panel. Most professionals use the largest panels that will fit into a room, and apply them horizontally in order to reduce joints which must be filled and taped. But this is usually impractical for the homeowner unless he has a well-muscled assistant to help him carry the huge panels and hold them against the wall. (A ½-in.-thick panel weighs about 2 lb. per sq. ft.) So you will be well advised to stick with 4x8-ft. panels, and install them vertically.

Other materials you will need are the following:

Gypsum board joint tape and joint compound. Figure 75 ft. of tape and 1 gal. of ready-mixed joint compound for every 200 sq. ft. of wall surface. (You can buy joint compound in powder form and mix it with water, but it is nowhere near as workable as the ready-mix. It is also hard to save what is left over after a job, whereas the ready-mix can be saved for a couple of years.)

NAILS. If the gypsum board is applied directly to the studs, use annular-ring nails only. These have ring-grooved shanks with exceptional holding power. Use 1⅛-in. nails for ¼-in. gypsum board, 1¼-in. nails for ⅜-in. board and 1⅜-in. nails for ½- and ⅝-in. boards. In all cases, you will need at least 1 lb. of nails for every 200 sq. ft. of wall.

If you install ¼- or ⅜-in. gypsum board over an existing wall surface, use 1⅞-in. cement-coated nails at the rate of 1¼ lb. per 200 sq. ft.

To apply ½- or ⅝-in. gypsum board over an existing wall or new backer board, use 2¼-in. cement-coated nails. You will need almost 2 lb. per 200 sq. ft.

You will also need gypsum board adhesive if you glue two layers of board together, and metal corner beads for each outside corner.

Equipment needed. One of the minor advantages of installing gypsum board is that you can get by with a very few common tools:

Hammer. The best type has a slightly rounded face, called a bell face, which dimples the gypsum board when you drive a nail home. Flat-faced hammers may break the paper surface.

Sharp pocketknife or utility knife.

6- or 8-ft. rule or steel tape.

Metal rasp or Surform tool for smoothing cut edges. This is not essential, however, since you can do a good smoothing job with a knife.

Keyhole saw for making cutouts.

4- and 6-in. wall scrapers for applying and smoothing joint compound; and if you want to save work, get a 10-in. joint-finishing knife, too, for making the last application of compound.

Pencil.

Stepladder.

Screwdriver for removing switch plates and the like.

Sandpaper.

Reciprocating sander (*optional*).

Preparing for work. When the gypsum board is delivered from the lumberyard, store it in a dry place where it won't be subjected to abuse. It's easily damaged. For long-term storage, the boards should always be stacked flat; but if you expect to use them soon, they can be set horizontally on edge. Stand them as straight as possible so they will have least chance of warping.

New stud walls require no special preparation.

If you intend to rip out old wall surfaces and apply the gypsum board directly to the framing, pry door and window casings, baseboards and moldings off carefully before attacking the walls proper. After the old surface is removed, hammer down protruding nails and replace unsound or badly warped studs.

Old walls which are to be resurfaced must be made level and reasonably smooth. Knock out areas which bulge outward; level large areas which bulge inward by gluing short, thin wood strips across the center. Electric boxes should be moved outward ¼ or ⅜ in., depending on the thickness of the gypsum board, so the rims will be flush with the new wall surface. In order to do this, you will probably have to knock holes in the wall to get at them.

Although I have known people who butted new gypsum panels against the edges of door and window casings and baseboards, this is not a good practice. It doesn't save much work, because fitting gypsum boards to an exact wall space is troublesome, and it is even more troublesome to seal the cracks around the edges of the boards. The best procedure is to pry off the casings and baseboards and let the gypsum boards extend a few inches into the spaces vacated. Before replacing the casings, insert ¼- or ⅜-in.-thick wood strips under the door-side edges, so the casings will lie flat.

If an entire wall is to be furred out, install furring, as in Chapter 3. Door and window casings and baseboards must also be furred out; and electric boxes must be pulled forward so the rims will be flush with the new wall surface.

The final step in all preparatory work is to make a faint pencil mark on the ceiling, showing the center of each stud. This will greatly facilitate fitting and nailing later on.

Installing a single layer of gypsum board over studs or furring strips. The temperature of the room should be maintained at 55° or higher from the time work starts until the last application of joint compound has dried. The room should also be ventilated sufficiently to get rid of moisture given off by the joint compound.

If you're covering the ceiling, put up those panels first.

Install the first wall panel at a corner. You can then work from this either in both direc-

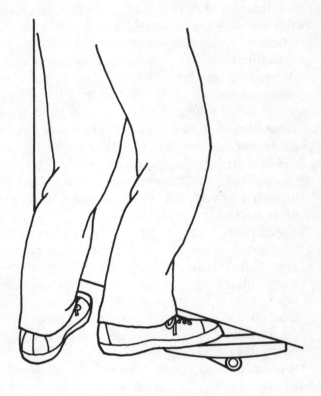

tions or in one direction all the way around the room. Check the corner for verticality with your plumb line. If it is more than about ⅜ in. off at top or bottom, the edge of the panel should be trimmed so it butts into the corner. (All other corner panels should be trimmed in the same way, if necessary.)

Measure the height of the wall at both sides of the panel and cut the panel to these measurements, so that it fits snugly between ceiling and floor. This helps to hold it flat against the studs. If a panel is too long, it may be impossible to force it into place without cracking the edges or damaging the ceiling or floor. On the other hand, a panel which is a little too short presents no problems, because after you butt it up against the ceiling and nail it, the gap at the bottom will be covered by the baseboard. The easy way to lift a short panel is to place a block of wood on the floor; lay a strip of steel or wood or a wrecking bar over the block and insert the front end under the panel; then step on the back end.

The width of the first panel (and all suc-

ceeding panels) depends on the spacing of the studs. Both vertical edges must bear on studs from floor to ceiling. If the studs are spaced 16 in. on centers and are straight up and down, the panels will fit over them neatly and do not require cutting. Cutting can also be avoided, in cases where the stud spaces measure 49 or 50 in., by nailing a board or 2x4 to the side of the end stud to provide a nailing base for the panel edge. But in every wall project it is almost inevitable that some panels must be cut into narrow widths or trimmed along the edge to fit the framework.

Gypsum board is cut by scoring the whitish paper on the front with a sharp knife. Only medium pressure is required; but make sure to cut completely through the paper into the gypsum core. Use a straight-edge for all straight cuts, but don't try to go too fast, as it is easy for the knife to veer off into the wild blue yonder. That simply makes for complications. If you are cutting on an irregular or curved line, take your time.

After the surface paper is cut, snap or bend the board backward. This breaks the core. Then slice the back paper with your knife and smooth the cut edges of the core with a rasp, Surform tool or knife.

When it's necessary to make an opening in a panel for an electric box, heating outlet or the like, there are two ways to go about it. First —in both cases—establish the exact location of the opening and mark it on the face of the gypsum panel. Then, with a pocketknife, poke holes through the panel at the four corners of the opening, and cut from hole to hole with a keyhole saw. The alternative—which is suitable mainly for small openings—is to drive an awl through the panel at the four corners of the opening. With your knife, score the surface paper along the lines of the opening, turn the panel over and score lines from hole to hole through the back paper. Then knock out the piece by rapping the front with a hammer.

Tilt the cut panel up against the framing and secure it with several nails driven through the top edge at the center of the panel. All nailing should be done from the panel center toward the edges. Now drop a plumb line from the pencil marks on the ceiling and mark the locations of the studs intermediate between the panel edges. By centering nails on these lines, you will always drive them into the studs.

The standard method of nailing gypsum board is to space the nails 6–8 in. apart all

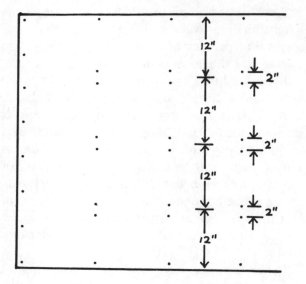

around the edges and up and down the intermediate studs. Drive the nails ⅜ to ½ in. from all edges and set them 1/32 in. below the paper surface. While driving each nail, exert pressure on the panel alongside, to assure that it is drawn up tight to the framing.

A newer and better nailing method is called double nailing. In this, nails are driven around the edges of the panel as in standard nailing; but on the intermediate studs they are inserted in pairs. The distance between the center of one pair and the center of the next pair down is 12 in. The nails in each pair are 2 in. apart. The idea behind this method is to prevent nail-popping—a common gypsum board affliction which occurs when nails loosen in the studs and pop head-first through the wall surface, causing unsightly blisters and holes.

The edges of adjoining gypsum panels should be snug, but not jammed together. If using panels with tapered edges, never butt a cut

edge to a tapered edge, because the joint is difficult to conceal.

Panels around doors and windows can be cut to fit the opening before they are installed. Normal professional practice, however, is to install an uncut panel right over the opening and then cut it out to fit.

Installing a double layer of panels. Multi-ply construction is used in the home primarily to reduce the transmission of sound from room to room or to deaden the sound of water racing through pipes in a wall. It also improves fire safety.

Ideally the panels in the two layers of gypsum board should be at right angles to each other; but this is not imperative. However, you should install the top layer so that the joints offset the joints in the bottom layer by one stud space or more.

After nailing up the first layer, apply the top layer either with nails or the adhesive recommended by the gypsum board manufacturer. Nailing is easier. Just be sure to use nails that are long enough to penetrate well into the studs. Gluing, however, makes a tighter, more sound-resistant wall.

The method of gluing depends on the adhesive used. For instance, the adhesive may be applied to the back of the face panel with a deep-notched spreader about 6 in. wide. This is used to apply a ribbon of ¼ x ¼-in. beads around the perimeter of the panel and down the center.

Another type of adhesive is applied either to the base layer or the back of the face layer in single ⅜ x ⅜-in. beads spaced 16 in. apart.

Still another adhesive is applied to the base layer in daubs 2 in. across by ½ in. thick. These are spaced 24 in. apart along the vertical edges of the panel and down the center.

After applying adhesive, tilt the face panel up against the wall and secure it with a few nails. Then go over the entire panel with a rubber mallet or with a board and carpenter's hammer and impact it tight to the base layer.

Installing gypsum board over an existing wall surface. First find the studs and mark their location on the ceiling. This is necessary because the nails used to secure the gypsum board should be driven through the old wall surface into the studs. (Exception: if the old wall surface is wood, plywood or particleboard.)

The actual installation of the gypsum board is similar to installation directly over studs. Don't make the mistake of thinking that, because an old wall surface is sound, the vertical edges of the gypsum panels need not fall over studs. Unless they are nailed into the studs, there will be some play in them and the taped joints may crack open.

Finishing joints. The process is the same for all walls which are to be covered with paint, wallpaper and the like. You can figure on the work running over three days. But the actual amount of time required depends on the size of the wall and on your skill in spreading the joint compound in long, thin, smooth ribbons.

There are just three things you should do to ensure that the walls, when completed, will be attractive and trouble-free for years to come:

1. Don't rush the work. The more carefully you apply tape and joint compound in the first place, the less sanding and clean-up you will have later on. You will also achieve better-looking joints, because even though gypsum board joint compound is very easy to sand, mistakes made in its application are surprisingly difficult to obliterate.

2. Use ready-mixed joint compound. I said this earlier, but it bears repeating. One of my sons-in-law is a thrifty fellow who doesn't believe in wasting anything; and when he moved into a new house some time ago and started putting up a gypsum board wall, I found that he was using some old powdered compound left over from a previous job. I remonstrated but got nowhere. So I bought him a gallon of the ready-mix before leaving town. He still can't get over the difference. When he heard I was starting this book, he told me: "Now be sure to tell 'em to use the cement that comes in the can." I've done my duty.

3. Don't try to get by with narrow wall scrapers as joint-compound applicators. All they do is make lots and lots of extra work because they apply compound in stripes rather than sheets. A 4-in. scraper is the smallest you should use.

The first step in taping a wall is to install corner beads on all outside corners. (Taping is the word used to describe the entire joint-finishing process.) The beads are long steel strips folded lengthwise to form a right angle and perforated along the sides. Cut them to the height of the wall and nail them over the corners to protect against damage. They also assure that the corners are straight and square.

Inside corners between walls, and between walls and ceilings, are reinforced with the 2-in.-wide tape used for all joints. The tape is simply folded in half lengthwise and embedded in joint compound spread into the corner. A special tape, reinforced with a thin ribbon of metal, may also be used, but is made primarily for reinforcing inside and outside corners of less than 90° or more than 90° (for example, the corner between a knee wall and a slanting wall).

Follow any sequence you like in finishing all the joints in a wall. You should, however, complete one joint before going on to another; otherwise the joint compound will begin to dry and become hard to work.

Starting at one end of a joint, spread a 4-in.-wide layer of compound over it to the other end. Then center the paper tape over the joint and roll it out gradually with one hand while you press it into the compound with your scraper in the other hand. Embed the tape firmly, but don't press down on it so hard that you force most of the compound out from under it. If wrinkles occur in the tape, pull it loose to a point behind the wrinkles and start over again. If the tape veers away from the joint, tear it in two and start a new strip just below the torn strip. At the end of the joint, hold your scraper squarely against the tape and tear off the roll.

Now go back over the joint once more and cover the tape with a skim coat of joint compound.

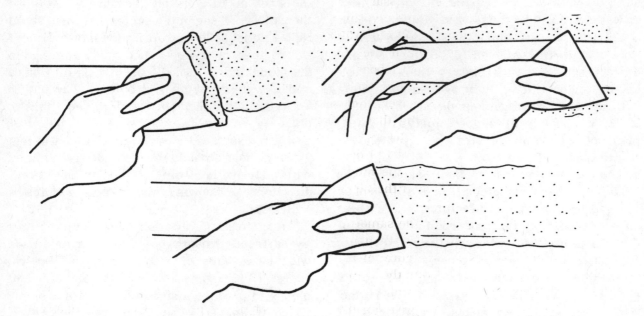

After taping all joints in this way, butter all exposed nailheads with compound and apply compound over outside corner beads.

Allow the compound to dry completely. This should take about 24 hours. Then sand it, to remove encrustations and to even out irregular areas, and apply a second coat. Use a 6-in. scraper for this, and spread the compound about 2 in. beyond each side of the first strip. Feather the edges.

Repeat this process once more over joints and corners (nailheads usually need only two coats of compound). If you have a 10-in. finishing knife, use it. The final strip should be 10 to 12 in. wide, but still very thin, even right over the joints. (Rubbing your hand across the wall, you should be only barely conscious of the hump formed by the joint compound.)

When the compound is dry, sand all joints and nail spots with medium sandpaper. A reciprocating electric sander is an excellent tool for the job; but since it stirs up much dust, close the doors to the room and stuff rags underneath. Then dust or vacuum thoroughly. If any depressed areas or scratches show up after cleaning (search for them by holding a light close to the wall), smear a bit more compound into them.

Walls that are to be finished with paint, wallpaper or other flexible coverings should now be given one coat of latex primer.

Installing moisture-resistant gypsum board as a base for ceramic tile. (*See chapter 16.*)

Installing vinyl-surfaced gypsum board. These prefinished panels are available in a number of solid colors and several textures, including stippled, grass cloth and burlap effects. Excellent "woodgrains" are also sold. The cost is generally a little lower than a wall built of standard gypsum board and later covered with vinyl; but the choice of patterns, colors and textures is vastly smaller.

Standard-colored vinyl-surfaced panels have beveled side edges which are covered with vinyl. Standard woodgrains have squared edges covered with vinyl.

Install the panels vertically directly to studs or furring strips or over a gypsum board base. Before starting installation, shade the panels like wallpaper and work out the best possible sequence of installation. As a rule, on a blank wall, it is best to arrange the panels from the center toward the corners, so that the end panels are of equal width. But if a wall has a door or window at one end, it is better to start paneling from the opposite end so that, if you wind up with a narrow panel, it will be more or less concealed by the door or window.

Panels at the ends of walls should be scribed to fit the corners (*see page 107*). Cut each panel a fraction of an inch shorter than the wall height and jack it up tight against the ceiling with the lever arrangement described on page 92. If a panel is fitted too snugly, the vinyl might be torn from the surface as you shoved it into place.

The easiest way to attach the panels to the studs is with color-matched nails supplied by the gypsum board manufacturer. Drive these on 8-in. centers all the way around the edges of the panels and up and down the intermediate studs. Use a soft-faced hammer.

An alternative attachment method is to apply a thick, wavy bead of gypsum board adhesive to the studs and plates, press the panel into place and nail it to the plates with color-matched nails. The middle part of the panel is then wedged against the studs with boards braced against the opposite wall, and held for 48 hours.

A somewhat more professional method of

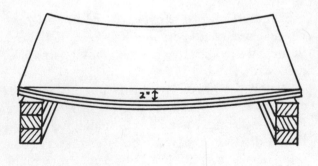

making glued panels stick tightly to studs is to lay them in a flat stack (after they have been cut to size) vinyl side up. Raise the ends of

the stack about 8 in. off the floor on 2x4s, so the panels will sag in the center. Let them stand for 24 hours or longer until they have acquired a permanent 2-in. bow. Then apply adhesive to the studs and plates, tilt the panels into place and nail them at top and bottom. The panels are thus held under tension until the adhesive dries.

If vinyl-surfaced panels are installed over a gypsum board base, they should be secured with adhesive according to the manufacturer's directions. Prebowing the panels assures a tight bond.

An interesting variation of the standard vinyl-surfaced gypsum board is a panel made with loose flaps of vinyl along the vertical edges. The flaps permit you to join adjacent panels to produce a smooth wall with a barely visible wallpaperlike seam between the two.

After cutting a panel to size, bend the flaps back over the face of the panel and secure them with masking tape. Apply a band of adhesive to the studs, which will be intermediate between the panel edges. Tilt the panel into place and nail the vertical edges to the studs with cement-coated nails spaced 8 in. on centers.

Put up the next panel in the same way and continue across the wall and around the room.

The joints between panels should then be filled with joint compound. No reinforcing tape is required. Simply apply several coats until you have a level, smooth surface.

For clarity, visualize two adjacent panels. The left has a flap along the right edge, which extends about 2 in. beyond the edge. The left-edge flap on the right panel is flush with the panel edge.

With a paint brush, spread wheat paste like that used for hanging wallpaper over the back of both flaps. Then smooth down the flap on the right panel with a plastic broad knife or its equivalent. Over this, smooth the wide flap on the left panel. Then center a straight-edge over the lapped joint and, with a razor blade, cut through both layers of vinyl from the top of the wall to the bottom. Remove the trim-

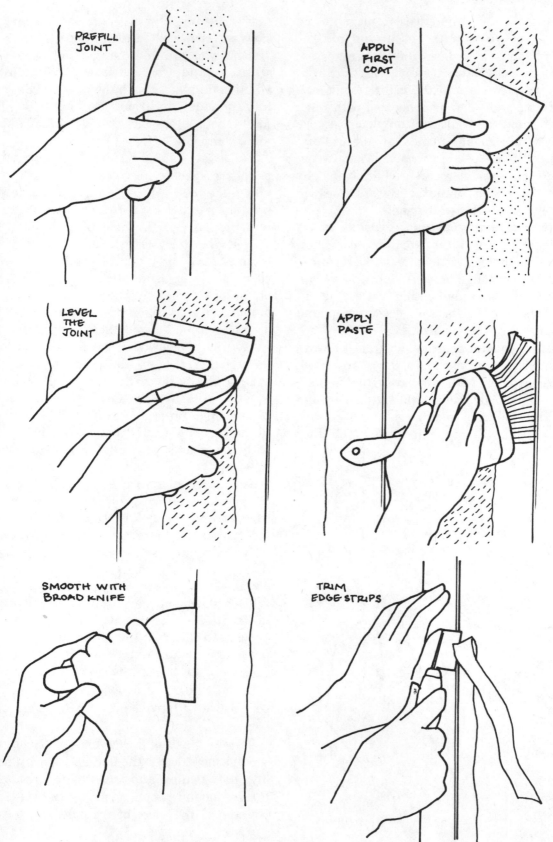

PREFILL JOINT

APPLY FIRST COAT

LEVEL THE JOINT

APPLY PASTE

SMOOTH WITH BROAD KNIFE

TRIM EDGE STRIPS

mings, smooth the vinyl edges firmly onto the gypsum core, wipe off the paste and roll the joint after the paste has set for 10 minutes.

Open cracks between any vinyl-surfaced gypsum board walls and the ceiling or in corners between walls can be concealed with wood moldings when the walls are completed. A cove molding is the usual choice at the ceiling; quarter rounds are used in corners. The alternative is to use special metal moldings sold by the gypsum board manufacturer. These are covered to match the wall panels.

Maintaining and repairing gypsum board walls. Nail-popping is the No. 1 problem, but, happily, it is the easiest to cope with. Hammer down the loose nail. Then drive in a new nail, preferably of the annular-ring variety, 2 in. away. Cover the heads with joint compound or spackle, and apply paint.

Cracks in gypsum board walls almost always occur only at the joints. If they are small, scrape them open with a screwdriver or beer-can opener and fill them with joint compound or spackle. You can treat large cracks in the same way, but if they reopen—as well they

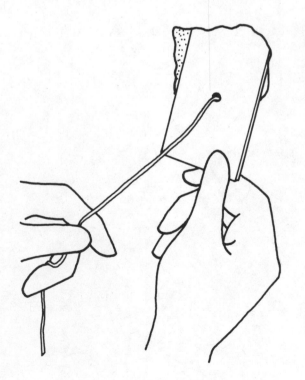

may—cut out the joint compound on both sides to form a wide ribbonlike channel. Odds are that you will find the tape is loose or badly wrinkled; and if so, cut it out, too. Then drive additional nails through the edges of the panels into the studs and refill the joint—like a new joint—with tape and two or three layers of joint compound.

Fill small holes and dents with joint compound or spackle. If you can't make the filler hold in a hole about 1 in. across, wedge a scrap of metal screen wire or coarse steel wool into the back of the hole before filling.

Holes between 1 in. diameter and the size of an electric outlet can be filled by wetting the edges of the gypsum with water. Cut a piece of cardboard slightly larger than the hole, poke a small hole in the center and thread a piece of string through it. Knot this on the back side. Then push the cardboard diagonally through the hole in the wall and pull it up against the back of the wall with the string. Fill the hole to half its depth with patching plaster and continue pulling on the string until the plaster sets. Then cut the string off flush with the plaster and fill the hole the rest of the way.

Very large holes are filled with patches cut out of a waste scrap of gypsum board. First trim around the hole with a keyhole saw, to make a square or rectangular opening. Add 2 in. to both dimensions of the opening and cut the gypsum board scrap to this size. This is the patch.

Turn the patch back side up, measure in 1 in. from all edges and draw an outline of the opening in the wall. Cut across the patch along these lines with a knife and bend the edges backward to break the gypsum core. Then trim the core edges away from the surface paper. You now have a plug with flanges on the front.

Trowel a thin layer of joint compound around the sides of the opening. Push the plug into the opening and smooth the flanges into the compound. Then apply a little more compound over the edges of the flanges. When this

REPAIRING A GYPSUM BOARD WALL

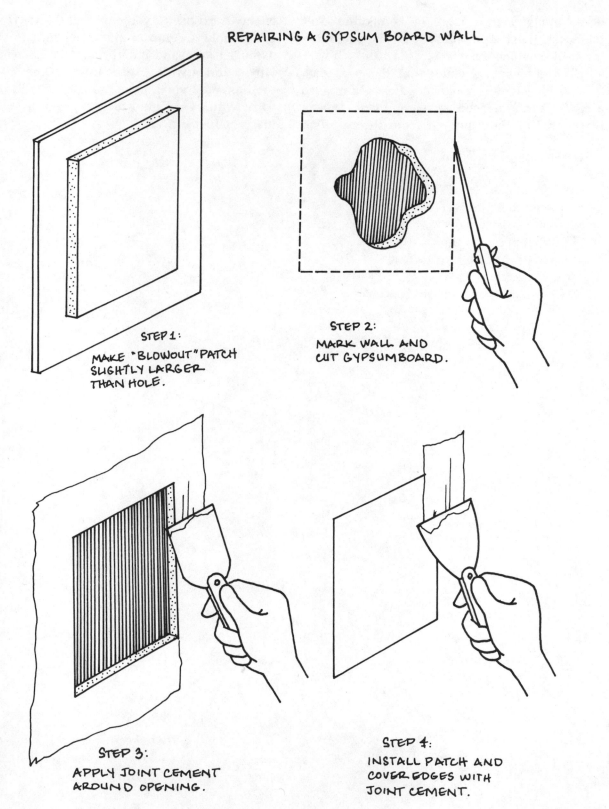

STEP 1:
MAKE "BLOWOUT" PATCH
SLIGHTLY LARGER
THAN HOLE.

STEP 2:
MARK WALL AND
CUT GYPSUMBOARD.

STEP 3:
APPLY JOINT CEMENT
AROUND OPENING.

STEP 4:
INSTALL PATCH AND
COVER EDGES WITH
JOINT CEMENT.

dries, apply a thin layer of compound over the entire patch and well out on the surrounding wall. Feather the edges. Finish the job with a still-wider coat of compound the next day.

In case you ever need to patch a damaged area in vinyl-surfaced gypsum board, save a few pieces of the flaps cut from the board or of the board itself (you can peel the vinyl from this). Hold a scrap of the vinyl film over the damaged area and cut through both layers of vinyl at once with a razor blade. Then remove the damaged vinyl, coat the back of the patch with white wood glue or wallpaper paste and insert it in the wall.

10

Plaster

Constructing plaster walls just isn't for the do-it-yourselfer. The work is entirely too demanding and finicky. As proof, consider the prosaic words of the Department of Labor's *Occupational Outlook Handbook*: "Most training authorities, including the national joint labor-management apprenticeship committee for the plastering trade, recommend completion of a 3- or 4-year apprenticeship as the best way to learn plastering. However, many workers in this trade have acquired some plastering skills by working for many years as helpers or laborers, observing or being taught by experienced plasterers."

But making repairs in a plaster wall is easy —especially if you are not a purist about technique. For instance, one of the walls in our living room had at one time been patched by a fellow who evidently either didn't know what he was doing or didn't take much pride in his work. Instead of making a neat, flat patch, he created a mesalike hump that was very prominent in certain lights. When I got around to repairing it, my first idea was to knock it out and start all over again. But then my lazy streak got the upper hand. "It may not look well, but the plaster's sound," I told myself. "So why not just spread the hump out wider and get rid of it that way?" And that's exactly what I did—with gypsum board joint compound.

Unorthodox? You bet. But it worked like a charm. To begin with, ready-mixed gypsum board joint compound is one of the smoothest, easiest-to-work-with fillers you can find. I don't use it as a rule for filling deep holes, because there are stronger materials for that kind of work. But if you want to obliterate cracks, smooth out rough surfaces, level uneven surfaces or hide bumps, joint compound is unbeatable. You can apply it in thin layers down to a feather edge; and when you're through, if there is any roughness in the surface, you can sand it off in a minute. Anyway, that's the material I used to get rid of the living room hump. I just kept applying joint compound in thin layers around the edges of the hump until I had feathered them out so far across the surrounding wall that you could no longer see the hump.

I see no reason why you shouldn't resort to trickery of this kind if it produces the results you're looking for.

Plaster-patching materials. In addition to gypsum board joint compound you will at some time or other need some of the following materials:

SPACKLE. This is the closest thing to an all-purpose patching material, because you can use it not only on plaster but also on gypsum board, wood, plywood—almost anything. Note, however, that it is good only for not-too-big holes and cracks. The material is sold in the form of a white powder which is mixed with water just before use, and as a ready-mixed paste in a can. Buy the latter. It saves time; is smoother and stronger. Apply it directly to plaster, gypsum board and other hard materials; but wood and plywood should first be primed with paint.

PLASTER OF PARIS. This is a white powder which you mix with water and apply to plaster or gypsum board. The holes in the wall must be well wet with water before they're filled; otherwise they will draw the moisture out of the plaster of Paris and cause it to shrink and crack.

Plaster of Paris is a perfectly acceptable filler; but it sets so quickly that you have very little time to pack it tightly into a hole and smooth it off. Setting time can be retarded, however, by adding vinegar to the water used to mix the plaster. Use about $\frac{1}{3}$ part vinegar to $\frac{2}{3}$ part water.

PATCHING PLASTER. This is easier to work with than plaster of Paris because the powder contains a set retardant; so all you have to do is add water and go to work. Holes in plaster walls and gypsum board must be wet with water before filling.

WOOD PUTTY. This is also called water putty. It is another white powder which is mixed with water and then smeared into holes in plaster, gypsum board, wood, plywood and so on. It is a good enough filler but has nothing particularly to recommend it for wall work. It does, however, have a unique advantage in that it can be molded into intricate shapes. It is therefore the ideal material for mending breaks in moldings and wall plaques.

READY-MIXED PLASTER. This is the type of plaster used to construct new plaster walls and also to make major repairs in old walls. It is put up in rather large quantities ready for mixing with water. Some types are finely powdered mixtures which can be used in both the base and final plaster coats. Others (the type I prefer) contain wood fibers and are usable only in base coats. Take your pick or, more likely, take what you can get.

Repairing small cracks. Small cracks can be just as ornery as large cracks about reopening after they are patched; but until you have seen how they behave, you might as well assume they will not make further trouble. To do otherwise is simply to give yourself work.

First, you must scratch the cracks open with a beer-can opener or old screwdriver and brush out all the crumbs. Then fill them with spackle or gypsum board joint compound and sand smooth. For no particular reason, I generally use spackle when there are only a few cracks.

But when a sizable area is crisscrossed with cracks, I use joint compound and cover the entire surface.

Repairing large cracks. Unlike small cracks, which may be caused by shrinkage in the plaster or by warping and shifting of the house framework, big cracks almost always result from movement in the structure. Consequently, they are likely to continue to open until the house attains a state of equilibrium.

Happily, there is a pretty reliable new way of dealing with large cracks. It involves use of a rubberized paper tape called Super Crack Seal.*

Wash the area around the crack thoroughly to remove dirt and grease. Then scrape the crack open wide, blow out crumbs and fill it either with spackle or patching plaster. When this has dried completely, smooth it off with sandpaper and brush on a thin coat of wallpaper size. Cut the tape to the length of the crack. If the crack is crooked, you will need to cut several pieces of tape and trim the ends so they will butt together. Then immerse the tape in room-temperature water and smooth it over the crack with a damp sponge. When it dries, cover it with a thin 4- to 6-in.-wide layer of gypsum board joint compound or spackle. Sand once more lightly, and apply paint, wallpaper and so forth.

Cracks in corners do not have to be given the final coat of joint compound. Two coats of paint or wallpaper will conceal the tape.

Repairing holes. Except for small ones, which are filled with spackle, holes are usually filled with patching plaster. Cut the edges straight up and down or on a backward slant. Remove crumbs with a vacuum cleaner or brush. Wet the plaster thoroughly with clean water and trowel in patching plaster. To get a smooth, hard finish, wet a plasterer's trowel or wall scraper frequently with water. For sand-textured plaster, mix the patching plaster 50-50 with clean fine sand or Perltex.

If the hole is deep, don't try to fill it all at

* Custom Tapes, Inc., 3260 W. Grand Ave., Chicago, Ill. 60651

once, because the moist patching plaster will sag. Apply the plaster in two or even three thin layers. To ensure that the top layer bonds securely, score the surface of the bottom layer with the point of your trowel or a nail. The top layer should be applied as soon as the bottom layer has set but is still damp.

In very large—more than a foot across—deep holes, patching plaster is difficult to use, because it may set faster than you can work. Use a prepared plaster mix instead. Fill the holes to within ⅛ in. of the wall surface, and then complete the job either with the mix or, for a smoother finish, with patching plaster or gypsum board joint compound.

If the lath behind a large hole is broken or rusted out, cut back the plaster to the studs on either side. Then nail in a piece of plaster lath or metal lath and build up from this with plaster mix. To make the patch flush with the wall, draw a steel straight-edge or framing square across it while the plaster is soft.

If the lath is missing behind a hole not much larger than an electric box, make the repair described on page 98.

Repairing bulges. If the bulging plaster is firm and sound—the result simply of a poor plastering job—try my living-room trick. If the plaster is loose, however, cut it out and carry on as if you were filling an ordinary hole.

Repairing plaster cracked into large pieces which are loose from the lath but otherwise strong. This is the crazy problem that Tom Rooney, the government scientist, encountered in his new old house. I frankly had never seen anything like it; but other people who should know told Tom it is not unusual. One thing is certain: If you are unlucky enough ever to run into the problem yourself, your initial reaction will be utter dismay. Then, like Tom, you will snap out of it.

There is really only one proper solution: knock out the plaster completely and start over again—probably with gypsum board. But the shortcut Tom learned from his paint dealer works surprisingly well if the plaster has been applied over wood lath. Drill small holes here and there through the loose pieces of plaster and fasten them to the lath with 1¼-in. screws driven through nickel-size washers which are perforated to resemble sewing snaps. Then cover the screws and washers with a well-feathered-out coating of gypsum board joint compound.

Repairing powdery plaster. If plaster becomes soft and chalky soon after it's applied, there's something wrong with the way you handled it. Maybe the plaster had deteriorated with age. Maybe it set up and dried too quickly because of too much ventilation in the room. Maybe it dried too slowly. And so on. In any event, the only thing to do is dig it out and start over again.

If the powdering occurs in old plaster walls, however, it is usually because there's a water leak. Find and stop this first. Then remove the white surface coat of plaster—the one that is powdering. If you find the brown coats underneath are also crumbling, remove them, too, and fill the holes as described above. If the brown coats are reasonably sound and hard, however, let them dry for several days. Then fill in the surface gap with patching plaster or gypsum board joint compound.

Repairing hot spots. (*See page 59.*)

11

Wood Paneling

If there's one thing that makes me drool, it is a wall paneled with wood cut from trees in the days when trees grew to giant size. To begin with, the width of the boards and panels is astounding. Eighteen inches is common. Two feet and even three feet are not at all rare. But after I got over oh-ing and ah-ing about the size of the wood, the full impact of the wall is felt.

There is a beauty about a wood wall which is hard to describe. The color is mellow and warm and has the depth that is unique to natural materials. The grain ranges from quiet to exciting. The texture of the fibers is subtle. The imperfections of the knots, burls and bark pockets accent the perfections of the medullary rays, which appear in certain woods as shimmering flakes.

There is a faint smell to wood that adds distinction to the room in which it is used. When you touch wood, it imparts a sense of warmth. No material is so friendly.

And, of course, you can shape wood and carve it to your heart's content.

Installing board paneling. Most wood paneling today consists of boards which are installed vertically but very occasionally horizontally or at an angle. The cost is modest. Knotty pine paneling, for instance, runs about 50¢ per sq. ft., and the only additional materials required are furring lumber (perhaps), nails and stain

105

or paint. Installation is in the low-medium range of difficulty. As opposed to paneling made with large sheets of plywood or hardboard, board paneling is particularly easy to install when you're covering walls with many openings.

Softwood paneling ready for immediate application is available in almost all lumberyards. The boards are graded either knotty or clear, have a smooth finish, are a nominal 1 in. thick, have tongue-and-groove edges and are also usually beveled at the edges. However, boards with rough-sawn texture and boards with square or especially milled edges may also be available or can be supplied on short notice.

Other woods such as birch, oak or cherry must, as a rule, be run through the mill for you, although if you want to use random-width oak flooring for paneling, you can find it in stock in a few lumberyards.

Old lumber which has been salvaged from demolished buildings makes the most beautiful paneling; but you can rarely find any which was originally used as paneling (unless of the crudest type). This means you use the boards as they are—possibly with squared edges—or you make arrangements to have them re-sawn and/or milled. But how much success you will have in getting this done I cannot say. I once wanted to have some old rustic oak timbers ripped into boards but was turned down cold by the local mill. "Have they had nails in 'em?" the mill manager asked. "Yes. They were used for siding on a building," I answered. "Then I can't touch 'em," the manager said. "But I'm going to pull the nails," I protested. "No matter; still won't touch 'em. Too easy to wreck the saw blade on the rust and metal particles in 'em." So, beautiful oak went into the fireplace.

Estimating the amount of wood you need involves measuring the total length of the walls by the height and subtracting the area of the door and window *openings*. You should then add something for waste and trimming if the wall height is exactly 8, 10, 12, 14 or 16 ft. (These are the standard lengths of boards.)

Little if any extra is required, however, if the wall height is less than these figures.

Give the answer you come up with to the lumberyard to determine precisely how many board feet of lumber you need. Admittedly, you can work out the answer yourself; but it takes a lot of computation to make allowance for the facts: (1) That the actual size of lumber is less than the nominal size; and (2) that cutting tongues and grooves in boards further reduces the face width. The lumber dealer, on the other hand, has a convenient list of "area factors" for finding the answer.

Once the amount of lumber has been determined, don't leave its selection up to the lumberyard; otherwise you will almost certainly be given a few boards containing large knots, splits, warps or other defects. Pick out every board yourself, and don't rush the process. I always feel a little nasty about this because it means that someone, not I, is going to wind up with the bad lumber; so I usually salve my conscience by taking a few slightly less-than-perfect boards. But don't you be *too* magnanimous.

One other thing to remember in selecting paneling is that, unless you are going to cover it with paint, all the boards, as well as all the moldings and other trim, should be of the same species of wood. This is perfectly obvious if you are paneling a wall in, say, redwood; it would never occur to you to accept white pine moldings, because they have no resemblance to redwood and would spoil the effect of the wall. But it also applies if you use white pine for paneling: Moldings of fir or spruce would be equally unsuitable, for although they have the general tone and grain of pine, they don't finish in the same way.

Have the lumber delivered from the yard a couple of days before you go to work, and pile it carefully on the floor in a dry room and keep it covered. Some time before starting construction, if you plan to finish the wall with paint or an opaque stain, spot-prime the knots in the boards with stain-killer. Then apply a priming coat of the selected color to the entire surface *and* the edges. (Boards that are to be finished with a clear stain should also be primed on the edges.) The purpose is to color the edges so that, if the joints in the wall open, raw wood will not be exposed. If you're paneling a basement wall, it is also advisable to give the backs of the boards a precoat of shellac or aluminum paint to seal them against possible dampness.

Sand the face of all boards—regardless of the finish to be used—before putting them up.

Although it's possible to panel over any old wall by applying furring strips, it is far better to strip the wall down to the studs. You then have two choices: (1) Nail 1x2- or 1x3-in. furring strips horizontally to the framework. On an 8-ft. wall, apply one strip at the base, one at the top and two more equally spaced in between. (2) Nail two rows of 2x4 blocks horizontally between the studs and equally spaced between the soleplate and top-plate. This is more troublesome than applying furring strips, but reduces wall thickness.

On a masonry wall, you must, of course, use furring strips. If you have any doubt about dampness in the wall, staple heavy polyethyl-

ene sheets over the strips to protect the paneling.

Board paneling is usually installed without baseboards and shoe moldings at the bottom or cove moldings at the top. The boards must therefore be fitted carefully. On the other hand, if you want baseboards and if you are using paneling which has deeply beveled or grooved edges, make the baseboards of 5/4-in.-thick lumber and install them before the paneling. The paneling is then butted to the top edges of the baseboards. This eliminates the dark, dirt-catching pockets which you would otherwise have if baseboards were nailed to the face of the paneling. (Note that this construction requires installation of a furring strip or blocking just above the baseboards, so you have something to nail the bottom ends of the paneling boards to.)

Ceiling moldings should be handled in the same way. But for some reason, pockets between paneling and surface-applied ceiling moldings are not so objectionable as those at baseboards.

Paneling is applied from one end of a wall to the other. Before starting to put it up, figure out the placement of the boards so you don't end with a sliver at the second corner. This is unattractive. It is easy enough to adjust the boards—whether they are random-width or same-width—so that those at opposite ends of the wall are more or less equal in width.

To ensure that the paneling is vertical and fits tightly into the corner, cut the first board to the height of the wall; place it in the corner groove first; and plumb it. If there is only a tiny crack along the corner edge, you're ready to start paneling. But if there is a wide or uneven crack, nail the board up temporarily, and scribe it.

Scribing means to mark a line parallel with another line and then to cut along it. In this case, the "other line" is the corner. To scribe the board to the corner, hold or nail it temporarily parallel with the plumb line. Open a pair of dividers or a compass slightly wider than the widest point in the gap. Hold one leg against

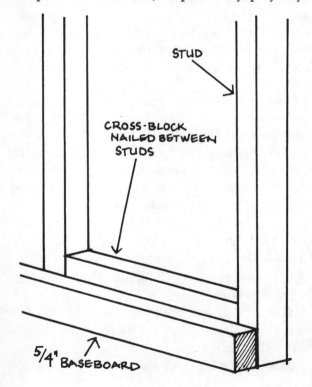

STUD

CROSS-BLOCK NAILED BETWEEN STUDS

5/4" BASEBOARD

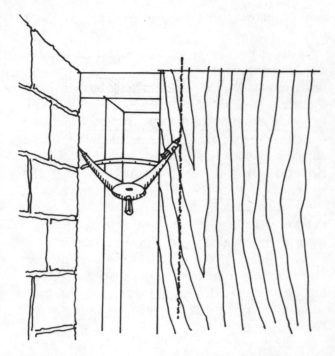

the corner and the other leg on the board and draw them down from the ceiling to the floor. If you do this carefully, you will mark on the board a line which conforms exactly to the vertical contours of the corner. Trim the edge of the board to this line with a saw, drawknife or plane, so that it will butt tight into the corner.

(Boards at all other inside corners are handled in the same way. At outside corners, butt the joints; or, if you have the skill and patience, miter them with a plane. The latter makes the more attractive joint, but it also tends to splinter more.)

As you panel across the wall, check every third or fourth board with your plumb line or carpenter's level to make sure you are maintaining vertical. Fit each board snugly against the other. You don't have to drive them so tight that you can't slip a piece of paper between them; but a close joint now will compensate considerably for the shrinkage that will inevitably occur in the wood. (In other words, it is very difficult today to produce a wood-paneled wall which does not develop rather open joints. This is especially important to remember if you use old boards with squared rather than interlocking edges. When these

spread apart, the larger cracks look very obviously open and may admit drafts. To guard against this, cover the wall framing with a layer of black building paper before installing the paneling.)

All paneling boards should be the full height of the wall. Piecing short lengths together is unattractive. (I don't know why it looks well in a floor but not on a wall.) However, if you are paneling a wall with horizontal boards, piecing out may be unavoidable.

Apply the panels with 2-in. finishing nails. If a wall is to be painted or finished with an opaque stain, these can be driven through the face of the boards. But on a wall with a transparent finish, drive the nails diagonally through one edge of each board. Avoid face-nailing as much as possible, especially in the middle of the wall. You probably cannot be completely successful in this effort, however. Boards in corners must be face-nailed; and boards more than 6 in. wide require some face-nailing as well as edge-nailing to prevent warping.

All nails driven through the face of the boards should be countersunk. On a painted or opaque-stained wall, cover the heads with spackle. On other walls, use beeswax or plastic wood which is colored to match the wood. (One manufacturer of plastic wood claims to produce the product in all popular wood colors.)

When the walls are completed, smooth them again with fine sandpaper or steel wool and apply the final finish. (*See Chapter* 5).

Other methods of paneling with boards. Board-and-batten paneling. This semirustic exterior siding is sometimes used for interior paneling. It is made of rough-sawn, wide (usually 12 in.) boards installed vertically about 1 in. apart. The joints are covered with 1x2-in. strips (battens) of the same rough-sawn wood. Construct the walls without baseboards or ceiling moldings.

Batten-and-board paneling. This is the reverse of the preceding. The battens are placed behind the boards.

Board-and-board paneling. Also similar to

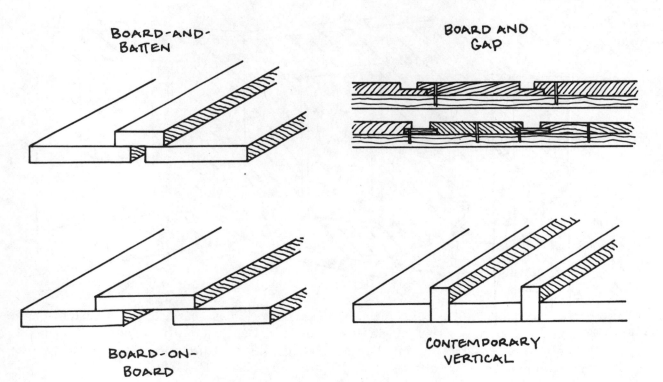

BOARD-AND-BATTEN

BOARD AND GAP

BOARD-ON-BOARD

CONTEMPORARY VERTICAL

board-and-batten except that the battens are replaced with boards. All the boards are the same width—usually about 8 in.

Board-and-gap paneling. This has much of the appearance of batten-and-board. It is installed horizontally as well as vertically. The wall is made with wide boards rabbeted along the edges. One rabbet is about 1 in. wide; the other only ¼ in. The wide rabbet faces the room and is overhung by the narrow rabbet. Thus there is a ¾-in. channel between each pair of boards. The depth of the channel equals half the thickness of the boards. By contrast, in batten-and-board construction the channel between boards is equal in depth to the full thickness of the boards.

Because it is only one board thick, board-and-gap paneling may be installed between a baseboard and cornice molding, though it generally is not.

Contemporary vertical paneling. In this, wide boards are separated by 1x2-in. strips installed with the thin edges facing front and back.

Horizontal paneling. Horizontal paneling may be done with square-edged or bevel-edged boards and also with boards molded in other ways. The boards are nailed directly to the studs in a framed wall. No cross-blocking or furring is needed. Over a masonry wall, furring strips are applied vertically 2 to 3 ft. apart. All outside corners must be made by mitering the ends of the adjoining boards; thus the porous, coarse end-grain is concealed. Baseboards are omitted, but shoe moldings and ceiling moldings may be used.

Diagonal paneling. In a conventional room with a flat ceiling the boards are usually installed at a 45° angle. But in other situations, the angle may be dictated by the pitch of the roof, the run of a stairway and so on. The boards are nailed directly to the studs; but some blocking between studs may be required in corners. Furring strips over a masonry wall can be applied vertically or horizontally.

In putting up diagonal paneling, take care to install the boards in the corners of the room so that they appear to continue from one wall to the other.

Herringbone paneling. In this arrangement, the wall is divided vertically into two or more

equal sections and the boards in adjoining sections come together to form a V or an inverted V. Because the effect is busy, use boards which are not shaped in any way along the edges.

No furring is necessary; the boards are nailed directly to the studs. Some blocking between studs may be needed behind the shortest boards.

Wainscots. Except for the fact that a wainscot is only about 30 to 48 in. high, it is no different from a full-paneled wall. The boards, which are applied vertically or horizontally or sometimes in herringbone fashion, are usually smooth-finished and have beveled, rounded or otherwise ornamented edges. You may or may not install a baseboard; but it is customary to top the wainscot with a narrow horizontal board which projects slightly out from the paneling (like a shelf).

The wall above the wainscot is normally smooth plaster or gypsum board which is painted or covered with a flexible covering. A very attractive all-wood wall can be made, however, by constructing a wainscot with horizontal boards and paneling above this with vertical boards. This arrangement requires installation of cross-blocks between the studs behind the vertical paneling.

How to panel a wall in the formal Colonial and Georgian manner. For sheer beauty and dignity, few wall treatments come close to this

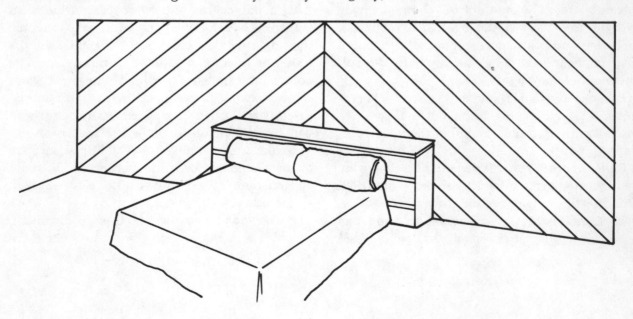

type of paneling. But design and construction are far from easy.

The walls are made with rather large panels set into a framework of stiles (the vertical boards) and rails (the horizontal boards) just as a conventional paneled door is made. The panels may be "raised" or "recessed." The former are the handsomer. They are beveled on all four sides to make them appear recessed; but the flat central area is in the same plane as the surrounding framework, or sunken slightly below it. By contrast, a recessed panel is a completely flat panel sunk about ¼ in. below the surrounding framework.

Don't try to build this kind of paneled wall until you have worked out the design for the entire installation in full detail. Actually, you would be smart not even to attempt the design. Turn the job over to an architect.

If you're using raised panels, have a good local millwork shop produce both the panels and the framework. The panels are designed so the edges fit into rabbets in the back of the stiles and rails and are held in place with cleats. (The panels are not fastened in any way, but allowed to "float.") The front edges of the rails and stiles are usually beaded or molded in some fashion.

A wall with recessed panels may be constructed in the same way; and if so, it should also be made by a millwork shop. Many handymen, however, cheat on this type of wall with very good effect. The flat panels are made of plywood or, if you prefer to be a purist, of solid boards edge-glued together. The front edges of the rails and stiles are rabbeted to receive the panels. And the edges of the panels are then covered with small ornamental moldings nailed and glued to the rails and stiles.

Installation of either raised or recessed panels is a tricky process for which I have no useful specific directions. The panels and surrounding framework may be attached to furring strips or directly to studs and cross-blocks. In either case, the placement of the strips or blocks is dependent on the design of the panel-ing. A rather complex arrangement is usually called for.

Building a cedar closet. Red cedar boards made specifically for lining closets are ⅜ in. thick, 2 to 4 in. wide and 2 to 8 ft. long. They are tongue-and-grooved along the sides as well as at the ends. The boards are sold at most dealers in random lengths in bundles which cover about 30 sq. ft.

It is a simple matter to line an existing closet, as long as the walls are level. All you have to do is remove the shelf, shelf supports, rods and other trim; locate the studs, and strike plumb lines over them.

To construct a new closet, frame the walls with studs spaced 16 in. on centers. *(See Chapter 3.)*

The cedar boards are installed horizontally. Cover one wall at a time, working from the floor up. Scribe the first board to the floor, so that the top edge is level, and fit it tight between the corners. Fasten it to each stud with two finishing nails. The nails should be positioned ¾ in. in from the edges of the board, to prevent splitting. In an existing closet, use 1¾-in. nails, which will penetrate through the old wall surface into the studs. In a new closet, where the boards are applied directly to the studs, 1-in. brads are large enough. (Thin cedar is very easy to split.)

After the first board is in, the next (and all others after it) is tapped down over it and secured with one nail per stud driven ¾ in. down from the top edge. When two boards in a row meet end to end, slip the tongue firmly into the groove to make a secure joint. Nailing is unnecessary; consequently, there is no need to make the joint over a stud.

If you scribe the ends of the boards carefully to the closet corners, the joints in the corners will be tight enough to discourage marauding moths. You can, however, make sloppy corners bugproof by nailing quarter rounds into them after the wall is complete.

For maximum protection of stored woolens, the floor and ceiling of the closet and the back of the closet door should also be lined with cedar boards. Weatherstrip the door.

The cedar should not be finished. With time, as it loses some of its aroma, it can be refreshened by sanding with fine sandpaper.

Maintaining and repairing wood paneling. Remove fingermarks, grease and other soil with a soft cloth or sponge wrung out well in a mild detergent solution; or use white appliance wax. Paneling with a natural finish benefits—just like wood furniture—if you go over it once every year or two with furniture polish. For a more durable finish, use a paste floor wax.

Small scratches can usually be concealed—but not removed—by rubbing them with paste wax or the meat of a nut. If a bad scratch occurs, sand it carefully and touch it up with the appropriate finish. Don't try to fill a deep scratch except in paneling covered with paint or an opaque stain. In natural-finish paneling, the filler is likely to look worse than the scratch.

If paneling with a natural finish becomes badly scarred through abuse, restoring it to its original condition and appearance is hopeless unless you remove it and run it through a planer and sander. But there is an easy solution and a good one: Wash it thoroughly to remove grease, polish, dirt and so on. Fill holes, dents, gouges and scratches with spackle, and apply two coats of paint (a primer and an alkyd flat or semigloss enamel). Painted paneling lacks some of the beauty of natural wood; but it is beautiful nonetheless. It is easy to maintain. And when it gets beaten up, it can readily be restored.

12

Plywood

Aggressive merchandising has made plywood paneling one of the most popular finishes for interior walls. But the product has been degraded to some extent by the effort.

Plywood paneling has two unique virtues: (1) It is available in a vast range of native and exotic woods. This is made possible by the fact that the surface veneer is very thin; consequently, one rare log of, say, bubinga, ebony or Brazilian rosewood can be made to cover hundreds of square feet of wall, whereas if it were cut into boards it would go nowhere. (2) The large smooth panels, when skillfully arranged, give a wall rare drama. There is nothing to which I can liken the effect, and

I find it hard to describe. The impact is felt, I think, because we are accustomed to seeing wood in relatively small pieces and here it is in great unbroken sheets.

You will note that I have said all this in the present tense, which might seem at variance with the last sentence of the first paragraph. But the reason I have put it this way is that what was possible with plywood in the past is equally possible today. However, plywood is no longer commonly used in homes to produce these dramatic walls, and that is why I am a bit mournful about it.

What happened? The panels were grooved to resemble boards. I don't know all of the reasons why this was done, but an important one was to make it easier for do-it-yourselfers and building contractors—people without any great design skill—to handle the joints between panels and the nailing across the face of the panels. The grooves hide both the joints and the nails, and I have to admit that that is all to the good. But, very much to the bad, the grooves also destroy the unbroken smoothness which gave plywood paneling its second unique virtue.

Nothing is to be gained by dwelling on this, however.

Except when it is tricked up for greater sales appeal, plywood has the same character as wood. Its one shortcoming is something its makers boast about: It is too perfect. Looking at a plywood wall, you have no doubt that it's made of plywood. Unlike the joints in solid wood paneling, those in plywood are straight as arrows (and also very shallow). And unless the paneling is meant to be rustic, it doesn't contain knots and splits and other defects.

Still and all, as a wall-surfacing material, I have to admit that plywood at its better or best is beautiful. (At its cheapest, it isn't beautiful; but neither is solid wood.)

Building walls with plywood falls into the moderately difficult category. This is because, like any rigid sheet material, plywood is awkward to handle and work—and because it needs to be carefully fitted, it gets considerable handling. You must also give it kid-glove treatment, because it usually comes with a factory-applied finish and doesn't react kindly when you hit it with a hammer or scratch it with a nail. However, because of the factory-finish, you don't have to go to the trouble of finishing it yourself. That's an obvious plus.

Compared with board paneling, plywood is easier to install on unbroken walls but more difficult on walls with openings, because the big sheets are troublesome to fit. On the other hand, plywood is no more difficult to install than other finished rigid-sheet materials.

The cost varies all over the lot. The cheapest hardwood paneling costs less than $5 per 4x8-ft. sheet (16¢ a sq. ft.). Textured softwood

panels run from about $9 up (almost 30¢ a sq. ft.). At the high end of the scale, if you buy, say, a pearwood or harewood panel with perfectly matched veneers, you can expect to pay over $100 a panel.

To the cost of the paneling, you must add nails, a little filler for covering nailheads, furring strips (perhaps) and moldings (perhaps).

Types of plywood paneling. The plywood most often used to surface interior walls is an interior-grade panel put together with glue which can be guaranteed to prevent delamination only if the panel is used in reasonably dry locations. In other words, it is safe to use almost everywhere in a house except very damp basements or bathrooms which are used by a lot of people who take a lot of long, hot showers.

The normal size of the panels is 4x8 ft., but you can also buy 4-ft. panels in 7, 9 and 10-ft. lengths. The standard thickness is ¼ in.; and I am sorry to report that there are some panels only ⁵⁄₃₂ in. thick. Using these is like covering a wall with cardboard; and the appearance isn't much better.

The patterns, textures and colors in which interior plywood is available are a major part of the reason for the material's zooming popularity. The wide selection you will find in any big lumberyard is only a fraction of what is actually on the market. Almost all the panels, as I said earlier, are grooved to resemble boards; but that's where the similarity ends. Some panels are as smooth as satin; others are textured like rough-sawn lumber, driftwood, timbers shaped with an adz and so forth. Most are good honest hardwood or sometimes softwood. That is to say, they are made of three plies of wood of which the surface ply is exactly what it purports to be: oak, cherry, pine, walnut and so on. But increasing numbers of lower-price panels are tricks of the production engineers. They are made of wood, all right; and they look like wood; but the surface is a fake. It is wood which has been embossed or printed or even covered with a film of wood-grain-printed vinyl. Somehow, the effect is amazingly real. But I for one prefer the honest product.

Because there are so many kinds of plywood paneling, and because it is labeled for interior use, there's a tendency for most people to overlook the possibilities of using exterior-grade plywood on inside walls. Don't make this mistake. If you want a rustic or semirustic effect, some of the siding panels are excellent choices. And you must use them in very damp locations.

All the exterior panels are made of softwood. Sizes are 4 ft. by 8, 9, 10 or 12 ft. Thicknesses are ⅜ and ⅝ in., which means the panels are more sound-resistant and stronger than interior panels. All but one type comes unfinished. This exception* is fascinating. It is a ⅜-in. sheet covered on the front with a tough epoxy coating in which small stone chips of various sizes, colors and shapes are thickly embedded. The total thickness of the panel ranges from about ½ to ¾ in. The resulting wall (just like a wall finished with certain kinds of glaze coatings described in Chapter 6) looks like handsome textured concrete and is just as durable. But unlike concrete, you can cut the panels with a carbide-tipped saw blade and nail them up with ordinary nails.

But stone-faced plywood is a gimmick, just as so many plywoods made for wall surfacing are gimmicks. If you want plywood wall paneling at its very best, don't go to a lumberyard. Call the nearest sales offices of the big companies that make plywood and ask to see their architectural-grade plywoods. They are gorgeous materials.

Estimating plywood paneling needs. Measure the length of the walls to be paneled and divide by four. Then subtract one-half panel for each door, one-half panel for a fireplace and one-quarter panel for each window.

Getting ready for work. Have the panels delivered to your home at least 48 hours before you start the installation and store them in the room where they will be used. Lay them flat, in a stack, with full-length strips of furring or

* U.S. Plywood, 777 Third Ave., New York, N.Y. 10017

boards between each pair. This allows the air to circulate freely around them. Don't remove the paper sheets which cover the panel faces. They're needed to protect the finish, and you may also want them later to cut out templates to guide in sawing panels.

While waiting for the panels to become acclimated, check your saws to make sure they are as sharp as can be. For straight cuts you need either a cross-cut hand saw—preferably with 10 teeth to the inch—or a power saw with a fine-toothed blade. Scribing and inside cuts are done with an electric saber saw or a compass saw—both with fine-toothed blades. When cutting with a handsaw or an electric table saw, always place the panel faceup. When using any other saw, the panel should be facedown.

Even with a sharp saw, cutting plywood—especially thin interior grades—is difficult because the panels are so large and because the saw binds as the panels bend. It is therefore necessary to support the plywood firmly on a pair of sawhorses. For added support, lay two or three 2x4s over the sawhorses and put the plywood lengthwise on these. I also advise bribing someone to hold large pieces you cut off.

Installing plywood panels. Except for ⅝-in. panels, plywood has little resistance to sound. It follows that, while you can apply it directly to studs spaced no more than 16 in. on centers, the resulting wall won't be pleasant to live with. To make the wall more soundproof, it should be covered first with ½- or ⅝-in. gypsum backer board. This obviously adds to the cost of the wall as well as to the work of building it.

If an existing wall is level, apply plywood directly over it. You must, of course, remove the trim. Then double-check the levelness of the wall by drawing a long straight-edge across it. Sand or chip down high spots; build up low spots with gypsum board joint compound. These steps are especially important with $\frac{5}{32}$-in. plywood, because it conforms closely to the wall base. Standard ¼-in. plywood is better in this respect, though not perfect.

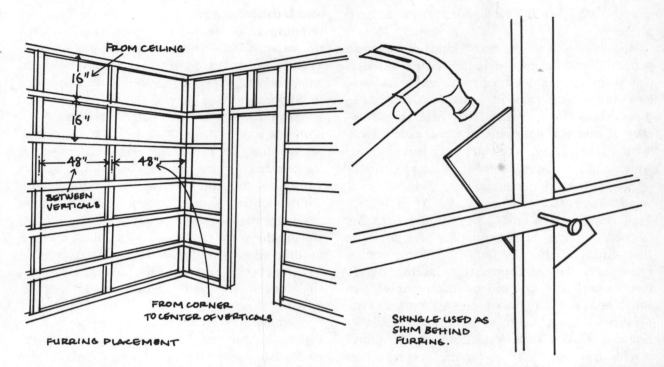

FROM CEILING

16"

16"

48" — 48"

BETWEEN
VERTICALS

FROM CORNER
TO CENTER OF VERTICALS

FURRING PLACEMENT

SHINGLE USED AS
SHIM BEHIND
FURRING.

Once the wall is leveled, find the studs and strike plumb lines over them to facilitate fitting and nailing of the plywood.

Old walls that are very uneven or in poor repair must be furred out with 1x2- or 1x3-in. strips of wood. Whether the plywood is to be put up vertically (the usual way) or horizontally, the furring should be installed horizontally at the top and bottom of the wall and on 16-in. centers in between. Then install strips vertically from floor to ceiling at all corners and under the side edges of the panels. These strips should be nailed over studs.

Take pains to see that the furring doesn't follow the contours of the old wall surface but is perfectly flat. Where the wall is too high, chisel out channels for the strips. Where the wall bends inward, shim out the strips with pieces of cedar shingle.

Fur out masonry walls in the same way, after making sure they are watertight. Covering the furring with heavy polyethylene film helps to protect the panels against moisture which may penetrate the walls or pass through the plywood and condense on the masonry.

As the last step in preparing the base, paint the studs or furring strips where two panels will come together a dark color, so that contraction of the panels will not reveal the raw wood.

If the plywood you install is grooved to resemble board paneling, apply it from corner to corner. If you use ungrooved panels, however, they must be carefully positioned for effect; and the panels at the two ends of each wall should be almost equal in width. In either case, before starting work, stand the panels against the wall and shade them like wallpaper.

Cut the panels to the height of the wall as you progress around the room. If you are not using a ceiling molding, scribe the panels at the top to the ceiling and subtract ¼ to ½ in. at the bottom. If you do use a ceiling molding, subtract ¼ in. at both top and bottom.

Set the first panel in the starting corner, plumb it and fasten it loosely with a couple of nails. Then scribe it to the corner and trim the edge along this line. (See Chapter 11.) Because it is so thin, plywood should always be scribed at corners to assure tight joints.

Plywood is usually put up by nailing. Use ordinary brads or finishing nails or the colored nails provided by the plywood manufacturer. For sheets up to ⅜ in. thick, you can use 1-in. brads if nailing to furring strips or studs. You will need longer nails if the plywood is going up over an old wall surface. The exact length of the nails depends on the thickness of the old surface. For ⅝-in. plywood, use 1½-in. or larger finishing nails, depending on the nailing base.

Nail the panels from the center toward the edges or from one edge to the other. If you nail the opposite edges first, you may buckle the panels. Space the nails 6 in. apart around the perimeter and 12 in. apart through the center. Drive them diagonally through the beveled edges and grooves, countersink the heads with a nailset and fill the holes with colored filler sticks available from the plywood maker. The grooves through the center of the panels are spaced 16 in. apart so that they should fall squarely over the studs, provided the latter are also spaced 16 in. on centers. If the studs and grooves don't happen to line up, you must drive nails through the face of the panels; but the filler sticks should conceal the heads well enough.

Plywood can also be installed with adhesives recommended or sold by the manufacturer. Some of these require a few nails through the panel—especially over porous plaster—but others do not. If you install panels with a smooth, ungrooved surface, by all means use the latter.

Like caulking compound, the adhesives come in cartridges and are applied with a caulking gun. Apply a single bead to all furring strips or all studs and plates under a panel. Use roughly the same pattern on solid wall surfaces; however, it is not necessary for the edges of the panels to fall over studs. Then tip the panel against the wall, position it, press it down tight and go all over it with a hammer and cloth-padded 2x4 block.

Contact cement can also be used, but is difficult to work with because you must position the panels perfectly the first time. Once they are stuck down, you can't move them.

Butt each succeeding panel snugly to the preceding; but don't fasten it into place until you are sure it is plumb.

When you have to fit a panel around a window, door or the like, it is helpful to cut it to the proper height and then hold it to the wall alongside the opening and make your measurements on it. This way it is easier to visualize exactly what has to be done than if you transfer measurements from the wall to a panel lying across sawhorses. Measure carefully once; then, for safety, do it all over again.

Making cutouts for electric boxes can be done in the same way. Another method is to chalk the edges of the boxes and press the panels against them. A third method—and the most accurate for making *all* cutouts—is to hang one of the paper sheets that protects the panel finish on the wall and draw the cutouts on it.

Prefinished moldings of wood, aluminum or vinyl are available from plywood manufacturers to match the panels. All are of simple, modern design and peculiarly unlovely; but you are almost forced to use them because it's the only easy, inexpensive way to get a perfect color and grain match with the plywood. Use as few as you can get away with. I see no reason for moldings in inside corners unless you

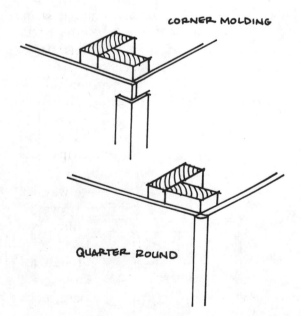

CORNER MOLDING

QUARTER ROUND

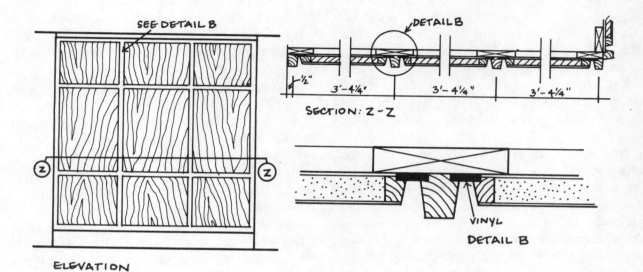

SEE DETAIL B

DETAIL B

½"   3'-4¼"   3'-4¼"   3'-4¼"

SECTION: Z-Z

VINYL

DETAIL B

ELEVATION

botch the scribing job. Outside corners, however, should be treated in one of the ways illustrated, to conceal the raw, unstained edge grain. And the top edge of plywood in a wainscot must also be covered with some sort of cap molding.

Joints in walls made with smooth, ungrooved panels are more conspicuous and therefore harder to treat successfully. The simplest approach is to bevel or round the vertical panel edges with sandpaper just enough to improve resistance to splintering, and then to butt the adjacent panels. Before butting, apply a stain of approximately the same color as the surface to the raw edges and to the studs or furring

strips underneath so that, if the panels do contact, the light-colored wood will not be revealed.

Other easy ways of treating joints are to cover them with attractive battens or moldings; and to separate the panels about an inch and set moldings between. One treatment which often seems particularly effective involves recessing a plain flat strip of a contrasting color between the panels (as in a batten-and-board wall—*see page 108*).

Other than a large expanse of smooth wall with almost invisible butt joints, what really delights my eye is a plywood wall paneled in the traditional manner (although the com-

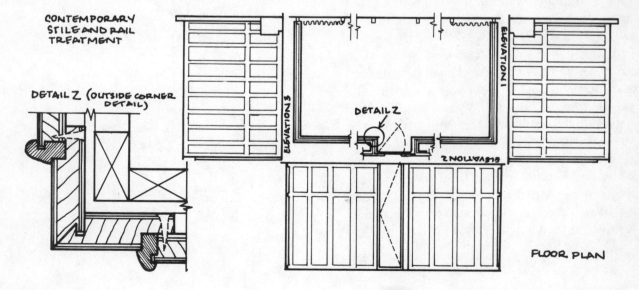

CONTEMPORARY STILE AND RAIL TREATMENT

DETAIL Z (OUTSIDE CORNER DETAIL)

ELEVATION 3

ELEVATION 1

DETAIL Z

ELEVATION 2

FLOOR PLAN

pleted wall need not be traditional). In this the plywood panels are frequently cut into smaller sections which are surrounded with an ornamental framework of solid wood or solid wood and plywood strips combined. Two examples are illustrated.

Mind you, I don't claim that this sort of installation can be made by anyone. Unless you enlist the support of a millwork house, you'll need shop tools, skill and patience. But the result is often well worth the effort.

(Note that the trickiest part of many such installations is to conceal the raw edges of the plywood. For this purpose, you might consider the flexible real-wood tapes which are available. They are easy to glue to any well-sanded edge and then to trim to size.)

Finishing unfinished plywood. After thorough sanding or steel-wooling, apply any finish you might use on wood. *(See Chapter 5.)*

Maintaining and repairing plywood paneling. Keep the walls dusted, and remove soil as it occurs with a cloth or sponge well wrung out in mild detergent solution. Or clean the walls with white appliance wax.

Prefinished panels should not require waxing, but there is no harm in going over them every year or so with furniture polish or paste wax.

Small scratches can be concealed with a clear wax or the meat of an oily nut. If scratches go through the finish into the veneer, patch them with the filler sticks made for nail holes. Use the same sticks to fill dents and holes.

The worst thing that can happen to plywood of $5/32$-in. thickness is to have someone kick a hole in it. Oh, yes, it's easy enough to do, but not at all easy to fix. In fact, it might be better to tear out the wall and start over again with some more durable, attractive material. If you dislike that idea, the best solution—if you can find a matching panel at the lumberyard—is to pull out the damaged panel and replace it *in toto.*

13

Hardboard, Particleboard, Fiberboard, Acoustical Board, Velvet Board and Asbestos-cement Board

The only reason for lumping these materials together is that all are made in sheets measuring 4 ft. wide and, usually, 8 ft. long—but sometimes 7, 9, 10 and 12 ft. long.

Hardboard. Hardboard is the most popular of the materials for interior paneling; and this frankly is something I can't fathom.

Hardboard is a superb material. Made of small wood fibers bound together under heat and pressure, it is dense, strong, durable and has good dimensional stability. It doesn't split, crack or check; has considerable resistance to moisture (this is particularly true of tempered hardboard); is easy to work; and takes paint well. I use it for numerous purposes in prefer-

ence to other materials; and I couldn't get along without it very well. But for covering interior walls—?

It's not that the panels don't produce a tough, wear-resistant, easy-to-clean-and-maintain wall. They do. And because of their density, they also are better sound barriers than many other materials. But in their most commonly used forms, they are less desirable than other products.

Most panels are imitations of board paneling and are no more successful than the cheaper forms of plywood paneling, although they cost more. So their advantage is decidedly questionable.

The other common form of hardboard has a smooth, paintlike, wallpaperlike, marblelike or tilelike finish. The panels are good-looking—no doubt about it. But for use on bathroom walls (a favorite location) they are not as resistant to water and damage as laminated plastics. And for use in other areas, they don't afford the range of effects you can get with a flexible wall covering on gypsum board.

But I don't mean to be entirely negative. Several types of panel are top-notch.

The best known are the perforated panels called pegboards. You can get them both finished and unfinished. The former have a tough, baked-on enamel either in a solid color or patterned to resemble wood or fabric. Whatever the appearance of the panels, the perforations—spaced an inch apart vertically and horizontally—make them a uniquely valuable storage device. The man who dreamed up the idea deserves a medal.

Embossed hardboard panels are not so well known—but should be. They are available in several textured designs which have not been duplicated in any other wall-covering material. One looks like wicker; another like a basket woven out of wood splats; another like a louvered shutter; and a fourth like a sheet of prismed glass.*

Filigree panels are a third excellent type. They're discussed in a bit more detail in Chapter 19.

Installing hardboard panels. Covering a wall with hardboard is of the same order of difficulty as building with plywood. The technique, in fact, is almost identical, so I won't describe it again. Only the differences will be covered.

Panels 1/8 and 3/16 in. thick should be installed only over existing walls—assuming, of course, that they are smooth and level—because they do not have enough rigidity to resist warping of studs and might eventually develop unbecoming undulations. Use adhesive to fasten them. Quarter-inch panels—the type in widest use—can be applied directly to studs if you are not concerned about noise transmis-

* U.S. Plywood, 777 Third Ave., New York, N.Y. 10017

sion through them; otherwise they should be applied over an existing wall (either directly to the wall or to furring strips) or over 1/2-in. gypsum backer board. Application is best made with adhesive, so you won't have to worry about concealing nailheads. If you prefer nailing, however, use either 1 1/4-in. finishing nails or special annular-ring hardboard nails colored to match the panels. The latter are driven flush with the surface. For finishing nails, predrill the panels to a depth of 1/16 in., countersink the nailheads and cover with matching-color filler sticks. In all cases, space nails 4 in. apart around the panel edges and 8 in. apart through the center. Try to drive nails through the grooves (if any) in the panels. This helps to hide them. Never nail into the edges of panels.

Pegboard can be used in 1/8-in. thickness if it is to bear a light load; 1/4-in. is required for heavy loads because it is more durable and rigid. Regardless of the thickness used, the board must be applied to studs or furring strips at least 3/4-in. thick. Use strips with a nominal width of 2 in. under the panel edges. Those in the center should be 3/4 in. wide. These widths will not block any of the panel perforations, provided they are spaced exactly 16 in. on centers and are absolutely vertical or horizontal. Use nails to install the panels, and toss in a few screws for safety if the load will be heavy. Adhesive cannot be counted on and may squeeze out through some of the perforations.

All types of hardboard should be put up with a hairline space between panels. Leave the joints visible if the panels are a woodgrain design. Visible joints can also be used with most other panels. But those between smooth panels are usually covered with moldings sold by the hardboard manufacturer or with wood moldings of any design. In bathtub recesses, the joints must be made with special metal moldings into which the panel edges are fitted. (To minimize the number of joints, panels for the backs of tubs measure 5x5 ft.)

Corner joints are usually covered with moldings. However, since hardboard edges are easy to plane, it is a fairly simple matter to miter the joints.

Unfinished hardboard panels can be treated with any kind of paint or transparent surface finish which is applied to wood. But best results are obtained with an alkyd primer followed by one or two coats of alkyd enamel.

An unusual characteristic of hardboard is its bendability. This makes it useful for covering curved walls. Bending is done both without moisture and with. When using the latter method, scrub water into the rough backs of the panels and stack them in pairs, face to face. Separate adjacent pairs with wet rags or newspapers. Then cover the entire stack with a plastic sheet, to prevent loss of moisture, and let the panels soak—24 hours for standard panels; 48 hours for tempered.

Whether panels are wet or dry, they are then fastened to the wall framing with nails. Work from one side to the other.

Panels ⅛ in. thick can be moist-bent to a minimum radius of 7 in.; dry-bent to 12 in. The corresponding radii for ¼-in. panels are 15 in. and 27 in.

Maintaining and repairing hardboard paneling. Clean with mild detergent solution or white appliance wax. Scratches in the surface are best left alone. If a panel buckles or loosens because of warping of the studs, nail it with annular-ring nails.

Particleboard. Also known as chipboard and flakeboard, particleboard is made of small scraps of wood bonded together under pressure. The panels have considerable strength and durability and excellent dimensional stability. They are used primarily as a base for other materials—under laminated-plastic counter surfaces or resilient flooring materials, for instance.

One of the roles particleboard plays in wall covering is as the base for a 4x8-ft. panel covered with vinyl in simulated woodgrains and colors. The panel is V-grooved to resemble random-width boards. In other words, except for the way it's constructed, it is identical to most plywood and hardboard panels. Its only

claim to fame is its cost—$4.50. No other real-wood or fake-wood paneling approaches this.

But particleboard is deserving of a better fate, and I am happy to find that several firms realize this and are making ¼-in.-thick wall panels which feature wood particles as much as 2 in. long. When given a couple of coats of varnish, they remind me of some of the beautiful wood products of the Finns, although I don't recall ever seeing any Finnish particleboard. On the other hand, there is also a great deal to be said for ordinary ½-in. particleboard of the type used as a floor underlayment. In these panels, the particles are smaller, more homogenized and less flamboyant. And they cost only about $4.

Installing particleboard panels. Follow the directions for plywood. Apply with adhesive or finishing nails. Nails, however, are easier and, if you take pains to drive them between particles rather than through particles, they will be almost invisible. Any that do show up can be countersunk and covered with beeswax or plastic wood.

Quarter-inch panels should be installed over gypsum board for adequate sound control. But ½-in. panels can be applied directly to studs because they are so dense that they give good acoustical privacy.

Joints between panels look best if they are veed slightly, but you can treat them any way you like.

Maintaining and repairing particleboard paneling. Clean like plywood panels. Scratches and holes in painted panels are filled with spackle. If the panels have a natural finish, try plastic wood.

Fiberboard. The best-known type of fiberboard panel is a so-called insulating board with relatively little thermal insulating value. It was much more widely used 20 and 30 years ago than today—which is a good thing, because the only thing to recommend it is its very low cost.

The ½-in.-thick, grayish panels made of wood or vegetable fibers are lightweight and lacking in strength. You can cut them with your thumbnail; and it doesn't take much muscle to knock a hole in them with your fist. They definitely should not be used in children's rooms, halls or anywhere else that they might be exposed to punishment.

Installing fiberboard panels. Like other wood materials, fiberboard must be allowed to adjust to conditions within the house for about 48 hours before it's installed. Put it in a stack like plywood, or simply lean separate panels against the walls around the room.

Because the panels are made in smooth, un-grooved sheets, position them carefully before taking saw and hammer in hand. As a rule, the end panels on a wall should be of equal width.

Panels can be applied over an old wall which is level but are usually put up over studs or furring strips spaced 16 in. on centers. Cross-blocks should be installed between studs or furring strips approximately 3 ft. above the floor, to protect the panels against breakage when chairs and other furniture pieces are slammed back against them.

Install the panels with 1¼-in. galvanized nails. Common nails may be used along edges which are covered with moldings. Use finishing nails otherwise. Drive these at an angle to within about ⅛ in. of the surface; then set the heads flush with the surface with a nailset, to avoid hammer marks. Space nails 3 in. apart around the edges and 6 in. apart through the center.

To allow for expansion, the panels should be in very loose contact along the edges. Exposed joints are veed. Use a special fiberboard bevel-ing tool or, if you are very careful, a razor-sharp utility knife. But joints covered with moldings are neater and easier to make.

Fiberboard panels come with a factory-ap-plied priming coat. Even so, you should apply two coats of latex paint or a coat of alkyd primer followed by a coat of alkyd enamel to get complete coverage.

Maintaining and repairing fiberboard panel-ing. Clean the walls with mild detergent solu-tion. If they are scratched or develop holes, about the only thing you can do is fill them with spackle or gypsum board joint compound; but you'll hardly be overwhelmed by the results.

Acoustical board. This is a kind of fiberboard panel made to deaden sound within rooms.* It is used almost exclusively in commercial and public buildings, but might well be of value in certain home situations. One thing to be said for it is that, while the surface has little resis-tance to wear, it has a very attractive texture. If you can imagine a pan filled with a flat layer of vermicelli, you have the picture.

The 1-in.-thick panels are available in 2- and 4-ft. widths and lengths of 6, 7, 8, 9, 10, 11 and 12 ft.

Installing acoustical board. Follow the direc-tions for installing ordinary fiberboard, but use 2-in. finishing nails and countersink the heads slightly. Since the panels come with beveled edges, joints are most easily made in a V shape. But an especially attractive effect is achieved by spacing 2-ft.-wide panels 1 in. apart to give deep vertical shadow lines.

Paint must be applied with a spray gun. Use latex.

Maintain like ordinary fiberboard.

Velvet board. This is a ¼-in. plywood panel covered with velvet plush. It comes in an as-sortment of solid colors and is made not only in 4x8-ft. panels but also in 1x8-ft. strips. Since it is easily damaged and soiled, it should be used only where it is subjected to little wear. The cost is 50¢ a sq. ft.

Installing velvet board. Because of the thin-ness, the panels should be installed over a gypsum backer board to control sound trans-mission. Use adhesive to hold them in place. The edges of the panels are beveled and cov-ered with fabric, so the joints are supposed to be exposed. However, you can achieve a very pleasant effect by covering them with ornamen-tal wood moldings.

Maintain like felt (*see page* 78).

Asbestos-cement board. Here's a tough one. Made of asbestos fibers and Portland cement, it's fireproof, rotproof, moistureproof, rodent-proof, verminproof, moldproof; inert and sta-

* National Gypsum Co., Buffalo, N.Y. 14202

ble; resistant to abrasion and impact; easy to clean; never needs finishing but takes paint well. And it's flexible enough to bend around curving walls.

The panels are made in 4-ft. widths; 4-, 8-, 10- and 12-ft. lengths; and ⅛-, ³⁄₁₆- and ¼-in. thicknesses. The very smooth, hard natural finish is a stone-gray color, but you can buy primed and completely finished panels. The cost of ⅛-in. unfinished panels is a bit over 20¢ a sq. ft.; for ¼-in., a bit under 40¢. The obvious use for the material is in furnace rooms and other areas that may be the source of fire. But an excellent use for ⅛-in. sheets is in re-covering walls that have fallen apart.

Installing asbestos-cement panels. Despite the weight of the material (80 lb. for a 4x8 sheet ¼ in. thick), installation is on a par with the installation of gypsum board.

One-eighth-inch panels should always be used over a solid backing which is reasonably level and smooth. Thicker panels can be applied directly to studs. Maximum stud spacing is 16 in. for ³⁄₁₆-in. panels; 24 in. for ¼-in. panels. Because of the density of asbestos-cement, a backer board is not essential for sound control, but is desirable.

Install the panels vertically, working from one end of a wall to the other. Handle them like gypsum board.

Always cut asbestos-cement board with the smooth face up, except when using a portable power saw. For straight cuts, score a panel several times with a sharp awl. Use a board as a straight-edge. Then place the panel with the scored line along the edge of a sawhorse or workbench and, starting at one end, snap off the projecting strip. Make curving or irregular cuts with a fine-toothed keyhole saw or with a saber saw.

Small rectangular inside cuts are made by scoring the panel and knocking out the piece with a hammer. For round cuts, punch a series of holes ⅛ in. apart with a sharp nailset and knock out the piece.

Applied over studs, the panels must be put up with case-hardened steel nails having diamond points and flat heads. The nails should be 1¼ in. long. Space them 8 in. apart along the edges; 16 in. apart along the intermediate studs. They should be at least ⅜ in. in from the edges. Drive the heads snug to the panels, but don't try to countersink them. If you have to pull a nail, put a block of wood under the hammer head.

When ⅛-in. asbestos-cement is installed over an existing wall or backer board, cover the back of each panel with adhesive recommended by the panel manufacturer. This should be applied with a notched spreader held at a 45° angle. Press the panel firmly against the subwall and flatten it completely. Then nail around the edges on 8-in. centers. Over subwalls up to ½ in. thick, use 1¼-in. nails; but use 1½-in. nails for thicker subwalls.

By eliminating nails in the center of ⅛-in. panels it is possible to produce a smooth, seamless wall. This is accomplished by concealing the joints between panels—and the nails along the joints—with gypsum board joint compound and tape. (*Follow the directions in Chapter 9.*) Nails in the centers of panels cannot be concealed satisfactorily, however, because they are not countersunk.

To paint asbestos-cement board, use chlorinated rubber paint. Two coats are needed as a starter.

Maintaining and repairing asbestos-cement board. Wash painted walls with a mild detergent solution. On unfinished panels, scrub with detergent solution or a powdered cleanser. For severe stains, use chlorine bleach or one of the cleaners made especially for asbestos-cement shingles.

Gouges in panels can be filled with gypsum board joint compound or spackle.

14

Rigid Plastics

Plastic wall-surfacing materials haven't made as much progress as you might expect from such an aggressive industry. This in spite of the fact that the potential market just for bathroom wall coverings is enormous. The hold-up is traceable to the difficulty the designers and engineers have had in figuring out how to make joints between panels installed in tub recesses and shower stalls watertight. But several firms have now come up with satisfactory solutions, and it is reasonable to expect that you'll be using more rigid plastics on bathroom and other walls in the future.

Conventional laminated plastics. These are the same tough materials that counter tops are made of. Although they are not used to any extent on walls, except behind kitchen counters, there is no reason why they shouldn't be. They're available in innumerable attractive colors and patterns and several finishes. They can withstand endless abuse; and after you are through heaping this upon them, you can wipe them off as clean as a whistle with water or detergent.

The usual dimensions of laminated plastic sheets are 4x8 ft. But you can find widths ranging from 30 to 60 in., and lengths from 5 to 12 ft. The general-purpose sheets used on horizontal surfaces are $\frac{1}{16}$ in. thick. These are sometimes used on vertical surfaces. But a special vertical grade only $\frac{1}{32}$ in. thick gets the big play. Looking at it, you can't tell it from the general-purpose grade; but it has slightly less heat and impact resistance. And it costs less— about 30¢ a sq. ft.

Installing laminated plastics. Laminated plastic sheets must have a rigid backing to give them strength and hold them flat. You could glue them to an existing wall if that happened to be surfaced with smooth plywood, hardboard or particleboard from which all paint, varnish and the like have been removed. But the simplest approach is to glue them to $\frac{1}{2}$-in. particleboard in your workshop before applying to the wall.

Fill any holes or dents in the particleboard with plastic wood, and sand smooth. Then apply contact cement in even overall coats to the face of the particleboard and back of the laminated sheet. Allow this to dry according to the manufacturer's directions. Then align the sheet carefully over the particleboard and lower it into place. This is tricky, because once the two coated surfaces touch, they are bonded together for life. A good way to go about the job is to lay smooth sticks of wood across the particleboard and support the laminate on these until it is positioned properly. Then, starting at one end, pull out the sticks one by one and lower the laminate gradually into place.

Press the laminate down firmly with a flat roller. Work from the center toward the edges and take extra pains to press down the edges. The panel is now ready to be trimmed to fit the wall. Use a crosscut saw with 10 or 12 teeth per in., a circular saw with a fine-toothed blade or a saber saw. When using a handsaw, the decorative panel surface should be up; otherwise it should be down. Support the panel well to keep the saw from binding and the plastic from chipping.

Arrange the complete panels on each wall so that those at the ends are of equal width. Then install them like plywood, but with adhesive only. Since $\frac{1}{2}$-in. particleboard is a good sound barrier, the panels can be applied directly to the studs. They can also be applied to furring strips over an existing wall; but they are too rigid to be glued unless the wall is perfectly level.

If adjacent panels are butted together loosely, no further joint treatment is required. Moldings may be used, however.

Prefabricated laminated plastic panels. These consist of a sheet of plastic laminate bonded to $\frac{3}{8}$-in. particleboard.* They are available in 16- and 24-in. widths and 8 and 10-ft. lengths. The edges are grooved to receive a spline which holds them together and to the wall. The price is about $1 a sq. ft.

Installing prefabricated panels. Both existing walls and new stud walls must be furred out with horizontal wood strips spaced 16 in. on centers. If the panels are to be installed around a corner on two adjacent walls, it may be necessary to shim out the strips to assure that the corner is absolutely plumb.

Install the panels from the corner. Cut a $\frac{3}{16}$-in.-wide rabbet in the face of the first panel along the corner edge. Then set the panel into the corner and nail it to the furring strips through the rabbet. Use $1\frac{1}{4}$-in. finishing nails.

Insert a spline supplied by the panel manufacturer into the other edge of the panel and nail it to the furring strips. Then slide the next panel over the spline and insert a new spline in the other edge. Nail this to the furring strips and continue in this fashion to the end of the wall. The corner edge of the last panel must be rabbeted like that of the first.

In addition to providing a means of fastening the panels, the rabbets are used to receive the edges of panels on adjacent walls, thus assuring tight-fitting corners.

The splines used between panels are available in three widths to permit a choice of joint treatment. When the narrowest spline is used, the joints are butted and slightly veed. The next-wider spline gives a joint $\frac{1}{2}$ in. wide and $\frac{3}{16}$ in. deep. This can be painted or stained—

* Formica Corp., 120 E. 4th St., Cincinnati, Ohio 45202

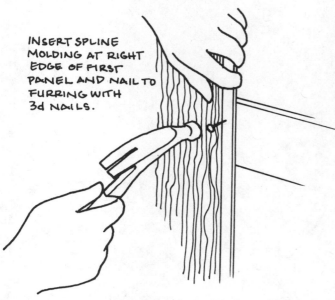

INSERT SPLINE MOLDING AT RIGHT EDGE OF FIRST PANEL AND NAIL TO FURRING WITH 3d NAILS.

SLIDE SECOND PANEL INTO POSITION OVER SPLINE AND CONTINUE PROGRESSIVELY WITH SPLINES AND PANELS.

usually in a color contrasting with the panels. The widest spline gives a ½-in. open joint. It is surfaced with plastic laminate.

Laminated plastic bathroom panels. The tub recess in the new bathroom in our present house is covered with these panels*; and despite the fact that we have had trouble with the panel at the foot of the tub, I recommend them. They are attractive, durable and easy to clean. And they don't have mortar lines which become stained and mildewed—which is the reason we switched from ceramic tiles to plastic. The cost comes to about $1.25 a sq. ft.

My complaint is not with the panels themselves but with the way they were put up. At the time I had them installed they were new on the market and the manufacturer had not worked out his installation methods and instructions very well. It was either that or my contractor didn't do as he was told. In any event, water got in under the end panel and softened the gypsum board to which it was glued; and the plastic has had an undulating look ever since. I don't believe this would happen today if new installation procedures are followed.

The panels consist of a decorative plastic laminate bonded to a thin layer of dense poly-

* Formica Corp., 120 E. 4th St., Cincinnati, Ohio 45202

styrene foam which conforms to small iregularities in the subwall. Thus it is possible to mount the panels on a slightly less-than-perfect base and still achieve a level, flat surface. The panels are available in seven sizes, so you can use them not only in tub recesses but also in shower stalls and on any other wall in the bathroom: 2½x5 ft., 3x8 ft., 4x8 ft., 5x8 ft., 5x5 ft., 5x6 ft. and 5x10 ft. Complete kits, which include panels plus moldings, adhesive and caulking, are available.

Installing laminated plastic bathroom panels. The work involved has a high difficulty rating because of the care which must be taken to fit and position the panels to ensure against leaks.

In new construction, after a tub is set into place between the studs, a ½-in.-thick subwall is nailed to the studs above it. This can be made of exterior-grade plywood with a smooth, knot-free face or of moisture-resistant gypsum board. If the latter is used, a 6-in.-wide strip of exterior-grade plywood should be installed immediately above the tub; and the gypsum board should be butted tightly to the top of this. It is unnecessary to tape the gypsum joints, and nail holes need not be filled if they are less than $\frac{1}{16}$ in. deep and only a little wider than the nailhead. But larger holes must be filled.

In an existing bathroom, the plastic panels

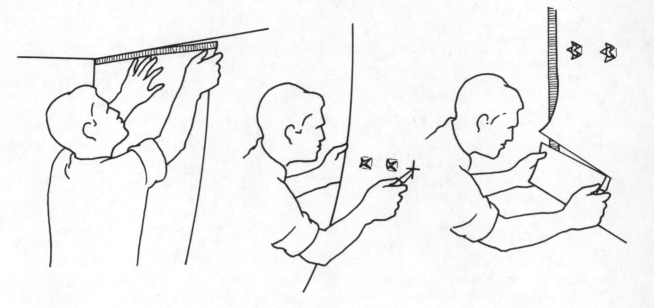

can be installed over any sound, smooth, level, clean surface which is free of loose paint, wallpaper or other flexible covering. Cut out gypsum board and plaster walls to 6 in. above the tub rim or shower pan, and put in strips of exterior-grade plywood. Plywood and hardboard which have been installed with adhesive must also be nailed. If any of these four materials has not been painted, it should be given a coat of urethane varnish or oil-base house paint to make it more moisture-resistant. The plastic panels may also be installed directly over ceramic tile, but not over metal or plastic tiles. Joints between tiles are not filled.

The first step in putting up panels is to cut and install the vertical corner moldings which seal the joints between panels against leakage. The moldings are in two pieces: a surface strip and a base strip which is concealed behind the panels. Nail the base strips into the corners with 1¼-in. galvanized common nails spaced 6 to 8 in. apart. Place the nails opposite each other in both sides of the strip. Similar moldings of somewhat different design are used for outside corners and between adjacent panels on long walls. The base strips for these are also installed at this time.

The most accurate way to fit the plastic panels—first the back panel and then the end panels—to the tub recess is to make templates out of rolls of wrapping paper and masking tape. Hang the strips of paper from the ceiling line with tape; smooth them down and join adjacent strips on the back wall with tape. Poke the paper over the pipe stubs. Then trim the paper away about 1 in. from the four edges of each wall and apply 1½-in. masking tape around the edges. The tape should be butted against the vertical corners, the tub and the ceiling. Then, with a compass or pair of dividers, mark a cutting line on all edges of each template. Allow $\frac{1}{16}$-in. clearance at the top and bottom; ⅛-in. at the sides. Mark the center lines for all pipes, and draw in the outline of a recessed soap dish.

Tape the templates to the face of the plastic panels and cut the panels to fit. Be sure they are well supported. You can use a crosscut handsaw for straight cuts, but a saber saw with a fine-toothed blade is handier and is needed for inside cuts. Make circular cuts with a hole saw or a brace with an expansive bit. All cutting must be done with the decorative face up.

Before smoothing the cut edges, chamfer the foam back slightly with a sharp knife or razor blade in order to keep your smoothing tools from getting gummed up. Then trim the edges to the exact shape of the templates with a block plane and smooth them with a file.

Cut a half dozen small shims out of general-purpose plastic laminate or cardboard $\frac{1}{16}$ in. thick, and tape these to the top of the tub rim close to the walls. Then dry-fit the panels to the walls and do whatever additional trimming is indicated. To assist in positioning the panels accurately after they are glued, draw a short line across the face of each panel and the tub rim with a grease pencil.

The backs of the panels are covered with an adhesive which must be liquefied with a special activator. Apply the activator with a 7-in., short-napped paint roller. Do not use a brush.

First apply a coat of activator around the edges of the wall behind the tub. Patched areas should also be coated. Then peel off the protective film on the back of the back-wall panel and roll on an ample coat of activator. Work quickly. The adhesive turns "money"-green. Press it frequently with a finger to test how tacky it is. As soon as it sticks to your finger so tightly that you can lift a corner of the panel

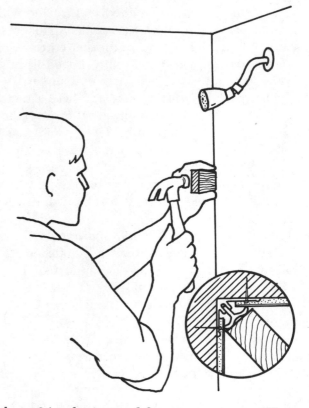

about 6 in., let it stand five more minutes. Then set the panel on the shims, on the tub rim, position it, tilt it up against the wall and press it into place. Go over the entire panel with a flat roller. Around the edges, tap it down tight with a hammer and a 4-in. square of 2-in.-thick wood.

Apply the end panels in the same way.

File the cut ends of the surface molding strips smooth and run a piece of paraffin up and down the tongues on the back of the strips. Then fit the surface strips into the base strips on the wall. Use a thin block of wood and a hammer to tap them in securely and tight against the face of the panels.

Conceal the exposed edges of the end panels with plastic-covered wood moldings. The same type of molding may be used as a cap molding on wainscots. Apply the moldings with white wood glue and finishing nails. Countersink the nailheads.

To seal the cracks between panels and tub rim, use the silicone caulking compound recommended by the panel manufacturer. The

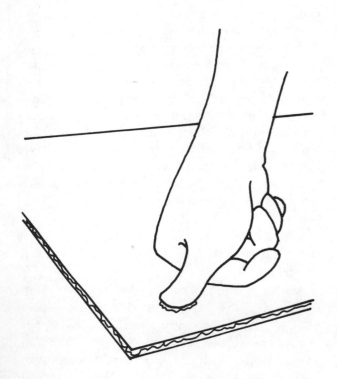

cracks should first be cleaned and treated with a conditioner used with the caulk. A ribbon of caulk is then squeezed into the cracks and smoothed with a lint-free cloth dipped in mineral spirits and wrapped around a finger.

Fiberglass bathroom panels. These panels* are sold in a $90 kit for installation over any standard-size recessed tub. They come in six solid colors. The two end panels are L-shaped, to fit around the corners of the recess and eliminate joints at those points. The flat back panel is 3 ft. wide and has a soap dish molded in.

Installing fiberglass bathroom panels. These are easier to work with than laminated panels because the fitting is less complicated if the wall corners are plumb. But if the corners aren't plumb, fitting the end panels can become an exasperating chore.

The end panels are fitted and cut first. Templates are of no help. Make careful measurements with a rule after establishing vertical lines for the outside edges of the panels and horizontal lines for the top edges. To double-check the measured positions of pipe studs, rub the ends with chalk and press the foot-of-the-tub panel against them.

The panels come with pressure-sensitive tape on the back. This holds them secure while adhesive, which you apply with a caulking gun, sets. The adhesive is applied in thick beads around the edges and in a figure S across the center. The backing on the pressure-sensitive tape is then removed and the panels are pressed against the wall.

The back panel has narrow flanges along the vertical edges. These fit over the end panels and are glued to them.

Methacrylate panels. These resemble marble of three colors.† other plastic and hardboard materials are made to look like marble; but compared with this material, they are pretty poor imitations. Methacrylate has the opalescent look of marble and the same apparent

depth because it is thick and has veining from front to back.

The panels, which are used not only for covering walls but also for making kitchen and bathroom counters, are very heavy, hard, rigid and strong. They are scratch- and stain-resistant; easy to clean.

To cover walls, use ½-in.-thick panels. These are 30 in. wide and up to 98 in. long. A special kit is available for surfacing walls around a recessed tub. The cost of the panels is approximately $4 a sq. ft.

Installing methacrylate panels. Because of their sound-stopping density, the panels can be applied to a framed wall; but the acoustical qualities of the wall will be better if a gypsum backer board is used underneath. In the latter case, cover the backer board with a mastic-type adhesive recommended by the panel manufacturer. This should be applied with a notched trowel. If the backer board is not used, nail horizontal furring strips to the studs on 16-in. centers. The strips must be of strong, knot-free lumber and almost smooth on the surface. Glue the panels to the strips with epoxy glue. The panels should be braced for about 12 hours after they are erected.

Arrange the panels so that those at the ends of each wall are approximately equal in width. Simple butt joints between panels are attractive and easy to make. However, joints which are veed or otherwise shaped can be readily formed with an electric router. In bathtub installations, the center panel overlaps the edges of the two side panels and is stuck to them with epoxy glue. The space behind the panel is filled with ¼-in. hardboard, to which the panel is glued.

Yet another way of handling joints is to cover them with 2-in.-wide battens of methacrylate.

Methacrylate is best cut with power saws equipped with fine-toothed, carbide-tipped blades. Bore holes with electric drills. If cut, shaped or drilled edges are to be exposed, smooth them with No. 80 to 120 aluminum-oxide sandpaper; then switch to No. 120 to 240;

---

* Swan Corp., 721 Olive St., St. Louis, Mo. 63101
† Building Products Div., DuPont Co., Wilmington, Dela. 19898

and finish with No. 240 to 600. Polish panels with a soft, damp rag dipped in rottenstone or pumice.

Plastic masonry. Wall coverings made to resemble bricks are truer to life than those resembling stones; but the imitations in both cases are pretty good until you get close up. Then you realize that no matter how artful plastic engineers and designers are, they can't make fiberglass or butadiene-styrene come out exactly like masonry.

Some of the coverings are fabricated in panels up to 4x8 ft.; others are only about 1x2 or 1x4 ft.; and still others are the actual size of individual bricks or stones. In all cases, L-shaped pieces are available for making outside corners. Prices range from 50¢ to $1.50 per sq. ft.

Installing plastic masonry. Because installation methods vary, I won't go into detail. Follow the manufacturer's directions.

Fiberglass coverings can be installed on actual fireplace walls as long as they are not directly exposed to flame; but other materials can be used only in areas where low temperatures prevail.

All the materials must be applied to some sort of backer board—preferably one dense enough to control sound transmission. In new construction, use ½-in. gypsum board. In an existing house, the composition of the wall is immaterial so long as it is sound, level and reasonably smooth.

Application is best made with adhesive in the manner prescribed by the manufacturer, but the larger panels may also be nailed. The latter are usually designed to interlock along the edges. In cases where a slight space is required between adjoining panels, the mortar joints are filled with a plastic compound and troweled smooth. The filler may then have to be colored with a touch-up preparation.

Maintaining and repairing all rigid plastics. Outside of cleaning these materials with detergent solution or a nonabrasive powdered cleanser, there isn't much you have to do to them. And you can't do anything if they are scratched or otherwise damaged.

15

Mirrors

Of all the ways to make a room look large, covering the walls with mirrors is the best. One mirrored wall doubles the apparent size; two adjacent mirrored walls quadruple the size. Try it in a tiny front hall and you may well wind up using the same treatment in every other cramped room in the house.

But be warned of two things:

1. Mirrors show smudges. They're easy to clean, of course. All it takes is a damp cloth and paper towel. But if you use mirrors on a wall which people touch or splatter frequently, the lady of the household is going to complain.

2. Mirrors can be dangerous. I don't mean you are very likely to break them if they have a solid backing. But I had an unpleasant experience which illustrates the point.

I was hurrying into a New York restaurant to meet a friend for lunch. I was late. As I came through the front door into a dark foyer I saw him sitting at the bar. Rushing toward him, I crashed into the mirror in which he was reflected. Everybody thought it was great fun. I didn't—even when the bartender admitted that it had happened many times before.

So be careful not to build a mirrored wall where the same fate may befall you. It should be far enough away from the main entrance into a room so you can see it and identify it.

Types of mirror. Mirrors are made of glass

and acrylic. Consider the glass type first. The best and most expensive (about $3 a sq. ft.) are made of ¼-in. plate glass. They are the best because they are free of distortion and because their thickness gives them extra strength. Ideally, you should use mirrors of this type if they are to be installed in large wall-high sheets. However, if the cost is a problem, you might settle for mirrors made of ¼-in. float glass. These are almost free of distortion; in many cases, in fact, you can hardly tell the difference.

Sheet-glass mirrors are ⅛ in. thick and as breakable as a windowpane (which is also made of sheet glass). But their main fault is that they are often wavy looking and distort the image. So they should be used only in small pieces—if then.

Whatever the glass used, you can buy mirrors which look like standard silver mirrors and others which are black, antiqued, veined, stenciled or whatever. But the standard type is the only one that is fully reflective and effective in magnifying room size.

Mirror sizes are also variable. If you make the proper overtures to a mirror manufacturer through a local dealer, you can get a plate-glass panel big enough to cover the average bedroom wall. But if you're going to make your own installation, you should think considerably smaller. Handling big sheets of glass is an extremely tricky, heavy business. Maybe you and a friend can install a 3- or 4-ft.-wide, wall-high mirror, but don't say I didn't warn you.

Acrylic mirror* weighs only half as much as plate glass and doesn't break, so there is no reason why you shouldn't be able to install the largest size available—6x9 ft. It also costs less and comes in six colors besides silver (but if you want a special pattern, as in glass, you'll have to apply it yourself). Its main drawback —in the manufacturer's own words—is that it "should be used where precise image reflectance is not required except in relatively small

* Rohm & Haas, Independence Mall West, Philadelphia, Pa. 19105

components." In other words, as a reflector it is more in the sheet-glass than the plate-glass category. It also has a combustibility comparable with wood.

Covering a wall with large plate-glass mirrors. I'm talking here about mirrors that extend from the baseboard to the ceiling. If you put in anything shorter, follow the installation methods given in Chapter 4.

Before having the mirrors cut (don't try it yourself), plumb the corners of the wall and measure the length between the plumb lines. Subtract 1½ in., to give yourself room to maneuver the end mirrors into position. This gives you the total width of the mirror installation. Then have all the mirrors cut to equal width. (Example: if the wall space to be covered is 11 ft. 6 in. long, you might have six mirrors cut to 23-in. widths; five mirrors cut to 27⅝-in. widths; or four mirrors cut to 34½-in. widths.)

Since the top edge of the mirrors will be covered with a ceiling molding, and the bottom edge with the baseboard, the length of the mirrors should equal the distance between these strips plus about 1½ in. This allows the ceiling molding to overlap the mirror ½ in.; the baseboard to overlap 1 in.

The subwall against which the mirrors are placed should be sturdy, level and smooth. Half-inch gypsum board is satisfactory. Be sure to install this with annular-ring nails, which won't pop loose and damage the back of the mirror. Countersink and cover the heads with gypsum board cement. Joints between gypsum boards need not be filled, however. The gypsum board should be cut away above the floor to a height equal to the height of the baseboard. Fill this space with strips of ½-in. plywood to provide a good nailing base for the mirror clips.

With a carpenter's level, strike a horizontal line along the plywood strip 1 in. from the top. Install the mirror clips just below this line with screws. Screw as many of the clips as possible through the plywood and into the studs for extra strength. Use clips made of steel, since they project only a fraction of an inch out from the mirror surface. The alternative—even better—is to use a continuous-steel channel.

Cover the plywood strip beneath the clips with another strip of plywood the thickness of the mirror. This serves as a nailing base for the baseboard.

Install the mirrors from one end of the wall to the other. The first should be about ¾ in. out from the corner. (Installing mirrors tight into the corners of a wall is a possibility if the corners are plumb. But the last mirror will be difficult to fit without chipping its edges or the edge of the adjacent mirror.) Hold the mirror upright and lower it carefully into the clips. Check whether it is vertical with a carpenter's level or plumb line. Then, while a helper holds it against the wall, screw two or three clips along the top edge. The screws should be long enough to penetrate well into the top-plate.

Edges of adjacent mirrors should just touch. When setting each mirror, allow about ½-in. space between it and the preceding mirror and then slide it sideways.

When all the mirrors are up, install the baseboard and ceiling molding. Be careful not to drive nails close to the edges of the glass. Then cover the gaps at the ends of the wall with moldings.

Installing glass mirror tiles. Ready-cut tiles with edges beveled or ground measure 1 ft. sq. They are made of both sheet glass and float glass. Larger tiles, or blocks, are available in plate glass.

The wall to be tiled must be strong, sound, smooth and level. It must also be dry, clean and free of flaking paint. Wallpaper and other coverings must be removed. If the height or length of the wall are not exactly divisible by 1 ft., you must decide whether to cut all the end tiles or the top and bottom tiles to the same width, or whether to cut only those at one end or at the bottom.

Cutting is done with an ordinary glass cutter. Cover a smooth, flat work surface with several thicknesses of clean newspaper, and lay a tile on this faceup. Use a yardstick as a guide and wet the bottom side with water so it won't slip on the glass. Hold it firmly and draw the cutter along it.

The cutter is held vertically between your first and second fingers, with the thumb under the handle. Start at the far side of the mirror just inside the edge, press down and draw the cutter in a continuous stroke toward you and off the near edge.

To break the mirror, hold it on opposite sides of the cut and bend it backward sharply. Or place a large finishing nail under the cut and press the glass downward. If the piece being removed is very narrow, place one of the slots in the cutter head over it and bend downward.

Unless your scheme for arranging the tiles calls for another approach, start installing the tiles from a corner. Check first whether it is vertical. If it is, butt the tiles tight against it. If it isn't you must either trim an edge of each tile to fit the corner or leave a gap and cover it later with a molding. If you elect the first course, measure 1 ft. from the widest part of the corner and strike a plumb line on the wall. Following the second course, measure 1 ft. from the narrowest part of the corner and strike a plumb line.

The first vertical row of tiles is installed along the plumb line. Subsequent rows should then be vertical, too, but it's a good idea to check every two or three rows anyway.

Install the tiles with double-faced adhesive tape. If this comes in long strips, cut them into pieces a little less than 1 ft. long and stick two of them to the back of each tile just inside the vertical edges. If the tape is supplied in small squares, stick one square to each corner of the tile.

Position each tile carefully and press it firmly against the wall. Once you get started, work goes fast.

Installing acrylic mirrors. The smallest sizes are 2x2 ft. If you use these, install them like glass mirror tiles. If you use floor-to-ceiling mirrors, the best way to install them is in equal-width panels; but this will probably necessitate waste because you must buy whatever widths are available and then cut them to size. To save money you may install the available width in the middle of the wall and cut the end panels as necessary. They should be equal in width.

Acrylic is easily worked. One way to make straight cuts is with a special scribing tool available from the plastics dealer. Place the panel on a table or workbench back side up, and, using a straight board as a guide, draw the tool repeatedly across the panel. Make at lease five passes on ⅛-in. mirrors; 10 passes on ¼-in. Then slide a ¾-in. dowel as long as the cut under it; hold the main part of the panel down with one hand and, with the other hand, press down firmly on the piece to be removed.

Cutting can also be done with power saws with fine-toothed blades. The mirror should be facedown. Edges are shaped with a router or a block plane. Use an electric drill for boring holes.

If cut edges are exposed, they can be scraped smooth with a sharp knife or sanded. Use No. 80 sandpaper to start, and progress to No. 400.

Mount the mirrors on a smooth, level, clean subwall free of flaking paint, wallpaper or other flexible coverings. Use 1-in.-wide, double-faced foam adhesive tape. On ¼-in. mirrors up to 3x4 ft., use at least 16 ft. of ⅛-in.-thick tape; on mirrors up to 4x8 ft., use at least 32 ft. of ¼-in.-thick tape; and on mirrors larger than this use ⅜-in.-thick tape four times the long

dimension. Cut the tape into mirror-length strips and apply one strip within ½ in. of each long edge and place the others in between. Then press the mirrors against the wall.

Acrylic mirrors can also be anchored with white silicone bathtub caulking compound or supported on clips like those used for glass mirrors. The latter should be used if there is any possibility that you will someday take the mirrors down. If tape or adhesive are used, they will pull the reflective film off the backs of the mirrors.

Because of the ease of cutting acrylic mirrors, the end panels can be scribed and butted to the corners and all panels can be butted to the top of the baseboard and the ceiling. But if you prefer to cover the edges with moldings, do so. Adjacent panels should be separated a tiny fraction of an inch. The edges are chamfered. Beveling weakens them.

Bending acrylic mirrors to conform to curving walls is easily done. Use double-faced foam tape to mount them, and gradually press them to the wall as you work from one edge to the other. During the process, the first edge must be clamped down with a wood batten. If the edges stand away slightly from the wall, fasten them with screws. The minimum bending radius for ⅛-in. mirrors is 22½ in.; for ¼-in. mirrors, 45 in.

Acrylic mirrors can be painted on either side with acrylic-base enamels applied by brushing, spraying, rolling or silk-screening. You can also decorate them by stenciling, engraving or appliquéing.

16

Ceramic Tile

Ceramic tile is beautiful. There's no need to tell you that unless you haven't taken a good look at it recently. Time was when it wasn't very beautiful. At least what we saw in most American houses wasn't. But today the beautiful tiles way outnumber the *un*beautiful.

And the variety is almost unbelievable. There are countless colors, several finishes, many shapes and sizes, numerous high- and low-relief textures and lots and lots of specially decorated tiles. The best way to find out what's available is to go to your nearest city library and leaf through the ceramic tile catalogs in *Sweet's Architectural File* (a series of thick books describing most of the building materials

on the market today). Then, having gotten an idea about which manufacturers have what you want, visit their showrooms or dealers' showrooms for a first-hand look. You won't find it easy to make a final decision about what to buy. In fact, you may be so carried away with the many possibilities that you'll start dreaming up fancy designs for your walls. This is where you can run into trouble, because when you get away from simple, more or less standard tile layouts, you move into the realm of the professional decorator, architect or artist.

Maybe you're capable of carrying on and maybe you're not. I'll have to leave that up to you. One thing I can assure you of is that tile dealers and installers are of little help. They are mechanics, not designers. Sometimes tile manufacturers have decorators in their largest showrooms who can steer you. But beyond that it's a case either of trusting yourself, hiring a professional designer or going back to a simpler scheme.

But enough of that.

Beauty is only one of the splendid features of ceramic tile. Water-resistance is another. In fact, you can't beat it here. That is why it has been the No. 1 covering for bathroom walls for decades.

It doesn't fade and is impervious to almost all staining agents.

It is tough as nails. It's one of the few wall coverings which you can scrub with scouring powder; and if little Willie scrapes his velocipede along it, so what?

Finally, it's easy to clean. The tile itself is, that is. The grout between tiles can be a problem if the wrong type is exposed to water containing heavy concentrations of iron or to kitchen grease.

The cost ranges from about $1 a sq. ft. up. Way up. I have a catalog which lists one type of decorated, hand-made Mexican tiles at $7.20; and I shouldn't be at all surprised if some manufacturers go even higher. These prices cover only the tiles in the main field of a wall. The trim units—that is, the border tiles—add further to the cost. So do adhesive and grout.

Installation is time-consuming and moderately difficult. Actual placement of the tiles on the wall is simple enough, but cutting and trimming are exacting.

Equipment needed. If you buy a so-called kit for tiling the walls in a tub recess, some of the special tools required may be included. In any event, you need the following:

Notched adhesive spreader.
Nippers for trimming tiles. You may be able to borrow these from the tile dealer. In a pinch you can use pliers.
Tile-cutter. If you can borrow this also, fine. If not, you can do perfectly well with an ordi-

nary glass cutter and a 5-in. finishing nail or piece of coat-hanger wire.
Coarse file or abrasive stone for smoothing cut edges.
Carpenter's spirit level.
Window-washer's squeegee. A 6-in. size is a good average, but use whatever is handy.
Old toothbrush with a handle rounded at the end.
Cloths.
Pencil.
Rule.

Estimating how much tile you need. Ceramic tile may be used to cover a wall from floor to ceiling; but it is often used to cover only part of a wall. If you go the latter route, your first step in figuring how many tiles you need is to decide approximately how high the tile will go. (I say "approximately" because you may have to adjust the height to suit the type of tile.) A few general rules will help you to reach this decision:

- In bathtubs used for shower bathing, the pipe for the shower head comes through the wall at a height of about 6 ft. Tile should be installed at least 6 in. above this.
- Wainscots behind lavatories and toilets and elsewhere in bathrooms are usually 4 ft. high.
- In kitchens, walls are usually tiled up to the bottoms of the wall cabinets. These are generally 54 in. above the floor; 18 in. above the counters.

The second step is to make an accurate measurement of the wall area to be tiled. This is done in several ways:

If you use 4¼ x 4¼-in. tiles. Square tiles of this size are the commonest type for wall installations. To determine how many you need, mark a straight strip of wood, such as a yardstick, into 4 ⁵⁄₁₆-in. segments. (The extra ¹⁄₁₆ in. allows for a joint.) Check the ends of the wall with your carpenter's level to see if they are vertical; and then, with the marked-off stick, measure the width of the wall at its widest point. This tells you how many vertical rows of tiles are needed.

Using your level, find the lowest spot on the

floor and measure up from this to the intended height of the tile to find how many horizontal rows will be needed. If the measurement indicates that one row of tiles will have to be cut, adjust the installation height up or down to avoid cutting.

Multiplying the number of vertical rows by the number of horizontal rows tells you how many tiles are needed for each wall. However, this may not be the correct answer if you want to install trim tiles along one or more of the edges of the field tiles. For instance, if the tile is not going to be applied all the way to the ceiling, the topmost row should be made with cap tiles which are rounded along the top edge. Similarly, if you tile only part way across a wall or to an outside corner (as is often the case in recessed tub installations), the last vertical row should also be made with tiles having a rounded edge. Or if you tile a wall from the floor up, you may want to use cove tiles in the bottommost row.

Trim tiles also measure 4¼ x 4¼ in. So, in order to determine exactly how many field tiles you need, subtract the number of trim tiles required from the answer arrived at with your marked-off stick. Then, to allow for waste, increase the number of field tiles about 5 percent and add a few extra pieces of each type of trim tile.

Field tiles are sold by the carton. This usually contains 40 pieces covering 5 sq. ft., but may contain 64 pieces covering 8 sq. ft. Trim tiles are sold by the piece or by the carton.

Trim tiles of various configurations are used on walls. The most common are:

Bullnose tiles having one rounded edge. They are used to cap a wall or trim it along a vertical edge.

Down-angles having two adjacent rounded edges. They are used to turn corners in cases where a wall is trimmed along the top and one edge. With square tiles, the same down-angle can be used at either the right or left end of a wall; but if tiles are rectangular, both right-hand and left-hand down-angles are needed.

Cove tiles curving outward at the bottom to eliminate a square, dirt-catching corner at the floor line. But they are used only when the floor is tiled, too. Special cove tiles are needed to go around inside and outside corners.

If you use mosaic tiles. Mosaic tiles are small tiles (usually 1x1 in.) which, as a rule, are sold in 1-ft.-square sheets. The sheets can be cut into small pieces and strips.

To find how many sheets are required, simply determine the square footage of the area to be covered and add a couple of sheets to allow for waste.

If sheets are larger than 1 ft. sq., divide the square footage of the wall by the square-foot area of a sheet and add one or two sheets.

The trim units used with mosaics are usually the same height as the field tiles. They are made in 1 and 2 in. heights and 1 and 2 in. widths. Bullnose tiles are sold in 1-ft. strips. Down-angles are sold by the piece.

If you use tiles of other sizes and shapes. Determine in inches the height and width of the area to be tiled; then let the tile dealer figure out what you need. He has figures which tell how many tiles of a certain size and shape cover a square foot of wall.

Adhesive and grout. Order 1 gal. of adhesive for each 50 sq. ft. of wall surface. Five pounds of dry cement grout cover 100 sq. ft. of 4¼-in. tiles, but only 15 sq. ft. of mosaic tiles.

Preparing the subwall. If building a new wall, cover the studs with ordinary ½-in. gypsum board. Joints and nailheads need not be plastered. If the tiles are over 5⁄16-in. thick, space nails 4 in. apart, rather than the usual 6 to 8 in., and install rows of cross-blocks between the studs about a third of the way up from the floor and a third of the way down from the ceiling.

In a tub recess, shower stall or other wet location, use ½-in. moisture-resistant gypsum board. Cover all cut edges and nailheads with a brush-on sealer supplied by the gypsum board maker. Leave ¼-in. space between the bottom of the board and the top of the tub rim or shower receptor. This is not caulked: the tile covers it. Reduce nail spacing and install blocking if the tile is over 5⁄16 in. thick.

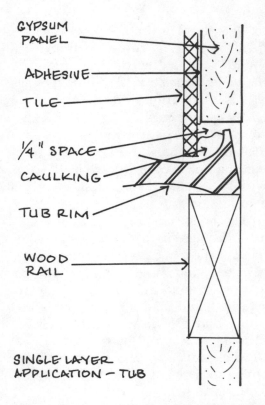

GYPSUM PANEL

ADHESIVE

TILE

¼" SPACE

CAULKING

TUB RIM

WOOD RAIL

SINGLE LAYER APPLICATION — TUB

If you're tiling an existing wall, remove baseboards, moldings, door and window casings, electric and plumbing fixtures, curtain rods and so on. It's also a good idea to take out recessed medicine cabinets if the mirror overhangs the sides, because it may interfere with placement of tiles close to the cabinet.

Tile can be installed on any wall that is sound, rigid and level. Patch plaster cracks carefully; but if a large part of the wall is weak and cracked, knock it out and replace it with gypsum board or cover it with ¼-in. gypsum board. Fill holes with spackle or patching plaster. Level sunken spots with gypsum board joint compound.

Scrape off loose paint. Remove wallpaper, vinyl and other flexible wall coverings. Wash off grease and dirt. If paint has a high gloss, sand it down a little.

If the wall is in a tub or shower area, apply a skin coat of adhesive with the smooth edge of your spreader, to help keep out water, and let it dry overnight. Pack adhesive into openings around pipes at the same time. To prevent

weakening of the subwall by water which may seep in under the tiles, gouge out a ¼-in. open strip just above the tub rim or shower receptor.

Establishing guidelines. The following discussion, through page 145, deals with installation of individual tiles. Mosaics are covered separately.

Wall tiles are best installed from the bottom up, so the first guideline you should establish is the base line. If you're using cove tiles at the foot of the wall, place one of them against the wall at the lowest point along the floor line, set one of the field tiles on top of it and mark the wall at the top edge. (This assumes that you are installing tiles that have spacer lugs on the edges. Most tiles are made this way. But if you happen to be using tiles without spacers, leave the space necessary for grouting between the cove and field tile. This is usually $\frac{1}{16}$ in., although some large tiles are spaced farther apart.)

If you're not using a cove, hold a field tile against the wall at the lowest floor point and mark the wall at the top edge.

With a carpenter's level, draw a line across the wall and across adjacent walls to be tiled. Then nail straight strips of wood along the line just beneath it. Don't drive the nails home, as the strips will be removed later. Their purpose is to hold the tiles secure as they are applied. Without them, the tiles might slip down the wall.

Follow the same procedure above bathtubs, shower receptors and counter tops. Don't take it for granted that these are level; always check them with a carpenter's level. Then lay one field tile against the wall at the lowest point along the tub rim and so forth, mark the top edge and draw a horizontal line.

Then draw another horizontal line to mark the top of the installation, if it is below the ceiling.

Tiles are sometimes laid from one corner of a wall to the other. When this is done, you start with a full tile in the first corner and usually end with a cut tile in the second corner. But for appearance's sake, this arrangement should be

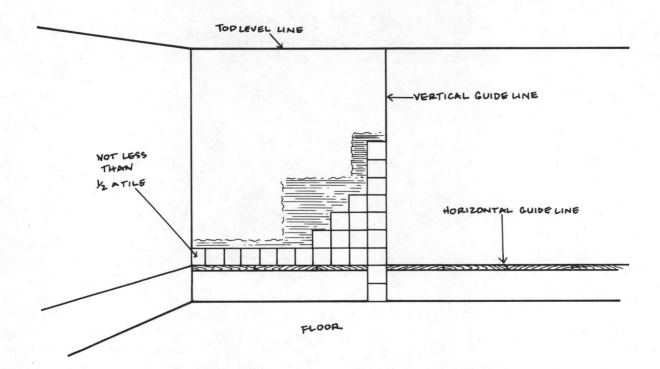

used only when the cut tiles will be inconspicuous. If you decide this will be the case, your next step in laying out the wall is to plumb the first corner and measure out from the widest point the width of a tile. Strike a plumb line at this point.

Tiling from the center of a wall toward the corners is preferable; and you must do this if both ends of the wall are equally visible. To lay out the wall, find and mark the exact center and lay a row of tiles from this point to either end of the wall. If this leaves more than half a tile in the corner, strike a plumb line at the center of the wall. You will start tiling from this line.

If the end tile is less than half width, however, the starting line must be adjusted. To do this, center a tile on the mark indicating the center of the wall, make a pencil mark along either edge and strike a plumb line there. You will now have more than half a tile at each end of the wall.

Installing tiles. It used to be that ceramic tiles had to be set in Portland cement mortar. Luckily, this is no longer true because the work was too difficult for amateurs. Now you can do the job just as well and very much more easily with a masticlike adhesive. Use one recommended by the tile manufacturer or dealer. Read the directions on the can and note particularly how long the adhesive takes to set. Until you get the hang of tilesetting, cover only 2 or 3 sq. ft. of wall at a time.

Apply the adhesive in horizontal strips with the notched edge of your spreader. Hold the spreader at a 45° angle. The beads of adhesive should be thick; the valleys between them, almost bare. To check whether you are applying enough adhesive but not too much, slide or twist a tile into it. If the adhesive oozes out from under the tile, you've used too much and should remove the excess. Now pull off the tile and examine the back. If it is not completely covered, you have used too little adhesive. If it is covered 100 percent, however, you've done just right.

Set the tiles into the adhesive with a very slight twisting motion—this spreads the adhesive evenly over the back—and press them down firmly. The first tile should be placed at

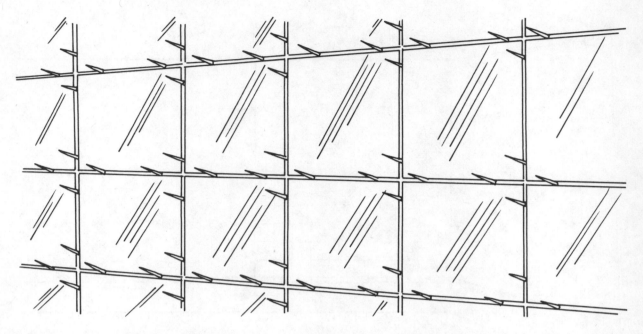

the juncture of the horizontal wood strips and the vertical guideline. Lay several more tiles along the wood strips, then build up along the vertical line and fill in between. If you butt the tiles together carefully, the rows should be perfectly straight. However, it's wise to check them now and then with your level.

If you're using tiles without spacer lugs, stick pieces of toothpicks vertically between them. These should be just wide enough to make $\frac{1}{16}$-in. joints.

After setting a lot of tiles, go back over them with a board and press them down once more. This helps to assure that all are in the same plane. (This can't be done with nonlugged tiles, of course.)

To set trim tiles, butter the backs with adhesive. It's easier than spreading adhesive on the wall to an exact line.

After completing the wall above the horizontal wood strips, let the tiles set for five hours or more; then pull off the strips and complete the wall. If you are installing a cove, set the cove tiles first and follow with the bottom row of field tiles. If the floor is uneven, cut the field tiles—not the cove tiles—and install them with the cut edges down.

If the field tiles are to extend down to the floor, they must be cut to conform to the floor.

When tiling around an outside corner, install a row of field tiles flush with the corner. Then conceal the exposed edges with bullnose tiles. Leave $\frac{1}{16}$-in. space for grouting.

Cutting tiles. Tiles usually have to be cut to fit snugly into corners; and they may also have to be cut to fit around doors and windows, pipes, medicine cabinets and the like.

To scribe a tile to fit into a corner, hold it (*marked* A *in the sketch*) squarely over the tile next out from the corner; and place a

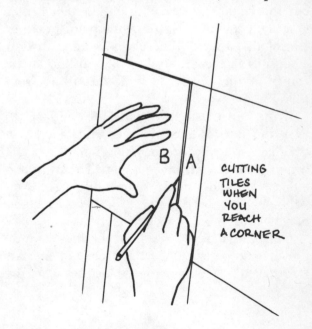

CUTTING TILES WHEN YOU REACH A CORNER

second tile (B) on top and slide it into the corner. Then draw a line on A along the outer edge of B. Cut along this line.

If you don't have a professional's tile-cutter, score the face of the tile with a glass cutter. (*For how to use it, see page 137.*) Then place the tile faceup over a large finishing nail or piece of coat-hanger wire, and press down on either side of the scored line. Smooth the edges with a file or abrasive stone.

In a corner, when the cut edge of a tile is butted to the face of another tile, be sure to allow space for grouting.

When it's necessary to make an irregular cut in a tile (around a pipe, for instance), trim a piece of heavy paper to the shape of the tile and mark the cut on this. Then trim it out with scissors and use the paper as a template to mark the tile.

Irregular cuts are made with tile nippers. Hold the tile glazed side up. Start from the edge and work toward the cut line, nibbling out less than ⅛-in. bites at a time. Finish by shaping and smoothing the cut with a file or abrasive stone.

If a hole must be made in the middle of a tile, cut the tile into two pieces through the center of the hole; then nibble out the hole in each piece.

Filling joints between tiles. Joints are usually filled with a dry cement grout which is mixed with water to the consistency of thick paste. If your water contains a great deal of iron, however, or if you're tiling a wall near the kitchen range, use mastic grout which comes in cans ready for use. It is more stain-resistant and easier to clean.

Let the tile installation set for the time specified by the adhesive manufacturer. Then, after making sure the joints are not clogged with adhesive, apply the grout over one entire wall. (Work on only one wall at a time.) Use a squeegee or rubber sponge. Go over the wall repeatedly, packing the grout into every joint. Scrape off the excess.

Let the grout set for 10 to 20 minutes, until it has begun to dry. Then tool the joints with the narrow end of a rounded toothbrush handle. Leave the joints concave.

As soon as the grout is firm, clean the wall with a sponge wrung out in clean water. You may have to go over it several times. Then polish with a clean, dry cloth.

To hasten curing of the grout, spray the wall with water twice a day for the next three or four days. The spray should be very light and fine, as from a good garden sprayer.

Complete curing takes two weeks. Avoid taking a shower in a stall or tub recess during this time.

Installing bathroom accessories. Ceramic bathroom accessories are made in two ways. The flush type is installed on the same plane as the surrounding tiles. The flange type overlaps the surrounding tiles. In both cases, some accessories, such as paper holders, are recessed in the wall; others are mounted on the subwall like the tiles. Similarly, some fixtures are the same size as the tiles, and some take up the space of one-and-a-half tiles—or even more.

Locate all accessories, so you don't have to cut tiles any more than necessary. It is also important to plan the location of recessed fixtures before you start tiling, in order to avoid studs and other objects inside the walls.

Install accessories after the wall has been tiled and the adhesive has set.

To set a surface-mounted accessory, spread adhesive into the gap between tiles and spread additional adhesive on the back of the accessory. Then press the piece against the wall and hold it with masking tape until the adhesive sets.

Holes for recessed fixtures are cut through the subwalls after the walls are tiled. Apply adhesive to the backs of the accessories and to the edges of the cavities.

Installing mosaic tile. The procedure is very much like that outlined. The major differences are as follows:

Install the sheets of tiles from one end of the wall to the other. After drawing a horizontal line across the wall one sheet up from the floor, check the starting corner for verticality and measure out the width of a sheet from the widest point. Strike a plumb line here. Install the first vertical row of sheets to this line (above the horizontal line) after scribing the edges to the corner.

Whether you nail wood strips along the horizontal line is a matter of choice. Because the sheets are so much larger than individual tiles, there is less chance of their slipping down the wall. On the other hand, the strips simplify alignment of the sheets to some extent.

Take care when applying each sheet to make certain that the small tiles line up with those in the sheets to the side and underneath.

Press each sheet of tile firmly into the adhesive by hand and then go over it again with a block of wood.

To cut mosaic tiles into strips, use scissors and snip between the tiles. The backing cuts easily. When trimming the tiles themselves, use nippers and nibble away small bites; then file and cut edges. It's not necessary to remove the backing when using nippers.

Grouted joints are generally not tooled. Simply strike them off flush with the surface of the tiles with a squeegee or sponge; and when they are firm, wash off grout remaining on the tiles with a damp sponge.

Maintaining and repairing ceramic tile walls. If water doesn't clean a wall, use detergent or a powdered cleanser. A cleanser is almost essential when the joints become coated with grease or stained by mildew or chemicals in the water supply. If it doesn't work, switch to a liquid cleaner made specifically for ceramic tile.

Rust stains are removed with naval jelly or any liquid rust remover. Use chlorine bleach on difficult coffee, mustard, ink or blood stains. Scrape off paint, varnish, nail polish and other films with a razor blade.

If the grout in a joint starts to crumble, scrape it out and regrout with the same material. But if a crack opens up between tiles and tub rim or shower receptor, don't waste time with grout. Clean the crack well and fill it with silicone bathtub caulking compound instead.

If a tile is loose, remove the grout around it and lift it out. Clean the adhesive from the back and scrape as much adhesive as possible from the subwall. If you happen to have the adhesive originally used to tile the wall and it's still in good condition, use this to reset the tile. Otherwise, spread silicone caulk on the back of the tile and stick it down. After letting the adhesive dry overnight, grout the joints.

If a tile is cracked, or if a bathroom accessory is broken, scrape open the joints around it. Then, working from the break in the center of the tile, chip it out in small pieces with a cold chisel and hammer. To remove a broken accessory, knock off the protruding parts; then break the base across the middle and chip it out. (Working out from the center of a tile or an accessory rather than in from the edges protects the surrounding tiles from accidental chipping.) Complete the job by removing the old adhesive and setting in a new tile or accessory.

17

Plastic, Metal, Resilient and Acoustical Tiles

Frankly, these are unimportant wall-covering materials. But they have their uses. And anyway, this wall book wouldn't be complete without them.

Plastic tiles. These things came on the market in the late 1940s when the do-it-yourself movement was beginning to catch on. At the time, the ceramic-tile people had not come up with a satisfactory adhesive for installing their product; so the plastics industry moved in with a substitute. Along with a lot of other people, I used it to cover the walls in a tub recess; and for a while I was going around urging everyone to follow suit. But eventually leaks developed and the tiles began to loosen;

and I finally ripped them all out and put in ceramic.

Although plastic tiles are still advertised for installation in tub recesses and shower stalls, I don't think they belong there. They just can't take the punishment. Use them in drier parts of the bathroom.

The tiles are made in 4¼-in. squares and narrow 6¼-in.-long strips for trimming around the sides and top of a wall. Although only about ⅛ in. thick, they're tough and durable. The colors, which are mainly pale pastels, go all the way through, so scratches which appear do not show up badly.

The two best things about plastic tiles are

their low cost and simple installation. A carton of 40 tiles covering 5 sq. ft. comes to only $2.75. A gallon of adhesive which covers 40 sq. ft. costs $5; a quart of adhesive cleaner, $1.25. Sears sells a complete kit for doing over a 50-sq.-ft. tub recess for $40 (80¢ a sq. ft.). That's only a third of what they charge for a similar ceramic tile kit.

You can make an installation in about half the time it takes to put up ceramic tile.

Installing plastic tiles. To estimate how many tiles you need, follow the directions given for 4¼ x 4¼-in. ceramic tiles. The main tools required are a notched adhesive spreader, carpenter's level, fine-toothed handsaw and coping saw.

You can install the tiles on any firm, level, smooth, clean subwall. Scrape off loose paint. Remove wallpaper or other flexible coverings. Wash walls thoroughly and roughen gloss paint. Fill cracks and holes. Level depressions with gypsum board joint compound (just because the tiles are thin, you can't make them conform to an irregular surface).

Lay out your work in the same way you approach a ceramic-tile installation. But there is no need to nail horizontal wood strips to the wall to keep the tiles from slipping.

Apply the adhesive recommended by the tile manufacturer over a 2- to 3-ft.-sq. area with a notched trowel held at a 45° angle. The beads should be full; the valleys between them, almost bare. Place each tile precisely; don't slide or twist it. Just set one edge into the adhesive and snap down the opposite edge.

Plastic tiles have beveled edges but no spacers. Butt them together tightly. After applying a section of tiles, go over them again one by one and press them firmly into the adhesive. Remove the adhesive that squeezes out of the joints while it is soft; it will save a lot of work later on. Use a scrap of tile cut in a V and follow with a cloth or paper towel. Leave only a very thin line of adhesive in the joints. Filling the joints full does not improve a wall's moisture resistance very much, but does make it unattractive.

Special tile-cutters may be available from the dealer on a loan or rental basis, but they are hardly necessary. The plastic is easy to cut with any fine-toothed saw. Smooth the cut edges by scraping with a knife.

Let the adhesive set for an hour or two before trying to thorough-clean the tiles, otherwise you may dislodge some of them. Use the adhesive cleaner recommended by the tile manufacturer, and dry with clean cloths.

Metal tiles. Most metal tiles are made of thin aluminum, but one design is solid stainless steel. Standard size is 4¼ x 4¼ in. There is also a long, narrow edging strip. Tiles in several colors are finished in baked-on enamel, which is rather easily scratched. Those with brushed or antique metallic finishes are more durable. Aluminum tiles cost between $3 and $3.50 for a carton of 24 covering 3 sq. ft. Stainless steel tiles cost $5.

Thirty years ago metal tiles were in competition with plastic for the do-it-yourself bathroom market; but their best use then—as it is today—is in kitchens. You might try them as a backsplash on walls behind ranges, sinks and counters.

Installing metal tiles. You can follow the plastic tile technique if you wish; but installation is usually made with double-faced adhesive tape. Apply this to the back of each tile in two strips along the vertical edges; or place small square tabs in each of the four corners. Then press to the wall, and the job is done.

Cut the tiles with tin snips or a hacksaw. A simple bending tool costing less than a dollar helps to bend tiles to form a cove base.

Resilient tiles. Covering walls with floor tiles made of vinyl, vinyl-asbestos, linoleum or asphalt isn't done very often; but if you see a color or pattern that strikes your fancy and you need a good, tough, washable wall surface, why not be unusual? The possibilities for an interesting and attractive decorative scheme are almost unlimited. Installation goes easily and quickly because the 9x9-in. or 12x12-in. tiles cover a lot of ground. Cost ranges from about 25¢ to $1 a sq. ft.

Installing resilient tiles. To order 12-in.-sq. tiles, simply determine the square footage of the wall to be covered and order a couple of extra tiles. To order 9-in. tiles, find the length and height of the wall in inches and divide by nine.

The wall should be smooth, level, clean and free of loose paint and flexible wall coverings. Lay it out with horizontal and vertical guide-lines, as for ceramic tile. Always tile from the center of the wall toward the ends. The end tiles should be more than half the width of an uncut tile.

Tiles with an adhesive backing are not recommended for walls, because they don't stay stuck down as well as they should. Use non-stick tiles instead, and install them with an adhesive recommended by the flooring dealer. Most of these are applied with a paint brush, but I still prefer the mastic type, which is combed on with a spreader. In any case, do not cover a larger area than the manufacturer's directions specify.

Apply resilient tiles by setting one edge into the adhesive and snapping down the far edge. Don't slide them. Rub all over the tile to firm it. If edges of adjacent tiles are butted tightly, you don't have to worry about maintaining vertical and horizontal lines.

Wipe off adhesive that gets on the surface as you go along.

To cut tiles to fit into corners, follow the procedure described on page 144. Many tiles can be cut with a pair of scissors; or you can use a sharp knife.

If you don't carry the tiles all the way to the ceiling, or if you cover only part of a wall, the exposed edges should be covered—and protected—with moldings. Tiles at the base of a wall can be curved outward slightly to eliminate dirt-catching cracks if you first nail a wooden cove strip into the corner.

Acoustical tiles. If you don't think resilient tiles belong on walls, you probably won't give the nod to acoustical tiles either. Well, it's not such a farfetched idea as you may think. Sometimes rooms are so noisy that the acoustical in-stallation on the ceiling is not large enough to reduce the sound to acceptable levels; and in that case, the easiest way to improve matters is to install additional tiles on one of the walls or on several walls above a wainscot. Conceivably, there may also be situations in which the wall, or walls, of a noisy room need renovation but not the ceilings; so why shouldn't you save money by using acoustical tiles on the wall and leaving the ceiling alone?

If there's a valid objection to acoustical tiles as a wall-surfacing material, it is that they are a little soft and therefore easy to damage; and because of their textured surface, they are not so easy to clean as other materials. Otherwise, there's little against them. They are good-looking—available in many textures and even in a few sculptured patterns. They are made not only in 12x12-in. and 16x16-in. sizes, but also in a number of larger squares and rectangles. They are paintable and repaintable. They are very easy to install. And you can get them for as little as 20¢ a sq. ft.

The selection of acoustical tiles should be based primarily on their ability to soak up sound—their "noise reduction coefficient," or NRC. As a rule, you can get by with a .40 to .50 NRC if you're covering a wall in a living, dining or bedroom. But in the kitchen, family room and bathrooms, use tiles with a .60 to .70 NRC.

Installing acoustical tiles. To protect tiles against damage from traffic and furniture, my inclination is to install them above a wainscot. But that's up to you.

Otherwise the tiles are installed like resilient tiles. Use the adhesive recommended by the manufacturer, and place it on the back of each tile in 1½-in.-diameter daubs about $\frac{1}{16}$ in. thick. Put five daubs on 12x12 tiles; nine on 16x16s. They should be far enough in from the edges so that when you press the tiles to the wall, the adhesive will not squeeze out from underneath.

Cut the tiles with a sharp utility knife or coping saw.

Acoustical tiles can also be installed over

horizontal or vertical furring strips. The center-to-center spacing of the strips should equal the width of the tiles. Fasten the tiles to the strips with $\frac{9}{16}$-in. staples or 1-in. common nails driven through the flanges on the tiles.

Maintaining and repairing all tiles. Wash with a household detergent solution to remove dirt. Most common stains will come off if you rub them with white appliance wax; however, this treatment should not be used on acoustical tiles. If you can't get these clean with detergent, repaint them.

Reset loose tiles with the appropriate adhesive. If a tile is badly damaged, replace it. When digging it out, always work from the center of the tile toward the edges; if you work from the edges in, you're likely to damage the surrounding tiles.

18

Masonry

Though I haven't admitted it before, you have probably detected that I am something of a purist. I just don't think that man-made imitations of natural materials are ever completely successful from the appearance standpoint. Certainly that is true when we come to masonry. As good as the plastic brick and stone surfacing materials are (*see Chapter 14*), they don't look like the real thing.

In short, if you want an authentic wall of brick, build it of clay brick. Or if you want an authentic wall of stone, build it of real stone. There are easier ways to do this than you may suspect, and they do not require construction of deep foundations or piers to support great weight.

Bricks. There are nail-on bricks* and glue-on bricks.† The former are about 1 in. thick, 2½ in. wide and either 7⅝ or 11½ in. long. They weigh 9 lb. a square foot. Several colors are available. The latter measure approximately ¼ x 2⅛ x 8 in. and there is one color—red. Bricks for use on outside corners are available in both styles.

Next to their true-to-life appearance, the big advantage of these clay bricks is that they are fire-resistant; consequently they are safe to use on fireplace walls and on kitchen walls behind the range.

* Ludowici-Celadon Co., 111 E. Wacker Dr., Chicago, Ill. 60601
† Sears, Roebuck

The cost of nail-on bricks comes to about $1.20 per sq. ft.; that of the glue-on type, $1.50. Both are quite easy to install—especially the glue-ons.

Installing nail-on bricks. To estimate the number of bricks required, measure the length and height of the wall to be covered in feet. (If you don't come up with even measurements, figure to the next higher foot.) Multiply the figures and divide by six if you are using 7⅝-in. bricks; four if using 11½-in. bricks. To this total add about 2 percent for waste.

Nail-on bricks must be applied over a nail-able subwall. Three-eighths-inch plywood is the minimum material allowable. As long as it is securely nailed to the studs, and level, it doesn't make much difference what condition it is in.

Use a running bond to lay-up the bricks. In this, the units in the even numbered courses are centered over the joints in the odd-numbered courses. Find the highest point along the floor line and establish a level line. Build the bricks up from this. The uneven space at the bottom can be filled with mortar.

To determine the best arrangement of the bricks within the courses, lay out two full courses on the floor before starting installation. If you're covering a wall with inside corners at the ends, the end bricks in each course should either be equal in length or one should be a half brick and the other a whole brick. However, if you're covering a wall with outside corners at the ends, you should construct or reconstruct the subwall so that the end bricks in each course are either whole bricks or half bricks.

Install the bricks with 1½-in. annular-ring nails driven through holes in the flanges on the top edges. Take care not to drive the nails in too hard. The nailheads should just touch the bricks.

Leave a ½-in. space at the ends of the bricks. A rabbet in the bottom edge of each brick fits over the top flanges of the bricks in the course below. This automatically provides ½-in. space between courses. Check each course with a level, to make sure it is horizontal.

When all the bricks are nailed up, point the joints with a mortar made of 3 parts sand, 1 part masonry cement, ⅕ part hydrated lime and 1 part water. This produces a stiff mortar for application with a trowel. Add more water if application is made with a caulking gun. Fill the joints completely; scrape the excess mortar from the surface; and when the mortar has set, strike it off with a piece of pipe to make a concave joint, or with a mason's trowel to make a beveled joint. Then wipe off mortar stains with a damp rag.

After letting the mortar dry for a week, you

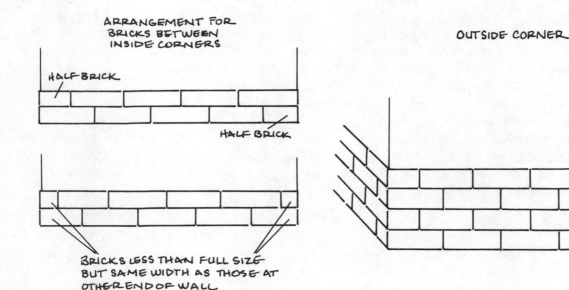

ARRANGEMENT FOR BRICKS BETWEEN INSIDE CORNERS

HALF BRICK

HALF BRICK

BRICKS LESS THAN FULL SIZE BUT SAME WIDTH AS THOSE AT OTHER END OF WALL

OUTSIDE CORNER

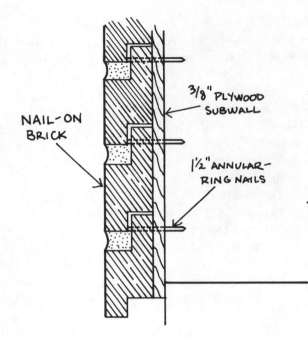

NAIL-ON BRICK

3/8" PLYWOOD SUBWALL

1½" ANNULAR-RING NAILS

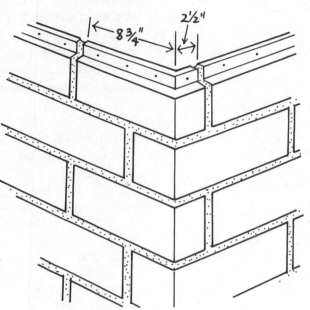

8¾"

2½"

can wash the surface again—if necessary—with dilute muriatic acid.

To cut the bricks, score a line on both sides with a cold chisel. Then crack off the piece with a hammer. Smooth the edges with a coarse file or abrasive stone.

Installing glue-on bricks. These bricks are sold in packages containing 35 pieces, which will cover 5 sq. ft. To order, measure the wall as above and divide the square footage by five. You will also need adhesive recommended by the brick manufacturer, adhesive cleaner and a notched spreader. One gallon of adhesive covers up to 20 sq. ft. It is either gray or black.

The subwall must be reasonably smooth, level, rigid, clean and free of loose paint or flexible wall covering. Lay it out as for nail-on bricks.

Cover 2 or 3 sq. ft. of the wall with adhesive. Use the notched edge of a spreader and hold it at a 45° angle. Then smooth the adhesive into an even, solid layer with the smooth edge of the spreader. Put three daubs of adhesive on the back of each brick and press it into place.

Leave a ¼-in. space (or a little more, if you prefer) on all sides of the bricks. Use little pieces of ¼-in. wood or plastic to establish the spacing. Check each course to make sure it is horizontal. The joints are not pointed; so when all the bricks are in place, your work is done except for going over them with the adhesive cleaner.

A kit containing a cutter and nippers for cutting bricks can be borrowed or rented; or you can simply score them with a cold chisel and nibble off the pieces with pliers.

Maintaining and repairing brick walls. Ordinary soil is removed by scrubbing with a strong detergent solution and rinsing. Use an abrasive cleanser to take off smoke stains; a mixture of 1 lb. of oxalic acid in 1. gal. of water to take off rust stains. Use paint remover on paint. For oil and grease, try a floor cleaner of the type used in service stations. The alternative is to make a thick paste of benzine and whiting; trowel it on a stain and let it stand till it dries. Then brush it off. Repeat until the stain disappears.

Loose mortar in joints between nail-on bricks should be scraped out. Then pack in a mixture of 1 part Portland cement and 2 parts sand; or use vinyl or latex cement according to the directions on the package.

Marble. Leave the installation of big slabs of

marble to a professional. But there's no reason why you shouldn't install marble tiles* yourself. They come in 8x8-in. and 12x12-in. sizes; are ½ in. thick, and weigh 6½ lb. per sq. ft. And being marble, they are beautiful. You have a choice of a dozen colors; a gloss or satin finish.

The cost is about $2 per sq. ft. up. The tiles are no more difficult to install than ceramic tiles provided you don't have to cut many of them.

Installing marble tiles. If you use foot-square tiles, simply figure the square footage of the wall to find how many are needed. If you use 8x8-in. units, divide both the length and the height of the wall by eight and multiply the answer. You may also need trim tiles.

The tiles are installed like ceramic tiles. Use an oil-free adhesive recommended by the marble dealer and a white cement grout or mastic grout. All adhesive and grout must be removed from the face of the tiles at once. Let the adhesive set for 24 hours before grouting; then moisten the joints with water. After packing the joints full, wipe them off at the base of the tiles' chamfered edges.

Space the tiles $\frac{3}{32}$ in. apart by breaking round toothpicks and sticking the fat ends vertically between the tiles.

* Vermont Marble Co., Proctor, Vt. 05765

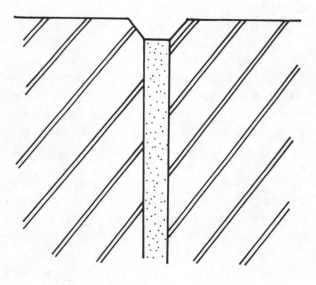

Cut tiles with a saw with a fine-toothed carbide-tipped blade. You can also score tiles with a glass cutter and then nibble away with pliers or tile nippers.

Maintaining and repairing marble tiles. You can help to prevent soiling and staining if you apply a special marble sealer to the new wall and every six months thereafter. This is available from marble dealers. Don't use any other polish or finish.

For ordinary soil and grease try plain water first; then a very mild detergent solution or solution of laundry soap.

For stains and smoke, use the special marble cleaners sold by dealers. It is very easy to discolor or etch marble by using the wrong cleaners. Anything containing an acid is particularly harmful.

If grout falls out, or is loose, scrape it out completely and regrout with the material originally used.

Slate. Blue-black slate* on a fireplace wall makes about as handsome an installation as anyone could ask for. The natural-cleft surface has a magnificent, vigorous texture and yet it isn't so rough that it's hard to keep clean. And what material is more durable?

Slate tiles cut especially for installation on walls measure 6x6, 9x9 and 12x12 in.; are ¼ in. thick, and are gauge-rubbed on the back to permit installation with adhesive rather than mortar. They weigh 3¾ lb. per sq. ft. If you want larger squares or rectangles up to 4x4 ft., you can have them but only in ½-in. thickness —which doubles the weight and makes for installation problems.

Sawed tiles are similar in all respects to natural-cleft tiles but have a less pronounced texture and are used primarily for flooring.

Quarter-inch tiles cost about $1.50 a sq. ft. They are no easier or harder to install than marbel tiles.

Installing slate tiles. Follow the directions for ceramic and marble tiles. Joints between the slates can be butted tight. If left open, they

* Buckingham-Virginia Slate Corp., 1103 E. Main St., Richmond, Va. 23219

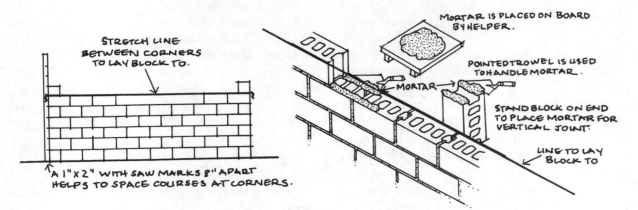

STRETCH LINE BETWEEN CORNERS TO LAY BLOCK TO.

A 1" X 2" WITH SAW MARKS 8" APART HELPS TO SPACE COURSES AT CORNERS.

MORTAR IS PLACED ON BOARD BY HELPER.

POINTED TROWEL IS USED TO HANDLE MORTAR.

MORTAR

STAND BLOCK ON END TO PLACE MORTAR FOR VERTICAL JOINT.

LINE TO LAY BLOCK TO

should be a minimum of ¼ in. wide. Grout them like nail-on brick.

Maintain like brick.

Concrete blocks. If you want a really good soundproof partition between you and your children, build it of concrete blocks. You are much more likely, however, to use this splendid building material for dividing your basement.

The standard block size is 7⅝x7⅝x15⅝ in., but innumerable other sizes are available. You can also get blocks in a variety of textures and sculptured designs. And I for one am particularly intrigued by blocks which are covered on one or both sides with a tough, glossy, resistant-to-just-about-everything, integral glaze. You can choose from almost 50 bright colors. Thus you have an unparalleled opportunity to put up a wall which will put the best of the cubist painters to shame.

A wall built with standard unfinished blocks costs roughly 50 cents a sq. ft. Because of the weight of the blocks, construction is arduous but not too difficult otherwise. Using blocks made with lightweight aggregates is obviously a smart idea.

Building a wall of standard-size blocks. You need 113 full-size blocks, 1 sack of cement and 2 sacks of sand to build 100 sq. ft. of wall. However, before ordering the materials, lay out the wall carefully on paper. You will find that the number of full-size blocks required is reduced somewhat and that you must also order a certain number of half-size blocks.

Concrete block walls are usually built with a running bond. The horizontal and vertical mortar joints should be ⅜ in. thick. To avoid cutting blocks—a tedious hammer-and-cold-chisel chore—plan the wall to be a multiple of 16 in. long and 8 in. high. If the height of the basement is a few inches less than a multiple of eight, the topmost course can be made of thinner blocks or of timbers.

If the basement floor slopes or has dips, level it before building the wall with latex or vinyl cement. These are special cements which, unlike Portland cement, can be troweled to a feather edge.

Block walls are built from the two ends toward the middle. That is, you should build up three or four courses of blocks at the ends and then fill in between them. To make sure a wall is straight, stretch a strong cord between the end blocks. A useful trick is to erect at one end of the wall a 1x2-in. wood strip marked off in 8-in. segments. This will help you to space the courses at the corners.

As the wall goes up, check it frequently with a carpenter's level, to make sure the courses are level and the wall is plumb.

Mortar is made of 1 part masonry cement, 2½ to 3 parts sand and enough water to produce a workable mixture.

The first blocks are laid in a bed of mortar on the basement floor. To lay subsequent blocks, apply continuous strips of mortar to the top front and back edges of the blocks in the course below. Do not apply mortar to the cross strips. Then apply strips of mortar to one end of the block you are laying, and set the block in place against the end of the previous block. Tap it into place with the handle of your mason's trowel. Lay a level at right angles across it to make sure it isn't slanting toward the front or back of the wall. Then scrape off the excess mortar and toss it back on to your mortar board.

To keep mortar from drying out and losing adhesive powers, apply the horizontal strips for only one block at a time. Your entire supply of mortar should be used up within 2½ hours if the temperature is over 80° F; within 3½ hours if the temperature is under 80° F. During this period, if the mortar in your mixing box should begin to stiffen, it can be retempered by the addition of water.

When the mortar joints become quite stiff, tool them with a piece of pipe or your trowel. The aim is to press the mortar into the joints so it is smooth, watertight and adheres tightly to the edges of the blocks.

Paint the wall, if you wish, with latex or Portland cement paint.

Maintaining and repairing concrete block walls. (Follow directions for bricks.)

19

Walls That Transmit Light

The main purpose of a wall that transmits light is to divide a room physically into two spaces but to give you the impression that they are still one.

Purpose No. 2 is to illuminate a dark room while assuring privacy for the occupants.

Clearly, one purpose is in opposition to the other. This is because of differences in the design and construction of the wall-building materials. But we'll get to that later. Consider here, in a general sort of way, the materials which come under the light-transmitting heading and the many ways you might make use of them.

Some of the materials are translucent glass or plastic. Most of these are made in large sheets; a few in small blocks. All transmit light and a few transmit sight; but they stop air and odors cold, and to a certain extent they also stop sound.

Other light-transmitting wall materials are large panels of metal, wood, hardboard or opaque plastics which are pierced with holes in a decorative pattern. These obscure vision and prevent your walking through them any more than you can walk through any solid material—but they are not barriers to anything else.

One of the commonest uses for light-transmitting interior walls in the home is between the living and dining areas of the living room —especially if it's a small living room. Here the walls (or wall) serve to spell out the functions of the two areas without making them feel as cramped as they might be if the walls were solid. The walls also allow the housewife to set the table and bring on dinner without feeling cut off from family and friends; and after dinner she can leave the table in a mess because it isn't clearly visible from the living area, and yet the living area seems to be almost as spacious as if the walls were not there at all.

A light-transmitting wall between kitchen and family room accomplishes more or less the same things. You get the impression that the two rooms are one; yet each is a separate entity. The jumble of pots and pans is obscured from the family room; yet the cook need not be isolated from everyone else.

If your front door opens directly into the living room, you can screen it off from the room without turning it into a dark pocket and without making a drastic change in the apparent size of the room.

If two children occupy a bedroom, you can largely satisfy their natural desires to have their "very own" rooms by erecting a partial light-transmitting wall between the beds. But the bedroom still looks like and functions as a single room.

One of the more intriguing uses of a light-transmitting wall is to create a sense of mystery about what is on the far side. Suppose, for instance, the doorway into a large room is flanked by pierced walls. As you come through the door, you can, of course, look through the walls but what you see is not very clear. And that immediately arouses your curiousity. You want to see more.

Finally, there is that ultra-practical purpose for this type of wall: to bring natural light into, say, an inside bathroom without destroying the privacy of the bathroom.

You can undoubtedly find other uses for these walls; and if and when you do, you will discover one more thing about them: Many of the materials are gorgeous. Not only do they have strong pattern, delightful texture and attractive color—they are also top-notch sculpture.

Unhappily, they are often priced accordingly. Ten dollars a square foot is not unusual. But don't let this scare you off. Other, simpler, but still lovely materials can be had for only 5 or 10 percent of this price.

What's available. I am not sure whether the first light-transmitting material was perforated metal or frosted glass. I don't go back anywhere nearly that far. But they are both still with us and going strong. However, they have a lot more competition.

Perforated metal. These are thin metal sheets stamped in innumerable plain and ornamental patterns. The materials in stock are made either of steel or aluminum in 3- or 4x10-ft. sheets. But as one of the biggest fabricating firms notes in its 178-page catalog: "We are prepared to perforate nearly every material which can be obtained in the form of coils, sheets or plates." It then goes on to list just about every common metal, as well as cloth, hardboard, paper, plastics, plywood and rubber.

The advantages of perforated metal are low price, strength and ease of installation. Sheets have to be painted.

Patterned glass. Under this heading comes any glass panel that isn't transparent. There is a vast array of patterns and textures; and if you want color to boot, you can have it. The glass is usually ¼ in. thick and comes in sheets up to about 4x10 ft. You could get larger sizes but probably wouldn't be able to handle them.

Patterned glass gives light with privacy, requires no finishing and only minimum upkeep. But if you want to use it where there's any chance of someone crashing into it, order patterned safety glass.

Glass blocks. When these were first marketed, many years ago, they were pretty unattractive and were almost invariably used in such unattractive ways that they rapidly lost popularity. But some of the blocks now on the market are handsome and interesting. Generally they are designed to obscure vision while transmitting light, but some are transparent. Used in interior walls, their outstanding advantages are their resistance to impact and noise. And you can get special designs for diffusing light or directing it upward.

Two-way mirror. This is a glass mirror made so you can see your reflection in one side, and see *through* from the other side. For the mirror to be fully effective, the area on the mirror side should be brightly lighted while that on the see-through side is dim.

Two-way mirror is made of both sheet and plate glass. The latter comes in stock sizes up to 6x10 ft.

Translucent plastic. These paneling materials are even more varied in appearance than patterned glass. You can not only get various textures and colors but you can also find laminated materials with dried plants and butterflies, filigree-work and so on sandwiched in the middle. Sizes and thicknesses are also variable.

Plastic panels are not so cleanable or abrasion-resistant as glass, but they are less likely to shatter—and less lethal if you bang into them. They're also easier to work and install.

Pierced opaque plastic. These are beautifully sculptured grilles. Although many are less than 1 in. thick (some are as much as 4 in.), they are more three-dimensional than any of the materials already mentioned (including glass blocks, which appear three-dimensional only when you see one alone). The few mass-produced panels measure only 2 ft. wide and 2 or 3 ft. high, and are used in tandem. Other panels produced to order can be made in almost any size.

Because of the intricacy of the designs, the panels collect dust and are rather hard to clean.

Pierced wood panels. Without belittling the best of the pierced plastics in the slightest, I must give the pierced wood panels top billing. The design is extraordinary. And since they are made of wood, they have all the color and warmth of that marvelous material. But their three-dimensional, intricate designs make them first-class dust-catchers. And they are even harder to clean than plastic because you're not supposed to wash them.

Several sizes up to 4x8 ft. are made.

Pierced hardboard panels. Made of ¼-in. material, these are much like the simpler metal stampings in appearance. Cost is low and installation easy.

Woven cane for seating, bamboo shades. There are a number of materials like these which are just waiting for your imagination to go to work. Don't let the fact that they are made primarily for other purposes steer you away from them. They can be used most effectively in light-transmitting walls, and you will be happily surprised at their low cost. Painting or varnishing is difficult, however; and cleaning's a chore.

Treillage. This is a fancy synonym for latticework; and with so many prefabricated, easy-to-use, light-transmitting materials to choose from, I doubt that you're going to build many interior walls with it—even in spite of the name. But if you want to be your own wall designer, then take a few strips of lattice or do-it-yourself aluminum and have at it.

Building paneled walls. Except for glass blocks and treillage, all the materials described come in panels that are either rigid or flexible. They have no load-bearing strength and cannot stand alone. Some sort of support is required.

In most installations, the panels are held in attractive wood frames built in one of the five ways illustrated. The actual method of securing the panels depends on their thickness, design, your skill with tools, the effect you aim to achieve and so on. You might, for instance, cut grooves in the four sides of a frame, set a panel into them, and then nail the frame together and erect it. Or you might cut rabbets in the four sides of a frame, set in a panel and secure it with square strips of wood or other moldings nailed into the rabbets. Or you might construct a frame (on the floor or in place), set it in a panel and hold it with quarter rounds nailed to the frame on both sides. Or, if the panel manufacturer also makes framing members, you might simply buy a knock-down frame

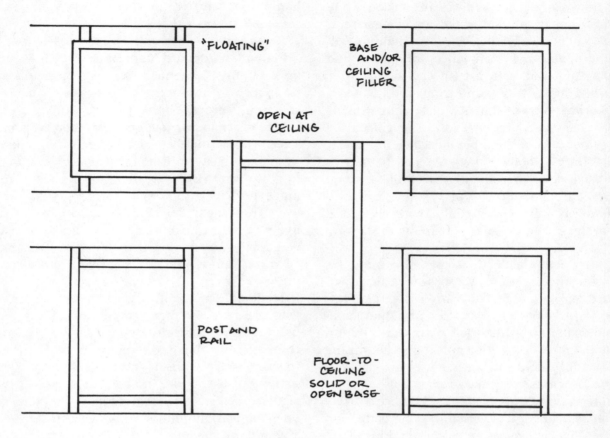

from him and put it together according to directions.

Whichever course you follow, remember that you must allow a fraction of an inch clearance on all sides of a panel to permit expansion and contraction. No fasteners or adhesives are used to hold the panel. It simply "floats" in the frame.

Other ways of installing light-transmitting panels are as follows:

1. Buy a pair of expansion poles which fit tightly between floor and ceiling, and fasten the panels in between. This method, however, is limited to panels that are thick enough to be held with bolts or screws driven into the edges.

2. If you use thick, sculptured panels, they can, in some cases, simply be set down into tight-fitting boxlike bases which are screwed to the floor.

3. Hang rigid, lightweight panels from ornamental chains attached to the top and bottom edges and secured to ceiling and floor. One maker of translucent plastic panels suggests using chains only from the ceiling.

Installing glass blocks. Most commonly used blocks measure 5¾x5¾ in., 7¾x7¾ in. and 11¾x11¾ in. All are 3⅞ in. thick. They are laid in a stacked bond with one block directly over another. The joints should be ¼ in. thick.

A wall can be any exact multiple of 6, 8 or 12 in. long. If it is to be built between two existing walls, locate the ends over studs so you can secure the block wall to them. If one end of the new wall is open, it should bear against a timber upright which is firmly secured to the floor and ceiling joists.

To facilitate construction of the wall, erect at each end a straight 1x2-in. strip of wood marked in 6-, 8- or 12-in. segments, depending on the size of the blocks. Stretch a cord tightly between the strips. This not only helps you to keep the wall straight but also marks the height of each course and helps to keep the courses level.

Blocks are laid with a rather stiff mixture of 1 part Portland cement, 1 part hydrated lime and 4 parts fine sand. First paint a strip of asphalt emulsion—available from the block manufacturer—on the floor and end walls. It should be about $\frac{1}{16}$ in. thick and a little less than 4 in. wide. When it is dry, trowel a strip of mortar on the floor and set the first course of blocks in this.

Lay the blocks from the ends of the wall toward the middle. Butter one side of each end block and set it firmly against the adjacent walls and into the mortar bed. When setting each succeeding block, butter one side with mortar and jam it up against the end of the block previously laid. The final vertical joint in each course must be made by troweling mortar down between the blocks.

Make sure each block is level—parallel with the guideline—and check it with a carpenter's level so it does not slant toward the front or back of the wall. If a block is set improperly, don't try to tap it into place with a metal tool. Work it into place with your hands.

To strengthen the wall, metal reinforcing available from the block manufacturer should be installed in the horizontal joint above the first course and at 2-ft. intervals thereafter. The reinforcing comes in 8-ft. lengths and consists of two long, heavy wires with short cross wires. To use it, cover the blocks with a half-thick bed of mortar; press down the reinforcing; cover with the remaining thickness of mortar; and set the blocks. For a wall more than 8 ft. long, install two strips of reinforcing and lap the ends 6 in.

To tie the block wall to the adjacent walls (or to the timber at the open end of the wall), use metal wall anchors which are also supplied by the block manufacturer. These are flat grid-like strips 2 ft. long. Bend them into an L and nail the upright arm to the adjacent wall, then

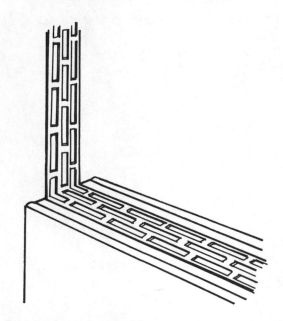

embed the horizontal arm in a horizontal mortar joint. The anchors are installed in the same joints in which you use metal reinforcing.

Mortar squeezing out of joints when blocks are set should be scraped off and returned to the mortar board. The entire batch of mortar should be used in about 2½ hours. If it stiffens too much during this period, it can be retempered with a little fresh water.

When the joints set slightly, tool them with a piece of copper tube. The finished joints should be smooth and concave. As you build up the wall, keep an eye on the previously finished joints to make sure they don't start to bulge. If they do, it means that the weight of the blocks is too much, and that you should suspend building operations until the mortar has set sufficiently to support the blocks above.

To make final clean-up easier, wipe most of the mortar from the face of the blocks after tooling joints. Then, at day's end, go over the wall again with a damp rag.

If there is a space between the top of the wall and the ceiling, don't try to fill it with concrete. Instead, conceal it with wood moldings nailed to the ceiling. You may also use moldings to cover the concrete strip at the foot of the wall. In both cases, the moldings help to hold the wall upright.

Maintaining and repairing glass-block walls.
A quick swish with a damp rag keeps the glass areas clean, but you may occasionally have to scrub the concrete joints with detergent solution or cleansing powder. Stains in the mortar are removed like stains on brick (*see page 153*). Loose mortar joints are repaired as in a brick wall.

20

Luminous Walls

A luminous wall is nothing more than a luminous ceiling set on edge. It's an interesting idea: very decorative but also very practical. Once you have seen several good installations, it's easy to become carried away with the possibilities for your own home.

Fair enough. But before committing yourself completely, back off a minute and take a hard analytical look at what you're doing. I'm not suggesting that you should change your mind. But luminous walls can't be slapped together in the same way you put up a wood-paneled wall or a fancy wall covering. You have to find the proper balance between the lights you install and the translucent paneling that forms the wall surface. And unless you have an illuminating engineer to advise you, you'll have to do this by yourself. That takes some experimenting, with equipment and materials that are not inexpensive.

What exactly is a luminous wall? It is an entire wall, a section of wall or only one large panel lighted from within, usually by fluorescent tubes, but sometimes by incandescent bulbs. It is surfaced on one or both sides with translucent plastic or glass which sometimes embodies decorative elements or is overlaid with decorative grilles.

The obvious effect of a luminous wall is to provide light similar to that coming through a thinly curtained window. It is, therefore, the perfect kind of wall to use in a basement playroom or any other dark room, hall or entry. But this is only one of its purposes.

My old associate Jim Jensen, a General Electric lighting engineer who has done a great deal with luminous walls, lists four other important things the walls can do in homes:

1. They can be used to display and silhouette decorative objects, collections and the like which are set in front of them.

2. They can be used to emphasize structural features of the house. For instance, in a room with a soaring ceiling, a tall, narrow, lighted wall panel directs the eye to the ceiling.

3. They can be used to affect mood and atmosphere. This is done by changing the patterns and intensity of light in the walls and by use of colored light.

4. They can be used to balance the light in a room and to create a luminous environment. By eliminating the sharp difference between the light and dark areas of a room, this makes the room more restful for the occupants. It also increases the apparent size of the room.

Building a luminous wall. To be effective, a luminous wall must be uniformly lighted. No harm is done if the light at the edges is a little less intense than that in the middle; or, vice versa, if it's a little less intense in the middle than around the edges. But if there are distinct light and dark areas, most people object.

The big problem in building a luminous wall is to achieve this uniformity of illumination. The lights must be placed far enough behind the diffusing panels so that they do not show through as bright spots. This almost always means that you must make the wall somewhat thicker than an ordinary stud wall.

In addition, you must hit on some way of controlling the light so that the entire wall surface does not seem uncomfortably bright. This can be done by installing a dimmer switch, by covering the wall with a panel material with rather low light-transmitting characteristics or by bouncing the light off a reflective surface.

Four methods of building a luminous wall are shown in the drawings.

Drawing below illustrates the best way to save floor space—by installing the lights within a stud framework. When this is done, however, you should substitute 2x6s for the normal 2x4s, so that the distance from the center line of a fluorescent tube to the diffusing panel is 4 in. This is minimum spacing. If the wall has diffusing panels on both sides, use 2x10s for studs. This is also minimum spacing.

The studs can be spaced 16 to 24 in. on centers. Two rows of fluorescent tubes are needed in each stud cavity for uniform brightness, and all surfaces of the cavities should be painted flat white. To reduce surface brightness, the lights should be on a dimmer; or the diffusing panels should be quite dense.

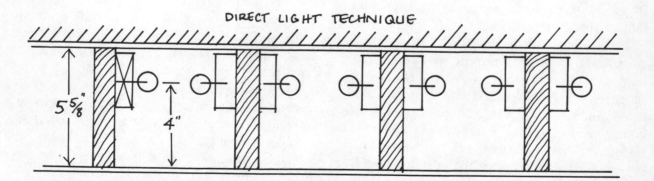

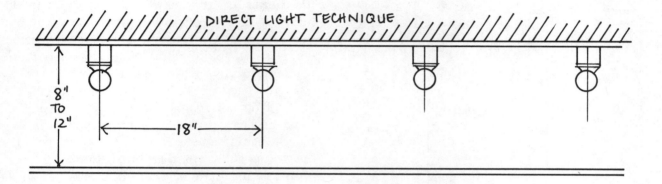

The completed wall will not, of course, appear as one large bright panel. It will, rather, consist of a row of narrow panels divided by the black lines of the studs.

Drawing above shows how to build a luminous wall in front of an existing wall which is painted flat white. The fluorescent lights are installed in vertical rows 18 in. apart. (A single row of tubes operated at full brightness will give more or less uniform light in a cavity 1 ft. deep and 3 ft. wide.) The diffusing panels are placed 8 to 12 in. out from the subwall, depending on their opacity. The unbroken expanse of the wall is limited only by the dimensions of the diffusing panels used.

To add drama to the wall, you can install small incandescent indoor or outdoor Christmas-tree lights midway between the fluorescents.

The installation in Drawing below solves the problem of brightness by mounting the lights on 1x3-in. boards just behind the diffusing panels and aiming them toward a white reflecting surface at the back of the wall. This permits a reduction in the thickness of the wall. However, the wall looks like a series of narrow luminous panels rather than one big panel.

Drawing on next page illustrates a way to build a luminous wall panel up to 4 ft. wide. One vertical row of fluorescent tubes is placed

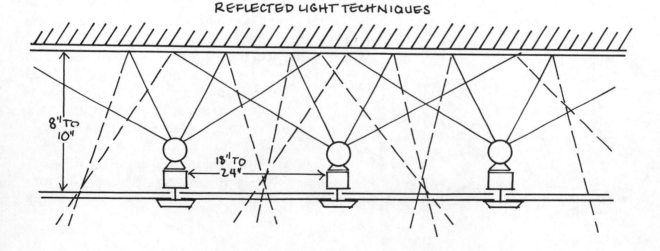

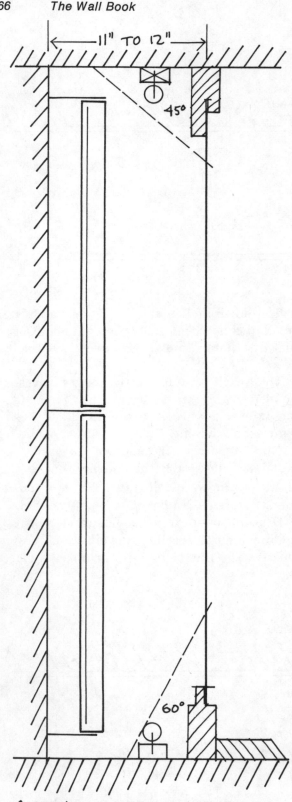

11" TO 12"

45°

60°

SECTION — INCREASE SHIELDING ANGLE
WHEN USING LAMP AT TOP OR BOTTOM
OR BOTH.

at each edge of the panel. This arrangement alone gives a surprisingly uniform effect, though the brightness falls off slightly toward the center of the panel. Adding horizontal lights at the top and bottom increases the light intensity or can be used to introduce other colors, such as gold or blue. Note, however, that when horizontal lights are installed forward from the back of the wall, they become more visible from the room. The depth of the shielding (the boards across the top and bottom of the diffusing panel) should therefore be increased as shown by the dotted lines.

In this installation, as in all others, all surfaces inside the wall are painted flat white.

Lights to use. The basic light fixture for luminous walls is a 4-ft., 40-watt unit using a warm-white or deluxe-warm-white tube. It should cost about $8.50 at most dealers complete with tube. Other size fixtures and tubes of other colors may be used.

Fluorescents are favored over incandescents because they give off more light for less money and with less heat. And they have a much longer life. If large incandescents are used, select the reflector type which is silvered on the inside. These are best for white light. But colored bulbs are not silvered. To carry off the heat generated by incandescents, you should devise some way of ventilating the wall. The ventilating holes should be screened so they do not form a silly-looking row of holes emitting light. The alternative is not to carry the wall panels all the way to the floor or ceiling, thus allowing a line of light—and heat—to spill out over the top and bottom of the wall so that the wall appears to be flat.

Diffusing panels. The same translucent plastic panels and patterned glass panels which are used for building the walls described in Chapter 19 are used for luminous walls. Whatever the design, you should set them into a wooden frame to hold them upright and rigid. To permit removal of a panel so you can re-lamp the lighting fixtures, rabbet the front edges of the frame on all four sides, set the loose panel in this and hold it in place with wood strips screwed into the rabbets.

Unlike luminous ceilings, luminous walls should never be surfaced with eggcrate or perforated materials alone, because they do not conceal the fluorescent tubes; consequently the walls are uncomfortable to look at. (It is also uncomfortable to look directly at luminous ceilings surfaced in this way; but the fact of the matter is that you rarely do.) If you want to cover a luminous wall with a decorative pierced panel of wood, plastic, metal or what have you, a simple flat diffusing sheet of plastic must be placed behind it.

Index